FRANK WERNER
COVERING + EXPOSING
THE ARCHITECTURE
OF COOP HIMMELB(L)AU

BIRKHÄUSER – PUBLISHERS FOR ARCHITECTURE
BASEL · BERLIN · BOSTON

PROJECTS DESCRIBED IN THIS BOOK

CONTENTS

"ARCHITECTURE IS INTERESTING BECAUSE IT IS FRAGILE, MUCH

MORE FRAGILE THAN TELEVISION, FOR EXAMPLE. TELEVISION IS

A VERY SYSTEMATIC, CLEARLY DEFINED SPACE, WHICH IS WHY IT

OFFERS SO MUCH SECURITY. A BUILDING, ON THE OTHER HAND,

IS RADICALLY UNCLEAR, AS CHILDREN, OF COURSE, KNOW

PERFECTLY WELL. WE TRAIN OUR STUDENTS TO NOT THINK LIKE

CHILDREN; WE TRAIN THEM NOT TO SEE GHOSTS, TO NOT IMAGINE

THAT THE LIMITS OF A SPACE ARE ENIGMATIC AND UNCLEAR. WE

GIVE THEM THE SENSE THAT ARCHITECTURE IS A SOLID, STABLE

INSTITUTION AND IT IS NOT, IT JUST IS NOT."

(MARK WIGLEY INTERVIEWED BY PETER LANG, NEW YORK 1995[1])

BACK TO THE ROOTS

It's a long time now since Austrian architects Coop Himmelblau were sold more or less under the counter as a "hot tip" on the architectural scene. Practically all international publications carrying specialist articles on "Deconstructivism" now see Coop Himmelb(l)au – the letter l has been in brackets for a few years now, suggesting less dreaming ('Himmelblau' – 'sky blue') and more actual building ('Himmelbau' – 'sky building') – as one of the leading international architectural practices. But this should not lead us to the false conclusion that the off-centre architecture built by this team now enjoys global esteem. Coop Himmelb(l)au's architectural language is simply too strange, too hard, too uncompromising, too uncomfortable to be woven seamlessly into the patter of current ideas, or even current theories, about architecture.

Coop Himmelb(l)au's thinking grew out of the "wild" Austrian cultural and architectural scene in the sixties. It still seems astounding today that such powerfully innovative ideas, at least for the European architectural scene, should have come from Vienna and other Austrian cities at that time. Hans Hollein and Walter Pichler were vociferously putting the case for turning away from one-sided, late-functionalist architecture in their fascinating exhibitions, campaigns and manifestos as early as 1963. And Raimund J. Abraham, Günther Domenig, Johann Georg Gsteu, Wilhelm Holzbauer, Eilfried Huth, Gustav Peichl, Ottokar Uhl and many architects of the same generation had tried to convert the distance they had put between themselves and exhausted Modernism into a programme of alternative ideas about space and form, long before Charles Jencks made his controversial proclamation of post-Modernism in Britain. Also, discussions centring around university lecturer Günther Feuerstein, one of the most prominent architectural theorists and influences on post-war Austrian architecture, were to provide a veritable reservoir of revolutionary cells of young architects, who intended to cock a much more aggressive snook at convention, and this included architectural convention. In the late sixties, fundamentalist "base camps" like this led to the formation of numerous young, furious agit-prop groups without a great deal of professional experience, including names like Haus-Rucker-Co, Coop Himmelblau, Zünd up, Salz der Erde, Missing Link, supported by committed "lone warriors" like Friedrich St. Florian, Franco Fonatti, Engelbert Kremser, Gernot Nalbach, Peter Noever and others. They all declared that they wanted to explore entirely new constructs and communication forms for architectural imagination, keeping well away from social and specialist constraints. Only one of the groups named has survived without losing any of its freshness, and that is Coop Himmelblau, keeping unbroken faith with these aims over the decades.

1 City with Pulsating Space, 1966, model 2–4 Wiener Supersommer, Cloud Setting, 1976, vertical superstructure, drawings

For this reason the work of the Coop Himmelblau team, founded in 1968 by Wolf D. Prix, Helmut Swiczinsky and Raimer M. Holzer (left in 1971) after a turbulent and interrupted course of architectural studies, deserves particular attention. The Coop Himmelblau "bad boys" are more rebellious, uncompromising and pigheaded than almost any group in recent architectural history. Over three decades ago they decided to take on the risky task of revealing the typical mechanisms used to suppress individual, emotional need by run-down cities and closed architectural containers, in other words they continually open up old wounds. What is more, they have until todayused the shock therapies developed in their own "lab" as a means of devising appropriate alternatives.

MAKING THE CITY ONE'S OWN

It actually sounded quite harmless in 1968 when the newly-founded group explained its name as follows: "Coop Himmelblau is not a colour but an idea – the idea of having architecture with fantasy, as buoyant and variable as clouds."[2] A good decade later, when trivial post-Modern architecture was at its height, the same group said: "We are fed up with seeing Palladio and other historical masks, because we do not want to exclude everything in architecture that makes us uneasy. We want architecture that has more to offer. Architecture that bleeds, exhausts, that turns and even breaks, as far as I am concerned. Architecture that glows, that stabs, that tears and rips when stretched. Architecture must be precipitous, fiery, smooth, hard, angular, brutal, round, tender, colourful, obscene, randy, dreamy, en-nearing, distancing, wet, dry and heart-stopping. Dead or alive. If it is cold, then cold as a block of ice. If it is hot, then as hot as a tongue of flame. Architecture must burn."[3] Finally, in the late eighties, they sounded somewhat more poetic again, more conciliatory: "When we speak of ships, others think of shipwreckage. We, however, think of wind-inflated white sails. When we speak of eagles, the others think of a bird. We, however, are talking about the wing span. When we speak of black panthers, the others think of predatory animals. We, however, think of the untamed dangerousness of architecture. When we speak of leaping whales, others think of saurians. We, however, think of 30 tons of flying weight. We won't find architecture in an encyclopedia. Our architecture can be found where thoughts move faster than hands to grasp it."[4]

If we compare these declarations of intention from three different periods it is clear how aggressively this young group of architects reacted, immediately after their foundation, to urban and environmental design of a kind that they denounced until well into the eighties as "Biedermeier architecture by a democracy of questionnaires and obligingness". But originally there was nothing more and nothing less behind Coop Himmelblau's theoretical concept than fulfilling an insatiable longing for "cities that beat like the heart, for cities that fly like a breath". Programmatic principles like these were first proclaimed openly in 1967, on the occasion of the "urban fiction" exhibition in Vienna. They were not intended so much as an unrealistic variation of early sixties metabolistic thought patterns, but as a direct reaction to the rapidly deteriorating urban development climate. At the same time as Haus-Rucker was designing its well-known pneumatic substitute worlds, the Coop Himmelblau studio was producing urban residential units with pulsating three-dimensional load-bearing structures (1966), the pneumatic "Villa Rosa" (1968) or the mobile, inflatable "Wohn-Wolke" (Living-Cloud; 1968–72). These were not – as was often supposed later - late-pubertal, uncritical glorifications of new space technologies for consumer purposes, but rather a *Sturm und Drang* attempt to work against current urbanism and architecture by de-materializing it and creating space for individual, nomadic dreams.

The quintessence of the European student revolts in the late sixties was present in all this like a tangible vision that was to be fulfilled immediately. It was not the individual who had to be changed so quickly and radically, but petrified late-capitalist society, to make it worth living in again. In this spirit, Coop Himmelblau, radically negating everything in existence at the time, demanded a fundamental transformation of urbanism and architecture, of tectonics and structure, so that future generations of urban nomads could be offered appropriate spatial configurations. They felt that the new approach to urbanism resulting from this and the three-dimensional structures constituting it should suit the human body, should pulsate, smell, sound, radiate colours, and be able to communicate with each other electronically. It should be possible to put mobile space units away in cases, then to inflate them within minutes to make air-conditioned coverings in which to live. It should also be possible to link them up with the aid of communications equipment. Coop Himmelblau's principal interest, like Pichler and Hollein before them, was centred above all on the changed, immaterial forms of communication within the society of new urban nomads they were aiming for. Chronicler Günther Feuerstein remembers all this as if it had happened yesterday: "Friedrich St. Florian was experimenting with rooms created by lights and laser, Hans Hollein denonstrated 'non-physical' environments; the extension of the university was a television set, an 'environment spray' created spaces of fragrance and the 'architectural pill', finally, had the power of simulating non-existing rooms: first presentiments of the idea of the electronic environment, an anticipation of virtual reality and yberspace. The same might be said about Coop Himmelblau, who employed their Soul Flipper and haptic vest in an attempt to transmit facial emotions and tactile qualities by simple electrical devices: their pioneering work dates back to 1969."[5] Coop Himmelblau's experimental set-ups for using the media to make heartbeats and movements of the face or body visible in the city, and for detonating explosives electronically from heartbeats, created sensations that can only be compared with those produced when under the influence of drugs. But above all they suggested new horizons for media to virtual forms of communication whose effects were largely unexplored at the time. Today some cyberspace experts are amazed that this pioneering achievement remained a brief episode without practical consequences.

Instead of moving further in this direction, their work in subsequent years seemed increasingly committed to Adorno's statement that art can only survive where it rescues its substance by denying its traditional form and thus renounces reconciliation, i.e. where it becomes surrealist and atonal.[6] But this quotation was referring exclusively to art, and not to architecture. And surely Adolf Loos, one of the supreme fathers of Viennese architecture, had offered his colleagues a way out of this dilemma decades before (though probably involuntarily)? Loos had already stated clearly in 1909 that people loved houses and hated art, so that only a very small area of architecture, namely tombs and memorials, were in the territory of art.[7] And so in the transferred sense it should be monuments, indeed sometimes gravestones, (alluding to the proverbial cultural and historical schizophrenia of the Viennese in their attitude to death), that would open up the narrowest possible corridor between art and architecture.

5

5 Wiener Supersommer, Cloud Setting installation, 1976

From the mid sixties at the latest Coop Himmelblau's work specifically stressed the principle of "atonality". In retrospect, the group's increasingly unruly appearances concentrated mainly on the "inhospitableness of our cities", something that the psychoanalyst Alexander Mitscherlich among others had complained about a decade before. Coop Himmelblau first attracted general attention in Europe in 1976, when Prix and Swiczinsky staged the legendary Viennese "Supersommer", an explosive mixture of "urban entertainment" and aggressive urban change under the cloak of art "actions". It was Günther Feuerstein who had linked city, architecture and art inseparably at the time: "City and art are 'considered' – not executed, people distance themselves … from cities even though people 'live' in them: but the city is only an empty, apparently semi-functioning covering for the banality of our everyday life, for the idleness of inert bodies: supermarket, underground, car-park, snack bar. And at home: tiled bathroom, infrared grill, television."[8] Feuerstein actually felt that the only way to overcome this inertia was by developing "processual architecture", using it to revive "human dimensions that had long been covered over, that are the only thing that can make the space, the object, the environment into what it is intended to be: into part of the human environment beyond conventions, free of all constraints."[9] Seen in this way, Coop Himmelblau's legendary "Wolkenkulisse" (Cloud Setting) for the "Supersommer" was intended less as a non-committal, temporary work of urban art than a highly symbolic occupation of socially contaminated communal territory as part of a "reconquista" of more human urban living-spaces. The initiators wrote at the time: "It is only outside impulses, and not acts of administration by the authorities, that can lead to an improvement on living conditions in the city. These impulses can be acts of self-help that repossess the urban space again. They will fill it up better than it has been filled up before by being

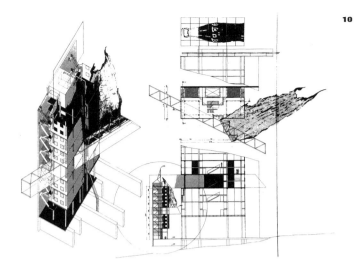

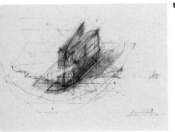

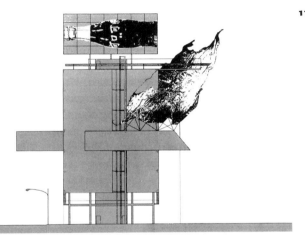

6 Vienna, Austria, Hot Flat, city apartment building, 1978, design sketch 7 Hot Flat, photo-montage 8 Hot Flat, model 9 Hot Flat, design sketch 10 Hot Flat, isometric drawing, typical floor plan, full and partial section, partial view 11 Hot Flat, elevation drawing

arbitrarily rampant and self-confident."[10] This led to a phase full of projects and campaigns involving symbolic occupations of public and private spaces that had been destroyed, complementing hard explosions, soft bubblings or uneasy mixtures of spaces like living cells and flying roofs.

URBAN POLEMICS

When transforming "dead spaces" into oases of self-determined nomadic life Coop Himmelblau, like many much more prominent comrades-in-arms (Archigram, Archizoom, Superstudio and others), very soon had to admit that the effectiveness of their criticisms of the city was in fact somewhere around zero. And so regardless of the first practical attempts at articulation, like the associative Vienna "Reiss Bar" (1977) or the Humanic Branches in Mistelbach (1979) and Vienna (1980/81), Coop Himmelblau's rhetoric and their projects became even more aggressive. The group now made a wildly dramatic appeal for an "emotional seizure" of the city and its architecture: "We have to discard everything that hinders this 'emotional act of using': the false aesthetic, sticking like smeared make-up on the face of mediocrity, the belief that everything that is disquieting can be beautified. Architecture is not a means to an end. Architecture does not have to function. Architecture gains meaning in proportion to its desolation. This desolation comes from the act of using. It gains strength from the surrounding desolation."[11]

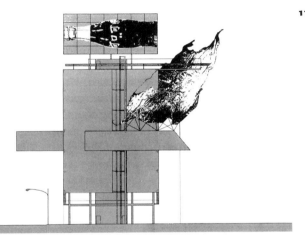

Following this theory of dilapidation, Prix and Swiczinsky, the terrors of the middle classes, launched countless projects to "injure the city", including "built angels of death", that owed less to Loos's reference to tombs than to Hans Hollein's reflections on death, and also "burning architecture". A key feature here was the "Hot Flat" residential project study, conceived in 1978/79 and ready for building. The block of flats, intended to provide five to ten units, was out of place to the extent of negating any urban context: it was intended to be built on the Hoher Markt, in other words right in Vienna's historic centre, to replace a multi-storey car-park by Karl Schwanzer dating from 1958. In principle the site was pure provocation, as strategically the building could have been placed anywhere else at all as an attack on the myth of the "mature city". Additionally, this block of flats was a "rough shell" in the best sense of the words, as all the rooms, which were about five metres high, were to be left as "rough shells", like abandoned factories or lofts, in other words without any interior decoration or furnishings at all, with the exception of built-in video and stereo equipment. The intention was to leave the old car lift in the core of the building when the conversion work was complete, which would have made it possible for residents to park their beloved cars outside their flats, on the balconies of the individual storeys. But the most striking feature of "Hot Flat" was the pier-like structure of the communal group space, which drilled diagonally through the complex at a precarious height and at night would have thrown gigantic flames – fed from countless gas jets – into the night sky of Vienna. The strategy was obvious: defeating "cold" urban architecture by emphasizing "coldness" and "roughness" and at the same time reinterpreting them as a poetically desolate time-signal, free of any contextuality, but deliberately intended to include ice and fire, the symbols of life. Flame-throwers in a military archaeology as intended by Virilio? Or just simply a similarly superficial spectacle to the Hundertwasser building?[12] At least one detail of the "Hot Flat" project was finally realized in the shape of the 15 metre high, actually burning steel "Blazing Wing" in the courtyard of the Technical University in Graz. The gas jets were lit on 9 December 1980 at 8.35 p.m. The noise of the flames was amplified by a sound system. Despite protective "water curtains" most of the panes of glass in the historic courtyard facades became so hot that they broke. "Burning Architecture" indeed!

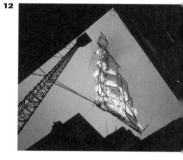
12

13

12 Graz, Austria, Blazing Wing, installation in the Technical University 1980 **13** Blazing Wing, sketch for the time sequence of the installation 8:30 p.m. – 8:45 p.m.

"Hot Flat" was intended to go beyond its actual purpose as a subversive urban development hypothesis or manifesto, but a further project dating from 1979 showed lack of piety with respect to urban development even more openly: the project devised with the Gerngroß-Richter team for redesigning the sacrosanct Karlsplatz in Vienna hit contemporaries like a threatening projection from another world. This provocative design proposed not touching the existing historic structures around the edge of the square, which were dismissed as "opportunistic", and putting a kind of lid on Karlsplatz instead in the form of a gigantic 158 by 556 metre slab suspended 15 metres above the level of the square. It goes without saying that this slab is intended as an implanted foreign body that would by its very dimensions reduce the Karlskirche and the Secession building to insignificance, and actually "bury" Otto Wagner's world-famous tram-stop. The increasingly dense residential development coming from the Wiental would have ended up in a Museum of Concept Art intended to climb diagonally above the slab as an urban vector; a 120 metre high steel wing on the slab was to have functioned as a new urban landmark. Ramps snaking out like an octopus were the only concessions to the existing city. The design proposed opening up the underground railway along the Wiental. The tracks were to be placed on high viaducts and taken right on to the slab in the form of a three-dimensional signpost in space and time. The arcades under the railway tracks would be avail-

15

able for multi-purpose use. It was absolutely clear what lay behind all this: the existing city was being refuted – Fischer von Erlach's Karlskirche and Olbrich's Secession building would have been nothing but toys in a shop window after an intervention of this kind – by obstruction and by introducing a charge of dramatically exaggerated space-time lines.

But buildings like the "Roter Engel", a wine and music bar completed in 1981 showed that Coop Himmelblau would be able to translate other projects than brutal ones of this kind into their own language. Even unrealized projects like the Elek House (1979–82), the extension to the Merz school in Stuttgart (1981), the proposals for converting and extending the "Alte Pumpe" in Berlin (1983), a second spectacular residential complex for Vienna (1983) or the theme of the "Open House", which has recurred constantly from 1983, seemed more positive, with a high professional quality in the models and drawings, and more concili-

16

atory than the agit-prop projects, despite all the gestural hardness. And then there were also two large-scale installations with a definite urban design thrust that could be seen as a rejection of the now exhausted agit-prop phase, but at the same time as a brilliant proclamation of new, non-domesticated urban energy fields. The Stuttgart installation "Architecture is Now" (1982) and its Berlin counterpart "The Skin of this City" (1982) were no longer intended to teach brutal lessons or to wag an admonitory finger. Instead, Coop Himmelblau concentrated on addressing the "unpleasant but real substance of the city, the urban building materials" in their relationship to space and time. Put more concretely, Prix and Swiczinsky were concerned that "those fields, the walls, roofs, and stable relations to ground and gravity that give us a false sense of security must be ripped open and something else, something alien, must be inserted."[13] – roughly as Frank O. Gehry, known to Prix and Swiczinsky only by hearsay at the time, had already demonstrated in California by "stripping off" his own home in Santa Monica, California. Real urban building materials like sheet metal, asphalt, tar and glass did their work in the urban model called "The Skin of the City", multiply layered and stretched over cross beams, three-dimensional in the space, while in "Architecture is Now" a crash barrier with a heap of steel and sheet metal moved in the simulated urban space "like a black panther in the jungle", resilient, penetrating interior and exterior, raising and lowering its backbone according to the level of strain.

159
160
161

THE CITY OF INTERACTIVE VECTORS

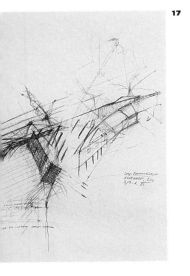
17

Reactive, mobile architecture should play a much more concrete role in the urban proposals made in "Skyline of the Media, Silhouette for a City Like Hamburg", created in 1985 as part of a workshop (Hamburger Bauforum). Coop Himmelblau tried to "make an invisible silhouette visible" by transposing two harbour edges and deliberately confusing the concepts of a harbour-town and a media-town. The project was in three sections called Skyline, Hamburg Buildings and Media Arc. The upper storeys of the Hamburg Buildings intended for the lively harbour edge were on stilts in the Himmelblau design, while the lower storeys were intended to float and move on the water, rising and falling with the level of the Elbe. Mobile "loft bridges" and a square hovering above the water linked the "floating objects". Several media towers were proposed for the container terminal right in the harbour, each over 300 metres high and linked up with each other. Coop Himmelblau offered the magazine editorial staff housed in the towers vector-like connections that swept out in all possible directions, to the media

18
19
20
21
22
23
24
25
26
27
28
29

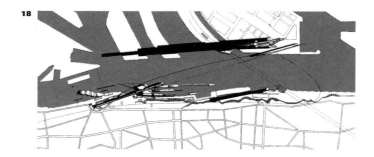

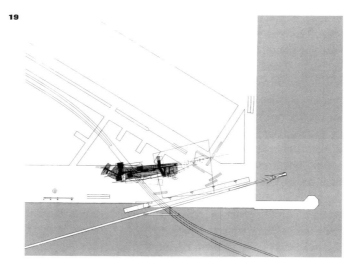

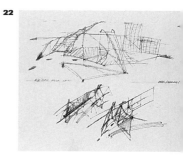

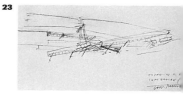

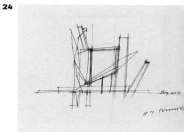

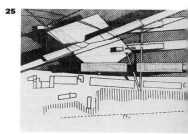

18 Skyline of the Media, Silhouette for a City Like Hamburg, site plan of the whole complex **19** Skyline of the Media, media tower floor plans in the port by the bank of the Elbe (+136m – +190m) **20** Skyline of the Media, ground floor plan **21** Skyline of the Media, section of the buildings at high tide **22** Berlin, Germany, The Skin of this City, 1982, first sketch **23** Hamburg, Germany, Skyline of the Media, project, 1985, isometric sketch **24** Skyline of the Media, section **25** Skyline of the Media, site plan of the Hamburg Buildings and the loft bridge with square floating above the water **26** Skyline of the Media, view of the 3 metre high model of a media tower

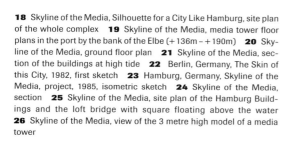

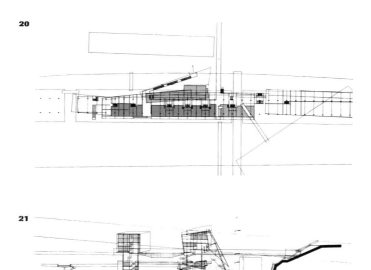

27

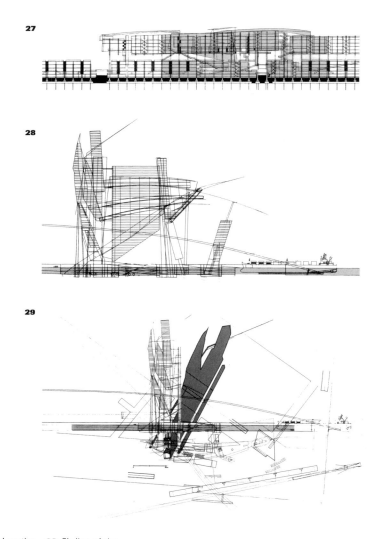

28

29

27 Skyline of the Media, longitudinal section 28 Skyline of the Media, "section A-A, the building seen through X-ray spectacles. 375 m high, 80 floors, 500.000 sq m organized three-dimensionally, occupied by 40,000 people." 29 Skyline of the Media, site plan, elevation, shadow of the first media tower

school, for example, to cinemas, hotels and shopping streets. But the towers themselves were the actual key to the project. They were narrow at the bottom, then spread out at the top as if struck by lightning, as if sliced vertically into bones, muscles and flaps of skin, built silhouettes of themselves, and yet entirely able to function, making up a breathtaking whole because kept just in balance. The surviving model of one of the high-rise media buildings is impressive not just because of its scale and hight of three meters. Long since housed in a museum, this vertical bundle of energy, literally bursting with dynamism, insists more than ever that it can be built and that its originators are proclaiming their will to build. There are some fine photographs showing Wolf D. Prix and Helmut Swiczinsky posing proudly by their "power package" trophy like head-hunters in old Hollywood films. With this project at the latest, Coop Himmelblau finally abandoned the detached urban utopian line of the sixties and seventies in favour of a criticism of conventional city planning for tomorrow's world. The approach is no less visionary but now markedly feasible and full of the will to be put into practice.

The recent extension of Himmelblau-style urban design – measured against the overall spectrum of the complex *œuvre* – was shown particularly strikingly in the competition for the new urban centre in Melun-Sénart near Paris, which won an international first prize for Coop Himmelblau in 1987. Starting with the first, rapidly sketched bundle of diverging urban directions of thrust and lines of actions, the urban texture, which at first seemed confused, became increasingly dense as it passed through numerous constructive (*nota bene* not "deconstructive") stages of transformation and transcription to become an impressive and entirely comprehensible urban vision for the 21st century. The starting-point was "Zoom City": finding hidden structures for the centre of three Parisian peripheries that were growing rampantly without any sign of a plan by gradually enlarging "an intensive drawing". Put more precisely, Prix and Swiczinsky used private "mental mapping" to research urban networks and vectors. The new town was to emerge from itself as a process, as it were, by the year 2010 in three planning phases and six thematic development stages: 1. Creating radial boulevards (fixing directions of movement), 2. working towards a little Los Angeles (installing networks of small residential buildings), 3. injuring the infrastructure (disturbing and overlapping the networks with long lines of lofts), 4. intensifying the infrastructure (introducing unpredictable dynamic elements), 5. breaking things up by the use of three-dimensional zoning (condensing and splitting up all the lines of lofts into 20 m high "sandwiches" to create a social and public area "in between"), 6. condensing the open city to the point of explosion (abrupt emergence of the provisional final state of the open city by increase of density and exaggeration). Post-Modern urban prettification strategies or ideas for reconstruction were thus countered vigorously, consistently and comprehensibly here with a neo-futurist urban organism, a regular maze. Walter Benjamin said that we should learn to lose our ways in the big cities.[14] And the design also incorporated dynamic elements like flexibility, speed, planting clues etc. just as skilfully as static elements of conventional town planning.[15] Rather like Zaha Hadid's Hong Kong Peak project or Bernard Tschumi's plans for La Villette in Paris, Coop Himmelblau's century-spanning plan for Melun-Sénart condensed to deliver an impressive lesson on the interplay of architecture and the urban layout in the form of a compressed metaphor of space and time. And didn't Daniel Libeskind's "City Edge" design for Berlin (1987) use astonishing analogies with Melun-Sénart at a later date? If one thinks in terms of Aldo Rossi's best-know "città analoga" the necropolis of S. Cataldo in Modena, it is scarcely possible to imagine a more systematic contrast than Melun-Sénart – a contrast that touches upon the core of the age-old conflict of "Gothic versus classical". But admittedly, unlike the "classical" necropolis in Modena, the "Gothic" counter-design for Melun-Sénart was so speculative, so unpredictable that it had to remain unbuilt.

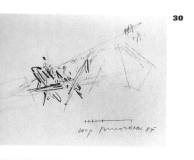

30

31

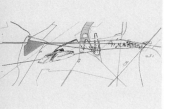

32

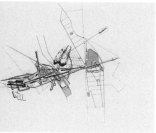

33

34

35

30 Melun-Sénart, France, The Heart of Melun-Sénart, project, 1st prize in international urban design competition, 1987, preliminary sketch **31** The Heart of Melun-Sénart, sketch of development pattern **32** The Heart of Melun-Sénart, drawing for key infrastructural facilities, site plan **33** The Heart of Melun-Sénart, site plan **34** The Heart of Melun-Sénart, preliminary model **35** The Heart of Melun-Sénart, model of the city centre

Prix and Swiczinsky went through two decades of architectural prohibition along the lines of "something like that could absolutely never be built", two decades with no money in them, and survived them with incredible doggedness and stoicism, but this competition success put an end to all that. It's true of course that the prevailing architectural and social climate had changed markedly: who would have wanted to risk even the smallest bet on "PoMo" in the late eighties? This had now been overtaken by "Decon" as the favourite in a scene that has always been hungry for "isms". It was a little surprising at the time to read that the French philosopher and structuralist Jacques Derrida more or less invented the concept of "deconstruction" because he was essentially doubtful about the authenticity of sacrosanct textures and the historically derived significance, and wanted the "*différences*" suppressed by these textures to be investigated. But surely architects like Peter Eisenman, Frank O. Gehry, Bernard Tschumi, Daniel Libeskind, Zaha Hadid, Rem Koolhaas or Coop Himmelblau had been advocating ideas like this for years, and even built them – and did all this without ideological support from someone like Derrida? This applies to Prix and Swiczinsky in particular, who had been "once bitten" and so were always on their guard against ideological takeovers by theoreticians of whatever hue!

36 Guadalajara, Mexico, JVC The New Urban Entertainment Center, The Simultaneity of Systems, 1999–2003, floor plan   37 JVC The New Urban Entertainment Center, floor plans   38 JVC The New Urban Entertainment Center, longitudunal section through the whole complex   39 JVC The New Urban Entertainment Center, cross-section   40 St. Pölten, Austria, Europaplatz, project, 1990, mass model   41 Vienna, Austria, Mariahilferplatz, project, 1990, mass model   42, 43 Mariahilferplatz, model 1:200

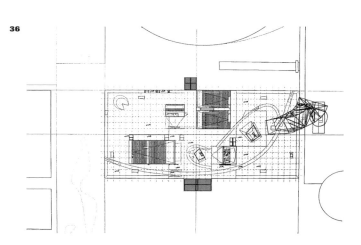

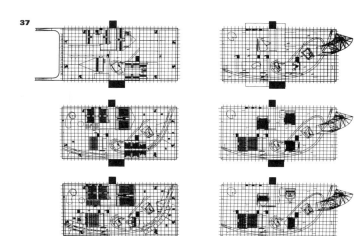

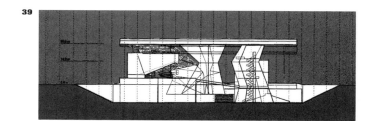

"Decomposition" was a concept that was introduced into the debate at the same time. It aims at deliberately fragmenting a familiar whole and then reassembling the fragments to form new patterns of thought and usage. But surely this "decomposition" was also an age-old phenomenon that has recurred cyclically throughout architectural history – we simply lost sight of it a bit because of all the trivial post-Modern rubbish? And surely this principle had also been advocated vigorously and committedly as a definite agenda by the same architects – with Coop Himmelblau in the vanguard once more?

In any case there were definite reasons why Wolf D. Prix, Helmut Swiczinsky and their Himmelblau comrades-in-arms were once more (or still?) attracting international attention. For decades the same old reproach had been trotted out that such complex, individualistic and rebellious three-dimensional pictograms or psychograms probably stood absolutely no chance of being implemented. This was now wide off the mark. More appropriate would probably be a version of a popular feminist song title of the eighties: "Coop Himmelblau come late, but come with a vengeance!" A story dating from 1988 is symptomatic of all this. The team had been accepted as part of the "Deconstructivist" pantheon at the suggestion of Joseph Giovannini and Aaron Betsky,[16] for the "Deconstructivist Architecture" exhibition in the Museum of Modern Art (under the auspices of the ageing *enfant terrible* Philip Johnson with Mark Wigley). When Coop Himmelblau presented plans and models for a spectacular roof extension in Vienna for the exhibition, their eminent co-exhibitors joked that probably such a "beautiful corpse" could never be built, unfortunate though that was. The response came back like a pistol-shot: "Come to Vienna, the roof extension is nearly finished!" In fact the team had been able to present "proper", that is to say completed, buildings for three or four years by then. Important projects like the Baumann studio (1984) and the Zugmann loft (1985) in Vienna, the Kon'yo Shen'the boutique in Tokyo (1986), the ISO Holding directors' suite in Vienna (1988) and the above-mentioned Falkestrasse rooftop remodelling in Vienna (1988) had been completed in the years immediately preceding the MOMA exhibition. These had again been followed by a large number of unrealized projects, but also spectacular completed buildings like the Funder Factory 3 in Kärnten (1988), the Follies in Rotterdam (1988), Osaka (1990) and Groningen (1990), the East Pavilion of the museum in Groningen (1994), the Research Center in Seibersdorf (1995), the Biennale Pavilion in Venice (conversion 1995), the UFA Cinema Center in Dresden (1998) or the SEG apartment tower in Vienna (1998/1999).

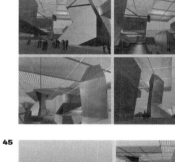

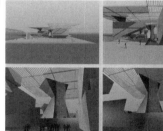

44 JVC The New Urban Entertainment Center, interior simulations
45 JVC The New Urban Entertainment Center, exterior and interior simulations **46** JVC The New Urban Entertainment Center, simulation of exterior view

But it was still the city that was more important than anything else for Coop Himmelb(l)au. There are clear signs of strategic changes that are not just verbal but also relate to design issues in urban development studies for a multifunctional service centre in the central Europaplatz in St. Pölten (1990), the new design for Mariahilferplatz in Vienna (1991), the redesign options for Prager Straße in Dresden (1993/1996), the design for the Place des Nations in Geneva and the centre for the new city of Guadalajara in Mexico (1999), where building was about to start at the time of writing. The proposal for the new centre of St. Pölten won first prize, and was effectively the last design that still contained echoes of Melun-Sénart. They will be discussed in detail in the chapter on "Design as Process". A chaotic tangle of invisible underground water arteries that could not be built over functioned here as a kind of random generator for their built counterpart above ground. In the Mariahilferplatz project Prix and Swiczinsky said that they wanted "to pull back the skin of the city to expose the nerve-bundles, thus making integrative architecture possible." This is a familiar strategy, but the combination they designed, consisting of a horizontal and a vertical tower with changing patterns of sound and light seemed more like a pragmatic intervention than a surgical one. But then in the design studies for

Prager Straße in Dresden they address transitory, i.e. temporary "condensers" as urban stimulants for the space between slab-built urban quarters. For the new town to be built on the periphery of the old city of Guadalajara – the whole "aristocracy" of the middle generation of architects are involved in this, under the direction of Rem Koolhaas – Coop Himmelb(l)au created a town centre that could hardly be less ambiguous or show more self-control for the sake of making it possible to build. Cinema centres, commercial, cultural and research facilities are assembled under a gigantic shady cantilevered roof and sunk into the ground to the level of several storeys to form a group around a spacious public piazza. The stupendous simplicity of the whole thing suggests reduced costs, but then this apparent saving is used to "sponsor" the "added value" in architectural terms. The details, like the tower sculptures and ramps, which are set diagonally, the incised media trench or the "exploding" media centre are only possible in the hard context of a profit-oriented project like this if the quality supports itself, as it were, feeds itself by economizing as an added value. Incidentally, a cloud formation crops up again at one point in the Guadalajara design and also in the proposal for the Place des Nations in Geneva.

"The city is like a field of clouds. The rubber-grid of a networked city," said Prix and Swiczinsky in a recent collection of theses on the subject of cities, in their usual simplistic and in part cryptic style. "The builders of the Tower of Babel were missing the material reinforced concrete. We are missing the material of the confusion of languages which we would need in order to complete it. There is no solution for the city. The strategies of urban planning operate on the matrix of diverging impossibilities. The architects have to choose one and claim responsibility for it. Clouds are symbols for conditions that change quickly. They form and transform themselves through the complex interaction of changing situations. Viewed in slow motion the architecture of urban development could be compared with patches of clouds. The vocabulary of urban planning should be placed in an architectural antique shop and replaced by phantasms still to be defined, which fluctuate and flicker like television screens after broadcast. The white noise of urban strategy, as a digitally networked system without hierarchy, is the play of suburb and periphery which will mold and determine the image of our cities and the quality they have to offer. The notions of centre, axis and spatial sequence will have to be replaced by tangent, vector and sequence of images. We should not regret the loss of public space, but reinterpret it as a fluctuating, networked media event. One which acts more like a semi-conductor than a sequence of spaces. The development of architecture is also furthered by strategies, which are compromised by searching for lines and fields of possibilities, tied together by chance, anti-logic and anti-authority. But the coincidence of systems – both as built space and as media space – becomes the basis for new designs and projects, the rubber-grid as the premonition of a dynamic design-net for cities like clouds. You cannot scare people more, than when you are going to dissolve form. That is almost an attempted murder on formalistic architecture."[17]

EFFECTS: CRITICIZING CRITICISM

Coop Himmelb(l)au's remark that they would be able (and willing) to complete the Tower of Babel only if a new form of linguistic confusion could be invented obviously refers to Jacques Derrida, who had said in an interview in 1984: "If the tower had been completed, there would be no architecture. It is only the fact that the Tower of Babel was made impossible that makes it possible for architecture and the whole diversity of language to have a history. And this history is always to be understood in relation to a divinity that is finite. *Perhaps it is a characteristic of post-Modernism that it takes this defeat into account.* If Modernism is distinguished by striving for absolute domination, post-Modernism is a statement or an experience of its end, the end of this plan to dominate."[18] Coop Himmelblau's chafing against the topos of the "Tower of Babel", which has recently become increasingly marked, obviously reveals injuries or "refutations" that they have suffered through the phenomenon of post-Modernism. The team had grown out of the heroic phase of the sixties and seventies, and had inadvertently stumbled into the middle of post-Modernism in the eighties. Fortunately they always avoided the troughs of vulgar semantics conjured up by Jencks and other shamans, and ended up correctly placed among the "*conditions postmodernes*". Today, in the "post-historic" age, no one doubts that these were real conditions. But for Coop Himmelb(l)au the arbitrary quality of the language and life games associated with this and practised everywhere meant that the team lost its comfortable revolutionary role from one day to the next and found itself pushed into the uncomfortable corner known as "house-trained" post-Modern exotic architecture or – even worse – the architecture of the orchid brigade. Thus they had willy nilly become an integral part of a movement that they had only recently denounced as "Biedermeier architecture on demand". And on top of this, what was the point of Coop Himmelb(l)au's aggressive designs when faced with the much harder aggression paraded on television screens day after day? And then all the fashionable drawing-room chatter about architecture! Surely the vain and conspiratorial revelations about how the New York MOMA exhibition on "Deconstructivist Architecture"[19] came into being are more like gossip in the gutter press than reasons that have been properly thought through? And were expressions like "PoMo" and "Decon" that tripped so easily from people's lips on these occasions, not absolutely disastrous as well? Disastrous because everything shown in New York had already been "labelled" before anything like a serious debate had even got under way.

Of course criticism of models for urban development in its hour of agony was growing in proportion to the increasing demand for non-conformist designs and consumable apocalyptic images, but so was criticism of the "triggers" suggested by Coop Himmelb(l)au for urban development alternatives. For example, Himmelb(l)au used the concept of "white noise", a pure, neutral hiss, as one of its many urban strategies. But Charles Jencks had criticized the team for this selfsame neutral hiss: "'white noise': the absolute saturation of information in Toyo Ito's liquid crystal architecture, or the extreme and violent complications of Lebbeus Woods' and Coop Himmelblau's work. Extreme reductivism, silence, is like extreme complication, noise, since both destroy narrative and organization; the former by a dearth of information, the latter by a glut."[20] But Jencks's reproach of creating nothing but a "neutral hiss" as a result of excessive splintering or dissolving came in principle from theses he was picking up from an older pamphlet attacking crooked architecture: "Deconstruction: The Pleasures of Absence"[21] – absence as a metaphor for the silence of architecture.

An almost forgotten seventies anthology called "Panik Stadt" (City Panic) seems much more revealing in this context. This deals with seemingly strange and entirely peripheral themes long before the current debate like "beneficial destruction", "cathedral shadows" or "staging destruction". The historian Michel de Certau wrote on the subject of the city as a linguistic metaphor: "Stories about places are improvisations. They are made from left-over bits of the world … The homogenous and traditional form of the report is made up of such heterogeneous, indeed contradictory elements. This shows us the relationship between the use of space and built order. On the surface this order appears to be hacked to pieces and perforated by omitted meanings, deviations and escapes: it is the order of a sieve."[22] The sociologist Henry-Pierre Jeudy countered the image of a perforated linguistic view of the city with his statement that making an aesthetic of bursting things apart and hollowing them out was definitely not an appropriate way of grasping the city properly. Jeudy says: "Analysing demolition … in the city cannot claim to have circumscribed the fact of the city more precisely, as though an aesthetic view of urban development was to be found again in the phenomenon of bursting apart, hollowing out the mythical presentation of the 'city as a work of art'"[23]

It certainly was important at the time to make this kind of interdisciplinary reference to the fact that every city effectively gives birth to an "anti-city" from within itself, and every order produces a counter-order, and that abundance always digs out a vacuum for itself. But how can all this be handled aesthetically, architecturally? The authors did not provide us with conclusions of this kind for a good reason. In this case a "left-wing" architectural theorist like Manfredo Tafuri spoke considerably more clearly when attacking experimental work by the so-called "neo-avant-garde" in the seventies. He was aiming principally at groups like Superstudio or Archizoom, but of course what he said also applied (although this was not expressed explicitly) to Coop Himmelblau's early work. Tafuri wrote: "The search for a possible avant-garde role for architecture – as in the 60s – while simultaneously using the analytical instruments of communications science (and here it is not even important how superficially or accurately this is done), causes a profound gulf to open up between some new experience and the Modern movement's traditional utopias. At the same time this means that the debate about architecture is reduced to dilemmas of the kind encountered by Russian formalism. It is therefore not surprising that Western European architectural theorists were stubbornly and uncritically interested in the Soviet avant-garde's experiences. Reducing architecture to an 'ambiguous object' within the total 'Merz' of the contemporary city means accepting the completely marginal role restricted to superstructure that current capitalist use of space allots to architecture today."[24] There we have it for the first time: the verdict that branded "atonality" in architecture as a confirmation of the capitalist system! We intend to show more concretely elsewhere how very much this verdict survive under entirely different general political conditions in the minds of those who are presently classified as "Deconstructivists".[25]

We are not really much cleverer today, but we do try to see social development, the city and above all the misery of the city in a different way: more productively, more soberly, more curiously, rather more like ethnologists approaching a "terrain vague". When Tilo Schabert says that Modernism made a monumental error because it thought that by telling the story of the world it was creating the world, and thus in fact achieved the opposite to what it intended, then this is just as objective a statement as the judgement that follows it: "The things from which it (Modernism) wanted to create its world – and it had to take 'things' – withdrew and in forms that emptied themselves depicted only a loss of the world, but not another world." But then it is interesting to see the conclusions that Schabert draws from this: "Anyone who says that there are no more stories to tell still tells them, of course. Anyone who says that cities are dissolving is still aware of the 'city'. It is not possible to describe the 'empty' mass of the modern metropolis without describing the architecture of the city. It is not possible to grasp the fact of the 'labyrinthine city' without the mythical image of the 'labyrinth'. There is architecture within all perceptions, especially in the perception of chaos, that 'yawning vacuum' in which 'nothing' is ordered. Something 'creative' is visible in the 'nothing' of the modern metropolis as it is in no other place. It is clear what this is: architecture and narrative. For the 'city' is an allegory of the 'world'. It is not about seeing nothing but nothing in the chaos of the metropolis. On the contrary, it is about seeing the creative something in this nothing that it shows so paradigmatically – and by no means paradoxically."[26] Perceiving and presenting chaos and labyrinth using architectural resources are not condemned either as an affirmation or as a post-Modern "language game", but even seen as real creative acts. Diana Agrest also requires us to "negate the city to affirm the city. It is the affirmation of the erasure of the city in order to reinstate its trace. The critical reading is taken from the subject: I am spoken through the city, through architecture, and the city is read through me."[27]

But other people take up the explosive force of counter-productive consummation of the city since the introduction of various new media and link the fragmented city or perception of the city resulting from this with our "fragmented bodies" or our "bodies in pieces". Thus Victor Burgin, in his essay "City in Pieces" is alluding in the first place to a passage by Walter Benjamin dating from 1936, in which Benjamin wrote: „Our taverns and our metropolitan streets, our offices and furnished rooms, our railroad stations and our factories appeared to have us locked up hopelessly. Then came the film and burst this prison-world asunder by the dynamite of the tenth of a second, so that now, in the midst of its far-flung ruins and debris, we calmly and adventurously go traveling." [28] Burgin spins this thread further by relating it to the omnipotence of the (TV) age of disinformation: "All the surfaces and all the pieces of the body form a complex puzzle we were once required to solve in order to become human. Like the elements of a building, the completed puzzle-picture holds together more or less provisionally: here, cracks may run wild under a calm facade; there, they may shatter a transparent carapace; and other structures may endure only in mute and fearful isolation. Today, the autistic response of total withdrawal, and the schizophrenic anxiety of the body in pieces, belong to our psychocorporeal forms of identification with the teletopological puzzle of the city in pieces."[29]

And what does all this have to do with Coop Himmelb(l)au's ideas of the city? One is tempted to say everything and nothing. In fact Prix and Swiczinsky had been handling the urban vacuum, the chaos of the city and its filmic fragments positively, that is to say productively for a long time. And they were always less suspicious of the "city in pieces" than of attempts at projecting questionable entities. As far as criticism by Tafuri and other representatives of the left wing are concerned, Coop Himmelb(l)au simply refused to come up with a general theory of urban development that was fixed unambiguously in social terms and thus open to attack. As counterpart to „sky building" Prix and Swiczinsky, as aging "angry young men" transforming the manner and messages of the Rolling Stones and other old rockers, indulge themselves by continuing to produce aggressive speech-bubbles, wandering to and fro between e-mail rhetoric and the emotionalism of old 68-ers. It remains undecided whether they are on the left or the right politically, to be taken seriously or ironically, understating or overstating, highly significant or oozing nonsense. The team's unspoken tactic of leaving the meaning of most things as undecided as possible, which we will have more to say about later, is the key to the fact that they have survived all these decades practically unscathed and "ageless". Scruffy buildings and surreal statements have been the self-defence tactics that have enabled Coop Himmelb(l)au to escape this or that "ism" with a "clean record" and to continue to produce an ideal combination of "crooked architecture and an upright gait".[30]

"There ought to be a surreal theory of the city," said Michael Mönninger, "that goes the whole chaotic way and picks up all the fragments that are inorganic, non-aesthetic, banal or completely invisible." He goes on to say that one could also see this surreal approach to interpreting the city as mourning or self-defence, "so that intellectually at least we can emancipate ourselves from the much-loved lucky showcases of medieval city vedutas, as there is unfortunately no way that leads back to them."[31]

Is it not true to say that Wolf D. Prix and Helmut Swiczinsky constantly addressed situations that initially suggested mourning or self-defence by trying to come to terms with urban topoi, long before theory declared these open for discussion? Would "Hot Flat" really have been suitable for urban marketing, or was it not one of the key attempts to present transitory, socially inefficient "non-places" as the "opposite of utopia",[32] long before the sociology and ethnology of Structuralism began to take an interest in it?

If Coop Himmelb(l)au were to be able to realize only fragments of their partially unambiguous, partially euphemistic strategies, then in fact that would have to be more than merely a spectacular change in the everyday business of planning. It should in fact be a historic opportunity shortly after the beginning of this century to make a start at least on settling all those vague promises (exploited aesthetically, and unfortunately only aesthetically to underpin Deconstructivism, up to the pain threshold of populist acceptance) that Futurists, Expressionists, "Organics" and Russian revolutionary architects gave us, effectively as outstanding accounts. "Open urbanism" in the spirit of Michel Foucault, what a vision! For in reality a museum pavilion, a UFA Cinema Center, a coach-house residential development, a high-rise block of flats are nothing like new urbanism. At best they begin to stimulate reading urban situations in a different way, and bring about unduly exciting discourses about the "*différences*" of the city. At worst– and even this would be achieving a great deal – they would be mere pin-pricks against the idleness of inert bodies in the urban space, thorns in the flesh of the city!

MASS AND TRANSPARENCY, CONSTRUCTION AND REMOVING BOUNDARIES – A LABORATORY REPORT

So far we have dealt mainly with urban development aspects, but we are now going to look more closely at individual "ingredients from Coop Himmelb(l)au's design laboratory", using selected buildings and projects; thus for example their work with contrasting pairs like mass and transparency, construction and deconstruction, lightness and heaviness, usefulness and "uselessness". Their radical commitment to "open architecture" produces specific processes in the course of which building structures that were originally hidden are understood, conventional static structures and ways of presenting things in plans are broken up, supposedly fixed components of a building become dynamic and imaginary spaces mutate into real time spaces as a result of Prix and Swiczinsky's particular design approach. As processes and design phases of this kind have changed in the course of three decades, they can only be seen and evaluated in the context of each particular group of works.

47 Heart Space, installation,1968   **48** Soul Flipper, installation, 1969

MIND-EXPANDING AND MEDIA PROJECTS

148
149
150

As mentioned above, Coop Himmelblau's early projects tried to investigate thoroughly plateaux of possible mind-expansion, configurations of spatial experiences with their boundaries removed and potential new communication horizons. Thus in the late sixties and early seventies they produced media projects that were often accompanied by actions and pneumatic prototypes. From today's point of view the mind-expanding media projects are interesting because they were real pioneering achievements. They include the "Heart Spaces" (1968), which were realized, in the form of mobile foil air-cushions stuck above the torso as well as stationary, transparent covers for space as "enlarged thoraxes". There was an electronic link with the torsos of the people taking part in the experiment, and their heartbeats were amplified in the form of acoustic and visual pulses. Or the "white suit" (1969) made specially for actions, with projection helmet and pneumatic jacket for amplifying recorded television images by temperature, smells and other tactile sensations. At the time this was a logical continuation of Walter Pichler's "Portable Living Room" (1967) and Haus-Rucker's "Mind Expander" (1967), which now admittedly seem like a visionary anticipation of fairly and very recent Cyberspace prostheses. Installations like the "Soul Flipper" (1969) are also legendary. This translated its users' current state of mind into colours and tones by electronically monitoring gestures and facial expressions. Experimental apparatuses like "Hard Space" (1970) and "Soft Space" were intended to reproduce this kind of experience on a larger scale. Thus for the "Hard Space", for example, three kilometre-long fuses with explosive charges were laid in the open countryside. Three guinea-pigs' heartbeats (Prix, Swiczinsky & Co) alone were sufficient to set off a series of explosions. In the short time occupied by twenty heartbeats this produced a body of explosions that could be documented only on film. It is an irony of fate that today, almost three decades later, artists like Roman Signer from Switzerland are following entirely successfully in the footsteps of the "Hard Space" with pyrotechnic installations and explosions triggered by people's bodies. The "Soft Space", a Viennese street "upholstered" by Coop Himmelblau in ten minutes with twelve thousand cubic metres of foam in toto, provided the necessary antithesis. Dynamite and foam as actionist metaphors, in the Freudian sense, for showing superiority and concealing? Günther Feuerstein felt that the essential difference between actionist tendencies on the Viennese scene and abroad in those years lay in wanting to realize things, being able to show them. Of course there are still echoes of ritual, liturgy and the fun of the Baroque theatre tradition in such installations. And of course the specific actionism of the Viennese art scene had a part to play as well. "The material actions by Otto Mühl, the slaughters by Hermann Nitsch, the subtle rituals by Brus and Schwarzkogler," Feuerstein remembers, "of course cannot be translated into architecture. But they are models, provocations calling for architecture that involves action. Hausruckers set up their 'Giant Billiards' in the *Museum des 20. Jahrhunderts* – and live in the museum. Coop Himmelblau fill the streets with foam and have their heartbeats trigger explosions. And Zünd-up dedicate themselves to the fetish motor-bike – while at the same time criticizing the machine."[1]

PNEUMATIC PROJECTS

After going through phases of hard or "incident" and "absolute" architecture,[2] it was Hans Hollein and others who gave some critical stimulus to the euphoric enthusiasm for new technology and mobile architecture. "Architects must stop thinking only in buildings," demanded Hans Hollein in the late sixties. While looking for buildings intended to be changeable and easy to transport without so much as a by your leave he came across "sewn" and "inflatable architecture" in 1968, and not just verbally. But he rejected even this kind of architecture, which for him was "fundamentally still (too) material" in favour of architecture that has to redefine itself as a medium from the bottom upwards: "Architecture means conditioning a psychological condition."[3] Although this did not prevent Hollein, who had tried out simple pneumatic objects even in the early sixties, from shifting his mobile one-man-office into a transparent inflatable – a "pneu" – for a time, to extraordinary effect in the media.

Regardless of all the euphoria about inflatable in those years, we should remember how great an influence Hans Hollein had both practically and theoretically on the subsequent generation and thus on Coop Himmelblau as well. "Form does not develop from the material conditions of a purpose," he stated categorically, "but from the nature of the purpose itself, from its spiritual significance, from the meaning of the physical reality. Spiritualization of the material leads to materialization of the spiritual. There is therefore no such thing as functional or functionalist architecture. There is therefore no constructive, structural architecture. A building should not express the way in which it is used, should not express its structure, its construction, should not be a wrapping or a refuge. A building should be itself. A building should show what it means."[4] Theses like these, which Hollein put into words as early as 1962, of course fell on fertile ground for most of the younger generation; but they tended to chafe against them rather than follow them directly.

49 Hard Space, installation, 1970 **50** Soft Space, installation, 1970

The late sixties' enthusiasm for pneumatic structures was stimulated and confirmed by great predecessors. Had not Buckminster Fuller, a "guru against his will" for the '68 generation, experimented with geodesic domes from as early as the fifties? These domed structures were simple to assemble and dismantle on any site, and could be made of practically any material – however inferior it might be. They were a kind of message of salvation in terms of mobility, transparency and minimalization of future structures. The system had even been developed further in the "Tensegrety Structure". And had Frei Otto not been addressing real "sewn architecture" for a considerable time, that is to say constructions and spatial enclosures in fabric? Warren Chalk of the Archigram group was therefore able to say in 1964, not quite out of the blue: "In this second half of the twentieth century, the old idols are crumbling, the old precepts strangely irrelevant, the old dogmas no longer valid. We are in pursuit of an idea, a new vernacular, something to stand alongside the space capsules, computers, and throw-away packages of an atomic and electronic age."[5] And so "bubbles" cropped up all over the place, and not just in Archigram's designs, in solid and soft, pneumatic units, supported by metal structures of a very high technological standard. The boundaries of anarchic architecture and retro-design were entirely fluid here.

Gernot Nalbach, for example, who like other Austrians had been experimenting with pneumatic structures since the early sixties, designed a wide inflatable armchair which in principle was made up of a field of "erect" pneus. In 1968 the designer Quasar Khanh built the prototype of a pneumatic apartment six metres high and wide, in transparent plastic, which had inflatable furniture and lamps as well as inflatable walls, floors and ceilings.[6] From 1967 at the latest prototypes of pneumatic balloons, transparent spherical architecture and urban "cell agglomerations"[7] started to appear in considerable numbers in Vienna. Legendary examples are the "Ballon für Zwei" (Balloon for Two; 1967), the "Gelbes Herz" (Yellow Heart; 1968) in Vienna or the "Oase Nr. 7" (Oasis No. 7; 1972) in Kassel, which Haus-Rucker-Co were able to put up almost as research stations. They were all bearing Günther Feuerstein's statement in mind, and wanted in the first place to realize rather than experiment, still less theorize.

Despite their boundless longings, utopia was not exclusively in the foreground for Coop Himmelbau either: "The city throbs like a heart, the city flies like breath. And an expanding feeling for life fulfills these imaginary cities. This urban poetry was sometimes confused with science fiction."[8] An abundance of vibrant sketches dating from 1968 and 1969, with titles like "Vertikale Stadt (pneumatisch)" (Vertical City (pneumatic)), "Pneumatische Stadt" (Pneumatic City), "Pneumatische Wohneinheit" (Pneumatic Living Pod), "Bewegliches Gebäude" (Movable Building), "Wohnzelle mit Kleidräumen" (Living Cell with Dress-Rooms) or "Architektur explodiert" (Architecture explodes) demonstrate how intensively the newly founded team addressed pneumatic analogies with architecture. The "Villa Rosa" (Pink Villa), designed by Prix and Swiczinsky in a number of variants, is still considered a key project in this phase of fresh starts and radical change. It was built on the scale of 1:1 in 1968, with a great deal of effort and expense, for an international architecture students' congress at the Technische Hochschule (now Technische Universität) in Vienna and later installed for a second time in the Museum für angewandte Kunst.

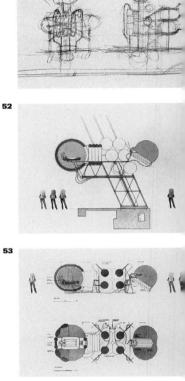

51 Vertical City, Pneumatic, project, 1968–69, sketch   **52** Villa Rosa, project, 1968, section, scale 1:20   **53** Villa Rosa, view and floor plan, scale 1:20   **54** Villa Rosa, prototype, scale 1:1   **55** Cloud, project, 1968–72, model

"The new forms," wrote Coop Himmelblau in the commentary on "Villa Rosa", "influence – supported through projections of colour, sound and fragrance – the quality of experience within the space. The pneumatic prototype is composed of 3 units: The pulsating unit with the revolving bed, projection and sound program. Through the ventilation system appropriate fragrances accompany the changing audio-visual program. The pneumatic transformable space. 8 inflatable balloons vary the size of the units space from minimum to maximum volume. The space in the suitcase – mobile space. From a helmet shaped suitcase one can inflate an air-conditioned shell, complete with bed. Neither pillars nor rafters, nor the construction itself is the goal of architecture. Since the erection of the first totem pole the goal has been dematerialization. The dream has always been release from the force of gravity. The pneumatic prototype in a maintainance structure."[9]

The core of the "Villa Rosa" was a slanting, three-dimensional load-bearing structure, distantly reminiscent of Lissitzky's speaker's stand, accompanied by a "clinical" labyrinth of tubes of various sizes. Large and small capsules or soft balloons were then fastened to these. The large ones were suspended on the supply framework drip, with sterile supply and disposal tubes, load-bearing ribs and "breathers", and contained revolving "pneumo-beds" with audio-visual installations above them. The smaller "pneus" worked like a kind of heart-lung machine with pulsating balloons, while the smallest housed the aroma capsules, the audio-visual programme unit and the "Indi-Heart". The exhibit was not accessible to the public, but Günther Feuerstein had repeatedly taken the opportunity of absorbing the full impact of the "Villa Rosa" and sensing the contradiction between the removal of borders and encapsulation, between embryonic secu-

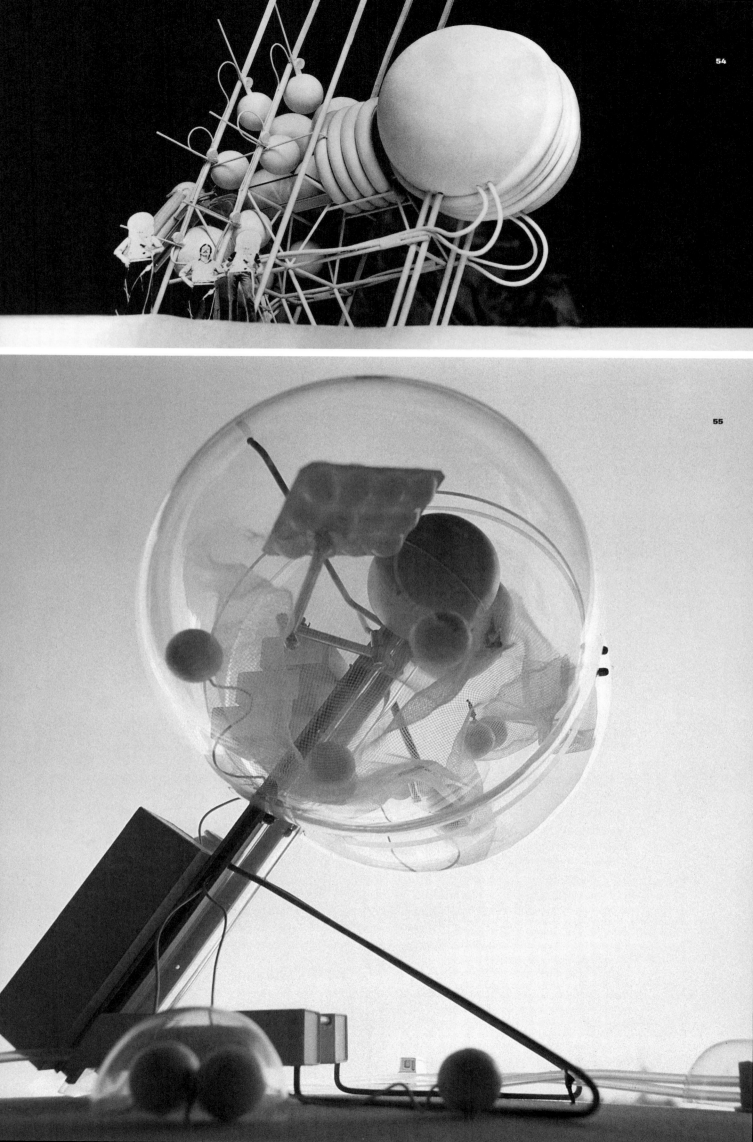

rity and painful exposure, between the Eros and the coldness of this clinical arrangement. "It is possible," Feuerstein noted, "to place yourself between the eight limp balloons and experience a sense of confinement increasing as the balloons fill with air, to the threshold of imprisonment. You can lie down among the balloons and experience a domed or spherical space directly – an age-old architects' dream – enriched by sounds and aromas."[10]

And so Peter Greenaway's "Belly of the Architect" had taken on three-dimensional form in the truest sense of the word long before its day. While most of the protagonists of those years bashfully dismiss designs of this kind as youthful peccadilloes, and distance themselves from them appropriately, Prix and Swiczinsky are still hugely fond of their "Villa Rosa". They identify a quite clear line of thought leading to their "Open House" (1983/1987), and they see themselves historically justified in their urge to make exciting buildings of imagination leap out of reality.

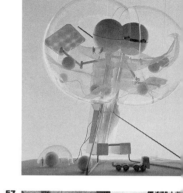

56 Cloud, project, 1968–72, model **57** Basel, Switzerland, City Soccer, action, 1971 **58** Vienna, Austria, City Soccer, action, 1971/72

55

The "Villa Rosa" was modified and perfected, at least on paper, in the form of more advanced projects like "Wolke" (Cloud) and "Wolke II" (1968–72). The concept now proposed a mobile support structure, similar to a fireman's ladder and hydraulically extensible, which could be put in (fighting) position at any time in any place; in other words it could be on the periphery, in the middle of a square or in a gap between buildings. Once in place, a labyrinthine, multi-storeyed structure of vertical steps, horizontal platforms, enclosing air cushions and skin-like bubbles could be unfolded. The particular location would have established whether this accumulation of clouds was a biomorphic, sociomorphic or technomorphic response to the existing site. So here there were at last: built clouds, or at least clouds that can be built! For some they are "carceri of the stratosphere", for others something like a promise. "Our architecture," and here Prix and Swiczinsky are identifying themselves with the clouds, "has no physical ground plan, but a psychic one. Walls no longer exist. Our spaces are pulsating balloons. Our heartbeat becomes room, our face is the building facade."[11]

58

It was fortunate that a model of "Wolke II" featured recently in the "At the End of the Century" exhibition (1999) in the Los Angeles Museum of Modern Art, as the only Austrian contribution from that epoch. Rather less fortunately the essay in the accompanying catalogue contained this statement: "Related designs for single buildings like Cedric Price's Fun Palace (1961), Michael Webb's Drive-In House (1963–66), and Coop Himmelb(l)au's "Cloud Project" (1968–72) probe the notion of the megastructure at the service of the utopian, and illuminate the roots of these ideas in the buoyant sense of possibility and experimentation that characterized the 1960s."[12] But designs of this kind had precious little to do with megastructures in the service of utopia. They were much more concerned with "housing for the future" and how it could be realized. For example, the "Cloud Project" was definitely intended for documenta V (1972) in Kassel, but then got stuffed away in a drawer, as so often happens.

But some temporary balloons were realized, like the "Unruhige Kugel" (Restless Ball), which trundled through Basel in 1971, along with the owners of the office in person, who had been welded into it. And in the same year the performance was repeated with a naked couple inside the "Restless Ball", trundling through the park in Schönbrunn. A paraphrase of Hieronymus Bosch's "Bridal Chamber in the Seed Capsule" in "Garden of Delights" triptych (ca. 1490–1500)? And at New Year 1972 Coop Himmelblau's "Stadtfussbälle" (City Footballs), six metres in diameter, trundled through the newly opened pedestrian precinct in central Vienna, greatly annoying the tradespeople, incidentally.

152

But then the gas-filled balloon called "Flying Roof" (London, 1973), intended to simulate removing (a roof) by lifting (a cloth), did not have the hard edge or the precision of the earlier projects. It seemed like a tired sign, a worn-out dramatic cliché. A seminar project with students at the Architectural Association had led to "mortally wounding" a terraced house, in other words it had been ruined by carefully calculated invasion and penetration; then a sheet of fabric was stretched over the roof of the torso, more or less like a shroud. A shiny silver balloon was fixed to it, intended to carry the roof away symbolically. But hadn't an artist like Gordon Matta-Clark's architectural splitting, punching and faulting in the sixties and seventies – received with a great deal of head-shaking at the time – not caught the explosive dividing line between destruction and deconstruction much more precisely and sharply? Aaron Betsky said that to Matta-Clark "building, the act of cutting and discovery is a process integral to knowing the world by living out its contractory orders.[13] Building as an act of incision and stripping, an important motif that is addressed for the first time here, was soon to affect Coop Himmelblau's thinking and actions.

The " Fresh Cell" project dates from 1972–73. It was the last repercussion of pneumatic architecture, and actually pointed to the field of socially conformist High-Tech architecture in a rather more conciliatory way. Coop Himmelblau were originally commissioned to develop a simple refurbishment model, but instead of an old-style roof they designed a horizontal glass and steel tube as a climatic envelope. The multi-storey tube in a densely built-up city area was intended to accommodate a "bio-climatic parking complex". If Coop Himmelblau had had their way, tubes like this would have sprung up to function as "green towers" in old and new building areas, rather like oases, "creating an autonomous biological climate". Thus the project was a kind of predecessor to the concept of ecological building that was to become fashionable later, but in a rather more diffuse form.

59

60

59 House with Flying Roof, Changing a Daily Reality, motion sketch
60 Vienna, Austria, Fresh Cell, project, 1973, model

FORM-MUTATION PROJECTS

The "pneumatic" chapter ended once and for all in about 1973, and was followed until about 1983 by an important working phase that is perhaps most easily described by using the title "Form-Mutation Projects". But we should not labour under the mistaken impression that these projects were exclusively about manipulating post-Modern colour. It goes without saying that this phase also involved social criticism, even though it was submitted to changed formal and structural codes.

The "Reiss Bar" in Vienna, completed in 1977, provided what some people thought to be a weak and others a brilliant start for this new approach. It could be seen as an interior decoration first for Coop Himmelblau. The brief was to convert the old Reiss Bar in a side alley off Kärntnerstrasse. The name says it all, thought Prix and Swiczinsky, and fished this quotation out of an issue of the National Geographic Magazine (1956): "The most fascinating thing about San Francisco is being in a city that is built on a crack in the earth's crust and never having that feeling." As the available 65 square metres were too small for the 66 clients the space was intended to accommodate, even in a bar without seating, but only 48 centimetres were needed to meet the legal requirements for this number, Coop Himmelblau decided that they would simply stretch the space by this 48 centimetres: "The stretched room, the crack ("Reiss" in the name of the bar suggests tearing or breaking), is the central concept of the room."[14] Even today, no one can agree about the way in which this concept was implemented. This was all solidified Pop architecture rather than a projection of symbolic faults, starting with its sheet metal-clad zig-zag crack via the two ceiling telescopes with giant screw fittings that span the space and break through the facade, and ending with the enormous nails above the bar. Typical Viennese "Neo-Mannerism" with an aesthetic exaggeration of the "Show me your wound" motif – or post-Modern decomposition architecture?

The next interior development immediately attracted very considerable international attention: it managed for the first time to regenerate these very qualities

61

62

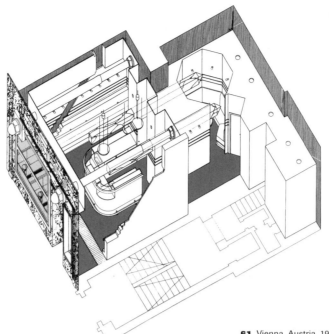

62

61 Vienna, Austria, 1977, Reiss Bar, interior **62** Reiss Bar, isometric drawing

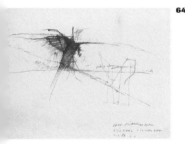

of architectural faults and mutations that are actually incomprehensible, and made it possible to understand them. This was the project for the "Roter Engel" wine and music bar, completed in 1980/81. Understandable in the sense that here for the first time we saw all the cuts, skeleton shapes, perforations and exposures that were later to be part of what could be called Coop Himmelblau's basic repertoire materializing in concrete form. An "angelic form", largely abstract, but entirely distinct in part, not only provided the complex structural framework for the rooms and the mythological references, but also worked as a large-scale, angular sound-box. "The angel of tone," said Prix and Swiczinsky, playing on the German word *Ton* which means both tone and clay, "is the concrete breath of the singer, the concrete melody of the musician, the materialized speech of the player on the stage. The formed vulnerability of architecture is the vulnerability of the singer. And above him – the Protector. The body of the angel is molded of plaster and glass blocks – who knows what an angel's body really looks like? – and is visible on the facade as well. The wings of the angel pierce the ceiling. They are distorted sheet metal rails with a stainless steel edge. And beween them, there is clay. The stainless steel tone line begins over the stage, ducks along the facade, breaks through the outside wall and ends inside in a needle point."[15]

155
156
157
158

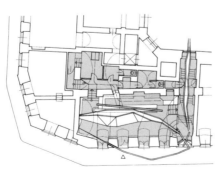

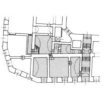

67

63, 64 Vienna, Austria, Roter Engel Wine Bar and Chanson Theatre, 1981, sketches **65** Roter Engel, sound line and angel from the outside **66** Roter Engel, extrior view **67** Roter Engel, floor plan after and before the conversion

33

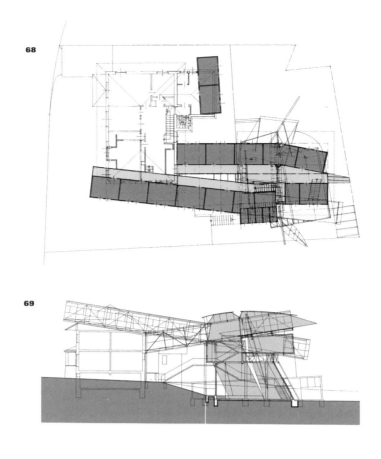

68

69

70

68 Stuttgart, Germany, Merz school extension, project, 1981, floor plan of the superimposed residential floor **69** Merz school extension, longitudinal section **70** Merz school extension, sketch

And they did something that they still love doing today. They quoted loudly from chapter 135 of Melville's novel "Moby Dick". They had found the image of the leaping whale there (which still fascinates them), but they had also found a passage that became their favourite: "Ha! A coward wind that strikes stark naked men, but will not stand to receive a single blow. Would now the wind but had a body; but all the things that most exasperate and outrage mortal man, all these things are bodiless, but only bodiless as objects, not as agents."And so there was their angel, captured in words: disembodied and yet distressing the body at the same time. And so "all" they had to do was built it. "Send me an angel" said a well-known pop song in the early eighties, and of course this angel was supposed to be absolutely bursting to have sex, and not transcendent like his Viennese counterpart. However, there was one faux pas involved that Coop Himmelblau were not ever to commit again: trying to achieve ethereal conditions of that kind by completely filling the storey above the boned-out ground floor with a banal kind of load-bearing structure.

The number of unrealized works continued to be large, and many of them were also dominated by winged beings; this included ambiguous works like the "Temperature Wing" for Munich (1980), or aggressive ones like the "Zer-schüttung" (Burial) of Essen University (1980). The 40 metre high "Temperature Wing" in a Munich park was supposed to sink when it was hot and rise when it was cold, while the potential liberation of Essen University from its urban isolation meant covering it up with coal clinker, a project devised in an "Ästhetik und Utopie" seminar, with Günther Domenig. Steaming mounds and blazing wings ("dampfende Hügel und flammende Flügel") would have provided an additional scenic boost for this return of the university to its original landscape.

Many of Coop Himmelblau's propositions were then dominated by technically inspired "nature analogies"[16] in the form of forked, winged or bird-like steel structures. Peter Blundell Jones, who found similar analogies in contemporary work by the "Graz School", offers a convincing explanation for this: "Animal figures are always interesting, for they are our biological cousins sharing our ancestry, sometimes our prey and sometimes a threat. For hundreds of thousands of years of our hunter-gatherer existence we shared the plains and forests with them, so it is hardly surprising that they inhabit our collective unconscious and play such major roles in our mythologies."[17] Scorpions, panthers and whales are still in Coop Himmelblau's intellectual repertoire today.

The emblematic project for extending the Merz school in Stuttgart (1981) should also be seen as involving this kind of nature-imitation analogy, as its originators pointed out that "the similarity of the plan to a bird is not accidental. It is intended." But far more important seems the emancipatory approach taken by this design for extending or rather building over an existing boarding school. The intention was that, rather like the educationally desirable way in which children grow out of the need for being looked after, veritable steel branches were to have grown out of the existing older building, and prefabricated residential wooden cabins would have been built into these. Isn't living in airy tree-houses like these an ancient childhood dream? "The apartment, the hall, the workrooms, the terrace etc." under the branches, said Prix and Swiczinsky, "are integrated, entweined areas, connected by steps, ramps, stairways. The static system complies with the concept of a differentiated disintegration of a house and thereby becomes a dynamic system. We called the project 'The Merz Boarding School or How A Fledgling Learns to Fly'."[18] Of course the name of the school suggests all sorts of wonderful but inadmissible intellectual games: from Dadaist Kurt Schwitters' "Merz-Bau" to the Viennese Merz – that would open up the floodgates to interesting speculations, but it would be going too far. Despite all that, this much publicized project was executed extremely professionally, which demonstrated Coop Himmelblau's ability to keep their subliminal architectural aggression increasingly in check, to reconcile it, mediate it, and indeed to give meaning; this was an ability that the team had first demonstrated with the "Roter Engel", and that they were to continue to develop in future, in particular for "educational" projects, for example the proposed conversion and extension for the "Alte Pumpe" youth centre in Berlin (1983). Berlin's ruinous degeneration, housing battles, Kreuzberg ghetto syndrome, crumbling Kurfürstendamm glamour and Wall claustrophobia were processed much more ruthlessly and openly to create a dialectical and didactic collage than was the case for declamatory architectural installations like "Architecture is Now" in Stuttgart (1982). Here an "undomesticated" hybrid architectural creature, locked in a museum and hurling itself against the bars like a wild beast created exotic shudders in the face of the grotesque.

The team still show unalloyed delight in more direct animal analogies, but it was to be expressed only by follies like "the long yellow legs of architecture" in Rotterdam (1988), "Folly 6" in Osaka, Japan (1990) or "Video Clip Folly" in Groningen, Holland (1990). The latter was set up as part of an international festival for the opening of the new Municipal Museum, along with other follies by Eisenman, Koolhaas and Tschumi. It consists of an imaginative rusty iron structure that has got slightly out of shape and is stalking on two legs, and thrusting out into the harbour like a crooked landing-stage. But the bridge comes to an abrupt end at a platform with a video installation on its front wall. A rusty iron box sliding up and down on a kind of third leg can shut in the platform and video machine as needed, that is to say black it out, so that the films can actually be watched, or open it up completely. At Coop Himmelb(l)au's express request "the box completely encloses the spectators, but only for rock video clips. It remains open for erotic videos, thus including the space on the bank and swapping round the conventional meanings of public and private.[19]

154

189
190
191

71 Berlin, Germany, Alte Pumpe youth centre, Project, 1983, perspective sketch **72** Alte Pumpe youth centre, model view from above **73** Groningen, The Netherlands, Video Clip Folly, 1989-90, side views when closed

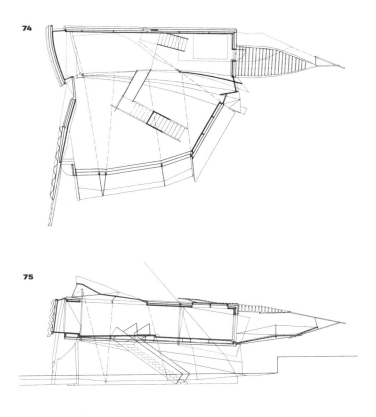

74 Open House, project, 1983, floor plan **75** Open House, section
76 Open House, first sketch

The provisional end and climax of the form-mutation series came with or comes with the "Open House" and the famous-infamous roof extension in Vienna's Falkestrasse. The "Open House" design, created in 1983 and revised in 1989, actually sums up Coop Himmelblau's credo better than anything else. The small dimensions of the house (100 square metres of living area spread over two storeys) tend to conceal the power package hidden behind it. It could also be called a buildable exploded diagram: ultimately the "Open House" derived in a completely concrete way from an emotionally charged sketch, further enhanced by being drawn with closed eyes. And that is exactly what this intellectual construct looks like, a hybrid mixture of ship and bird; in Himmelb(l)au's view it is "tilted body or curved skin". The condensed flow of forces hurled on to paper in the form of lines is reflected in the statics and construction. The building seems to float, as it is precariously supported and anchored at three points only. The anchor-point gave rise to the construction of a double-glazed skin with adjustable sun-protection slats. The tilt on the space encouraged the use of double wall and ceiling structures to adopt and adapt passive energy concepts and flexible fittings. There is no provision for dividing up the space, and the only access to the enclosed volume is by a staircase. If the client who wanted to build this project for himself in Malibu, California, had not died at an early age, the "Open House" could have seemed like a brilliant development of Bruce Goff's Bavinger Residence in Norman, Oklahoma (1955) or Herb Green's Prairie House in the same place (1961). But it would certainly have been a powerful development of Mies van der Rohe's Farnsworth House in Plano, Illinois (1950), and of its formal adaptation by Philip Johnson's Glass House in New Canaan, Connecticut (1949): a white time-space ship, suggesting that it was able to fly, positively bursting with optimism, but actually quite small (in terms of scale), and yet boundless. It curves gently forward into the space while stabbing into it at the same time, transparent and opaque, light and heavy, high and wide. The "feeling of the interior that is stretching the skin of the exterior",[20] made visible in this way, would have probably been a unique manifestation of the ambivalence that "open architecture" conceals within itself.

These contrasting pairs like transparent/opaque, light/heavy probably trip a little too easily from the tongue, and one could effortlessly add a few more, like constructive/deconstructive or useful/useless. But as they are very important both for the form-mutation projects and the "operations on the box" that we shall be looking at next, they should be differentiated by at least a hint of architectural theory. In fact even transparency ultimately turns out to be quite a tricky business. For a long time architectural theorists were afraid of a notion of transparency in which (as we can see happening today), "the object liquifies into a matrix of unstable yet constitutive relations."[21] Rowe and Slutzky, in their legendary essay on "Transparency" left the Modernistic trivialization of transparency well behind them by resisting equating transparency in a generalized and material way with "an inherent quality of substance". Instead, they suggested that transparency in the transferred sense should be seen as a visually intelligible organization of spaces stacked one behind the other.[22] So they continued to assume an axial perception from a static viewpoint. But given that glass facades have now long since taken on operative roles rather than having a merely illustrative function, the concept of transparency needed to be made even more precise. According to Dietmar Steiner it no longer means "clarity and openness, and not material translucency (any more). Transparency is (much more) a constant location of attentiveness and forgetting and everything in between. This makes transparency a perceiving movement that attracts attention to something indefinite at the appropriate moment."[23] The mind-expanding and pneumatic projects had scarcely any points of contact with Rowe and Slutzky's definition of transparency, but Coop Himmelb(l)au's buildings in the form-mutation phase and the subsequent series of works could definitely be read as "movement of perception towards the indefinite" in an extended sense like this. They could, if they had actually been conceived in the sense mentioned. But they weren't! With the exception of the most recent buildings, the eighties and nineties projects, including the "Open House", were in fact generated by the dialectic of "covering" and "exposing". This mean that transparency is only guaranteed to the extent that the covering will allow. Formulated on the metaphorical plane, transparency for Coop Himmelb(l)au is half surgical, half sensual in character. Only where the "skin" (and this is the word that Prix and Swiczinsky always use when describing buildings) is pushed back, opened up, folded away do we have an insight into the intertwined innards. So this is transparency as providing the "forbidden glimpse".

Thus voyeuristic, exhibitionist and similar aspects also come into play, via psychoanalytical conclusions about the design process and the way in which its results are received. It was no coincidence that Günther Feuerstein put a photograph of a wax figure dating from about 1800 from the famous-infamous display section of the Vienna anatomical museum in the Austrian catalogue for the Architecture Biennale in Venice in 1996. Presumably only a very few people have seen these life-size, amazingly realistic images of naked young women with their own eyes. Their jewellery on shimmering skin, loose hair and half-open eyes make the viewer feel that he has surprised them in an erotic day-dream. One blink later, from another angle, the image shifts: the belly of one naked beauty has opened up, one half of the face is cut away, another's trunk is sliced apart to create a sensation for the dissecting eye, an eye that is looking at an open body. The mixture of eroticism and coldness confronting injury and intactness is what is actually fascinating about these exhibits, beyond the medical and educational aspects.

"If there is a poetry of desolation," Prix and Swiczinsky had written as early as 1979, "then it is the aesthetic of the architecture of death in white sheets. Death in tiled hospital rooms. The architecture of sudden death on the pavement. Death from a ribcage pierced by a steering shaft. The path of the bullet through a dealer's head on 42nd street. The aesthetic of the architecture of the surgeon's razor-sharp scalpel. The aestetic of peep-show sex in washable plastic boxes. Of the broken tongues and the dried up eyes. And that is how the buildings have to be. Unpleasant, rough, pierced."[24] Of course they had moved some way away from these horror scenarios with the "Open House" (1983) and the rooftop remodelling in Falkestrasse in Vienna (1988). But what remained (and this is

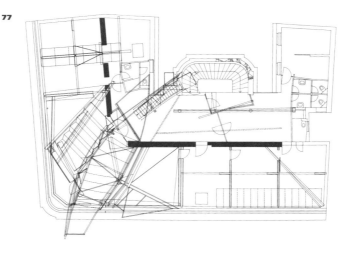

77

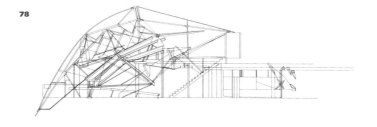

78

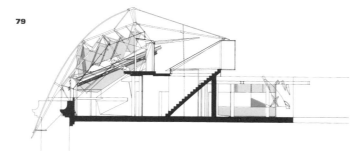

79

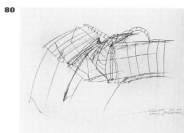

80

81

77 Vienna, Austria, Falkestrasse rooftop remodeling, 1984–89, floor plan **78** Falkestrasse rooftop remodeling, section **79** Falkestrasse rooftop remodeling, section trough the conference room **80** Falkestrasse rooftop remodeling, first sketch **81** Falkestrasse rooftop remodeling, exterior view

true to the present day, with certain reservations) was an emotional interlinking of covering and exposing, rather than using "naked", or better, neutral high-tech transparency. Coop Himmelb(l)au had never been concerned with neutrality: "Neutral architecture as a neuter, as putty in the hands of developers, challenges one to rethink the meaning of the term 'architecture' ... Architecture as a professional, lifeless product would be the holocaust of every spatial concept."[25]

Coop Himmelblau's spectacular rooftop remodelling in Falkestrasse in Vienna (1988) pushed emotional handling of covering and exposing just about as far as it would go. And in fact this extension or conversion project arose from something quite ordinary. A barristers' chambers, which already occupied offices in a multi-storey, listed Ringstrasse mansion in Falkestrasse on the mezzanine and first floors, wanted to expand into the roof space above a corner section of the building. As the conservation authorities wanted to put in a word it would have been easy to obey in anticipation and think up a post-Modern piece of bay-window camouflage adapted to the 1870s building stock. But not Coop Himmelblau. At a height of 21 metres, Prix and Swiczinzsky packed two floors, each 3.9 metres high and 200 sq m in area for the central conference room, offices and side rooms, under a "space-creating bow". The starting point for the "tight packing" was neither a bird nor a wing this time: the first thought was of a flash of lightning or a drawn bow. At the drawing stage the architects say that they developed this into a "visible energy line" aimed at the corner situation, "spanning the project from the street, smashing through the existing roof and thus opening it up … This space-crating, drawn bow – an element in our architecture that has become increasingly important since 1980 – is the steel backbone of the project. And that of (our) approach … The differentiated and differentiating construction system, a mixture of bridge and aeroplane, translates the spatial energy into built reality."[26] Even today this plasticized wound dressing on a corner of a roof that has been broken open seems almost as provocative as Le Corbusier's plastic work for the roof garden of the Villa Savoye and the roof gardens of other house projects did in its day. While Le Corbusier saw roof gardens as a coherent component of his Five Points and used the plastic roof structures to the same extent as a wind-shield and programmatic reference to the sculptural intentions of his cubist alter ego, Coop Himmelblau's roof solution is first and foremost a tangible piece of friction with the existing building stock. The injury inflicted does not produce – and this is different from Matta-Clark's approach – an open wound, but a surgical implant, a modern prosthesis. And so in contrast with adapted animal analogies, this is a high-tech project, appearing both self-consciously as an artistic installation, and also taking up the old Viennese game of covering and exposing. In addition, instead of intruding into the scarcely perceived, closed roof volume, it is transformed into an open, floating labyrinthine body that it is not easy to interpret, with a high symbolic quality. Coop Himmelblau also use a roof garden, or better, roof terraces. One of them even curves in the form of a balcony into the large conference room. It is only possible from this balcony to look over the curved "backbone" down into the street. Coop Himmelb(l)au have paid a great deal of attention, even in this apparently ephemeral project, to which views should be "released" and which "blocked".

A wild and expressive structure like this one, apparently light as a feather, would have to be very effectively connected with the existing substructure, and provided with a very consistent internal structure if it was to have the desired prosthetic effect. Thus this apparently chaotic "dental bridge" has a structure made up of four layers that are calculated entirely rationally. The first deals with the anchoring system. A refined steel and reinforced concrete structure conveys loads into the existing building, which avoids having to transmit central loads and transverse loads to non-reinforced sections, like the chimney and the exterior walls. The second level is the primary steel construction. The main support is the visual and structural backbone of the building. The prestressed hinged girder, which is bent through three dimensions and supported laterally, spreads over and spans the existing roof edges, thus providing the envelope for the conference room. The lateral supports define and differentiate the distorted glass pulpit in spatial and structural terms. The third level is made up of a system of secondary support structures. These are identical with the shape of sculpted areas and volumes that modulate the light and the space. The fourth and last level contains the lighting system. Daylight is controlled by complex systems of fixed and mobile membranes. This creates the unusual mix of cave and open perch. Points of light distributed throughout the space – halogen spots, neon tubes, indirectly lit areas and specially designed light piers – underline the spatial quality at night. At night this supposedly uncontrolled, anti-tectonic, rearing roof extension sparkles like a magic, theatrical crystal.

It was left to Charles Jencks to call a play of forces staged in this way a "Frenzied Cacophony". "Using leightweight tensile elements in juxtaposition, they have created that airy, scratchy filigree of complex lines and angles which architects as diverse as Peter Cook and Daniel Libeskind have projected in drawings. Thin white lines of steel jump about and cross in contradiction. Leaning or tilted structures play off each other achieving a dynamic balance. I-beams and diagonal cross-braces collide at a dissonant angle. These creations have an affinity with the 'tensegrity structures' of Buckminster Fuller playing compression versus tension, but they are rhetorically complex and redundant, not efficient."

173
174
175
176
177
178
179

Jencks called the roof extension in Vienna "a riotous *mélange* of twisted and warped shapes which resembles a dead pterodactyl that has crash-landed on the roof. There is no calm and perfection to set off the cacophony, unless it is the classical architecture below. Nonetheless the thin steel lines, which slightly bow and strech, have a taut beauty. Their counterpoint is so tense that it seems the architecture would explode into life if one tendon were cut. Perhaps it would. In any case this is the image of dynamic, moving, balancing forces frozen into architecture."[27]

We can still sense the fascination that even Jencks could not avoid in this sharply-worded criticism with its convoluted metaphors. Admittedly his remarkable reference to Buckminster Fuller's "Tensegrity Constructions" suggests more questions than answers. How is the roof extension constructed? Does that construction look light or heavy? Does it seem to float, or does it weigh down heavily on the corner of the building, filigree but immovable? Is this a triumph for the "avant-garde" in the form of floating dematerialization over the "restorative" weight of the historicist substructure? No hasty answers, please. Even the materials have a whole range of different visual qualities. An old master of structural analysis, Edoardo Torroja, does indeed say that the idea has its place before and above any calculation; i.e. that design intentions dominate its material conditions. But then he casually states that while natural stone, brick and solid concrete express stability, massive building style and calming through their statical qualities, steel creates a certain nervous carefree quality and also a highly developed sense of tension.[28]

In the course of the debate about the pros and cons of classical Modernism we quickly got used to defining and acknowledging a floating quality as a characteristic of the avant-garde. As statics experts usually confront the concept of floating with complete incomprehension, it would of course be more precise to talk about an impression, an architectural simulation of floating. Surely we had to identify with suggested situations involving floating, never mind whether they were expressed in utopias or realized buildings, simply because critics from the conservative camp tried to denigrate them as signs of cultural degeneracy? "Even if these tasteless phantasms are entirely meaningless for the architecture of the day," wrote Hans Sedlmayer in 1948, alluding to the work of the Russian Constructivists, "they also represent symptoms of a denial of the tectonic that here do not arise from the thinking of engineers, but from the spirit of Expressionist painting which makes everything unstable and makes tectonic forms tumble around in its pictures as if in an earthquake or an intoxicated state."[29] Sedlmayr put things rather more concretely in relation to Le Corbusier's "floating buildings, which always seem to get lighter towards the bottom". Starting with French Revolutionary architecture and coming right down to the masterpieces of classical Modernism, he felt that floating architecture, flying buildings, in short the will to stand out against in contrast with the primal ground were nothing but manifestations of the end of Western culture, and therefore to be resisted.

Later observers have seen the "floating syndrome in architecture" in much more subtle shades and like Adolf Max Vogt came to the conclusion that Corbusier and others, who were "already almost on the side of promenade sculpture" had actually looked for the floating experiment as "a long-prepared provocation, … a scandal that they sought for".[30] It was also Vogt who said that the cosmos was „scarcely open to being depicted statically any more", at the latest since Newton's theory of gravity, "but only dynamically. No artistic genre," he went on, "can manage without reflecting its own preconditions, that is its materials and working processes. It by no means does this merely verbally, as part of the accompanying theory, as discussion – it does it primarily in the handling of the materials themselves, which means that they are stamped into the product as an articulating force. For architecture this means: discussing its own 'physics', as a choice of material, as a calculation of forces, as a formgiving process. Wölfflin and his contemporaries called this kind of 'physics' a 'basic theme' of architecture … tracking down and perceiving a 'basic theme' does not happen only and above all not exclusively through the eye, but also through the other senses, which are in a position to set up an interplay between one's own physical experience and the artefact."[31]

The basic theme of an architecture that pretends to be weightless has obviously so fascinated us that in the course of the Deconstructivism debate historical examples of Tatlin, Leonidov, Melnikov, Le Corbusier and Hannes Meyer are quite unscrupulously exploited in terms of fatherhood or motherhood despite expert objections.[32] Despite a whole range of social motives for buildings projections or buildings from the heroic phase of classical Modernism, the floating or lightness syndrome is addressed only in terms of the fact that it can be reproduced formally and aesthetically. Adolf Max Vogt has emphatically pointed out how questionable such fallacies are in two recent publications. He has also asked why art, the humanities and architecture set off down this road. "This early deviation by Modern architecture: away from conflict and on to the utopia of harmony is doubly remarkable because it stands out so sharply against things that were happening at the same time in kindred arts and the humanities. Kindred arts: just think of Picasso, who was involved in conflict painting all his life – in complete contrast with his contemporary Le Corbusier, who indulged in utopian idealism from 1928 onwards and did not come back to articulating conflicts until after the Second World War. The humanities: their most important exponents turn to tracking down and revealing conflicts despite enormous resistance from the bourgeoisie. Four consecutive generations have worked on the idea, using the catchwords 'demythologization' and 'subversion', from Sigmund Freud via Rudolf Bultmann to Roland Barthes, from early women's studies, which opened up the way to demythologizing the patriarchate, down to the fourth generation of subversives, which includes Habermas and Theunissen as well as Kristeva and Derrida. Why did architecture, in complete contrast with painting, for example, scarcely pay any attention at all to this Freud-inspired work at the frontiers of conflict, but distanced itself by getting involved in floating dreams that get lost in a utopia of harmonized perfection?"[33] Vogt pulls even fewer punches in his criticism of Le Corbusier. "It is true of both artists, of the Russian (Lissitzky) and the Western European (Corbusier): they are celebrating lightness, and they are doing it to that finest degree of striking the balance where physical floating can be suggested – as a balance between (floating) body and aerial (surroundings) … It is clear that it was Le Corbusier's fascination with floating that made him blind to the disadvantage of lost space – and blind to … warming earth, fertile earth, which is not only rendered speechless in the Carpenter Center by 'cold cement', but even more so by the virile construct of taking off that is intended to secure the floating effect."[34] In this way Vogt addresses the problem of "lost spaces" for the first time, which are almost inevitably produced by arrangements of floating architecture. Coop Himmelblau had been responding to this intuitively for some time, and they had done it by tipping spaces up or twisting them round. Wolf D. Prix says: "This tilting creates spaces beneath the buildings that can be opened up to the surrounding area."[35]

But our assessment of architecture that seems to float or simulate lightness is threatened from a quite different side: the avant-garde hankering after weightlessness, transparency and speed seems to have produced a new need for repose, slowness and heaviness recently. So Joseph Hanimann says that "spatial concepts are imposing themselves that suggest that weight is not to be found simply at the bottom, by the foundations, and lightness high up above in the freely available sky. Spaces in which ground and horizon blend into each other, in the way that architectural theorist Greg Lynn suggested using Rudolf Arnheim's image of the cave as an example."[36] I shall return to this subject later. Hanimann alludes to Le Corbusier's thesis of the roof as the fifth facade, and puts in a plea for regarding the foundations as the sixth facade. This would render facade problems with their superficial alternative "stony heaviness" versus "glassy lightness" obsolete. "Norman Foster's design for Wallot's Reichstag building in Berlin," says Hanimann, " was originally based on a model like this of historically differentiated spatial density arising from convention and innovation, monument and instrument, base and zenith, lightness hanging low and heaviness striving upwards. But people pulled Foster's planned metal and glass baldacchino around so much that all that was left was the glass spiked helmet above the Reichstag and we were back to the old spatial convention: heavy at the bottom and light at the top. And in between, and people continue to believe this, the path of progress leads continuously upwards against the inhibiting force of everything that pulls back down into the depths of old-fashioned ideas in the form of mass resistance."[37] And so heaviness as a sign that has been used for decades for old-fashioned ideas is now seen positively again: "heaviness striving upwards" as a social corrective for "lightness hanging low". One might think here of the Berlin architectural dispute on this topic if removing the taboo from heaviness did not have a much more serious background. Heaviness is intended to offer a stay, support and new prospects to the gradual disappearance of architecture as expressed in Virilio's fears, but above all to a nomadism which is no longer more than loosely linked with "non-places". This would bring the shining concept of lightness proposed by ethereal Modernism back to the level of social reality, that it to say it would be restored to the robust dialectic of soaring up and bearing down.

The conclusions from all these considerations seem all the more important as even today Coop Himmelb(l)au's work still attracts descriptions like "light as a cloud", "filigree", "floating" or even "flying". The precise opposite is often the case. Anyone who has actually seen structures like the Falkestrasse roof extension and knows their building history in terms of materials will know what I am talking about: these are very robust machines. They are both light and heavy: light, where it is artistically feasible from a professional point of view, and heavy where it is inevitable, for equally professional reasons. Coop Himmelb(l)au do not have even a nodding acquaintance with the academic debate about lightness and heaviness, but for a long time now they have had an imaginative romantic idea at their fingertips to describe what the team understands by a balance of forces. "Have you ever seen a leaping whale?" asked Prix, and he doesn't only put the question to his American students. "I saw one in San Francisco and it was fantastic. I would like to compare this way of drawing with a leaping, chaping whale. I was in a boat and the water was very calm but I could feel that there was something moving under the surface. All of a sudden the animal emerged and jumped 15 metres high. You have to imagine it: a 30-tonne, floating, flying object."[38] It was even the most important motif in the 1996 Venice Architecture Biennale catalogue: "A jumping whale. A whale, a fish, that is not a fish, changes from one medium to the next, and in the moment when it moves from water to air, 30 tons fly."[39] This is what Coop Himmelb(l)au dream of: they want to be able to make something heavy float visually, even if it is only for fractions of a second, without denying its weight. The aim is not to invent "lightweight structures", but to see "open space" as "lightweight", individually and socially, in other words physically and psychologically, in terms of urban space and formal aesthetics. This leads to unmistakable "placings" and spatial and structural configurations that are not just a neutral backcloth, but want to involve all our senses.

And so the Falkestrasse rooftop remodelling to some extent marks a first modest triumph for "open space" over the old city, but another, much more capacious "roof extension" marked what is so far Coop Himmelblau's greatest defeat. This is their expert report on the revitalization of the Ronacher Theatre, which won the team a first prize in 1987, and yet fell victim to political despondency despite all the announcements that it was to be built. One fact that was perhaps not the most painful thing at the time, but still gnaws at their self-confidence, is that this project could have provided a clearly defined "visiting card" of the very first order a stone's throw from their own office. The Ronacher variety theatre, an 1870s building, was very run down at the time. The plan was that its facade should remain largely untouched. The extension work and new build would have concentrated solely on the raised roof storeys, as in the Merz school in Stuttgart. "We thought," the architects wrote in their report, "that we would 'publish' the main and rehearsal stages, which we achieve through multi-functionality (possible conversion, adaptable space). We thought of a roof terrace with open-air stage, we thought of restaurants in the basement and on the roof, of an open videotheque and bars in the foyers. But the Ronacher is not just a 'theatre building': the constant presence of television has made it into a gigantic media production machine for cultural exports. Publicity means seeing and being seen. The outer form of the building is a self-confident presentation of all these possibilities."[40] There we have it, the image of the production machine. In

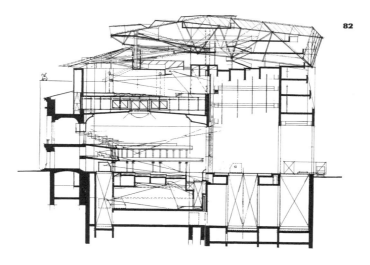

82 Vienna, Ronacher Theatre refurbishment, project, 1987, longitudinal section

fact the machine-like structural apparatus was intended to sit on top of the old building like a massive storm hood, to soar up above it. And incidentally here too we can see the ambivalent dialectic of light and heavy at work; here too we can imagine the metaphorical lines of a whale leaping over the silhouette of the city of Vienna.

"OPERATIONS ON THE BOX"

For the catalogue of their individual exhibition at the Venice Architecture Biennale, Prix and Swiczinsky drew a diagram that looks very serious, indeed almost scientific at first glance. It allotted individual projects and appropriate concepts to the individual letters of the "company name". It is only when you look again that it becomes clear that all the irony, verbal wit and language games on this diagram do nothing but paraphrase their own name. Trying to filter precisely outlined phases of work from three decades of architectural „cross culture", matched in terms of time, is a pretty tall order in this context, if not an impossible one. Particularly as Coop Himmelb(l)au constantly and frequently quite spontaneously go back to earlier "language particles". The team still identifies itself with its past works without exception, and so this does no harm to their architectural self-perception. And this kind of architecture seems to rule out literal repetitions (and also any suggestions of plagiarism). But there is one group of works from a certain phase that is still continuing that Coop Himmelb(l)au themselves define as "operations on the box". This title does not mean something like more conformist architecture, but new thinking and working approaches, whose roots go back to the team's beginnings, despite constant modification.

As friction with the closed box is a *sine qua non* for Coop Himmelb(l)au, the processes and instruments used to articulate this friction are at least as interesting as the results. Approaches like this had been mentioned before, perforating the box, for example. As early as 1978 a 54 metre long aluminium needle ("Vektor") drilled its way through a historical box, and that was Olbrichs Wiener Sezession building. And as already described, in 1978 an arrow-shaped, inflammable structure thrust diagonally through the box shell of "Hot Flat" as an extension of the communal floor. A happy find for those who see this in the Freudian sense as more or less violent erotic displacement activities: "A violent symbol of deflowering and penetration dominates the building's peak at the level of the golden section, where a girder-like element of glass and steel, a full two storeys in height, stabs right through the building at an angle. A leaping flame of glass springs from one end like a torch and cuts through the apartments on the upper floors."[41] Even Günther Feuerstein, a long-standing source of stimulus to Coop Himmelb(l)au who is truly above suspicion points out that in projects like "Hot Flat" the "theme of injury is modified particularly as a complex penetration process".[42] But seen in this way the whole history of art and architecture would probably consist of a complex knotted cord of artistic acts of sublimation. We therefore turn to more straightforward, but not less striking operations on the box that have been built or are about to be built. Let us make a start with the factory called "Funderwerk 3", which dates from 1988–89 and has been extremely widely published.

The commission was to design the finishing shop of a paper-coating factory in St. Veit, Glan in such a way that it would stand out from the anonymous container architecture of faceless industrial areas. Coop Himmelblau dismantled the box, sticking closely to its planned use, into three-dimensional units, and transformed the plain production shop into an unmistakable structure made up of head, torso and trunk. So there are three parts: an energy control room, an office and laboratory wing and the factory hall, which is immediately adjacent. This would not be particularly exciting if it did not include the power control room's "dancing chimneys", the "media bridge" as a connecting element between energy and production, the wide span of the "flying roof", the corner of the lab and office wing, which dissolves into glass to the south or is tipped up diagonally, and finally the finishing shop. It is studded with garish, ironical sculptural fittings (Wolf D. Prix likes entertaining his lecture audiences with quirky explanations of these). It has a flat roof, designed with a "red comb" that is visible for

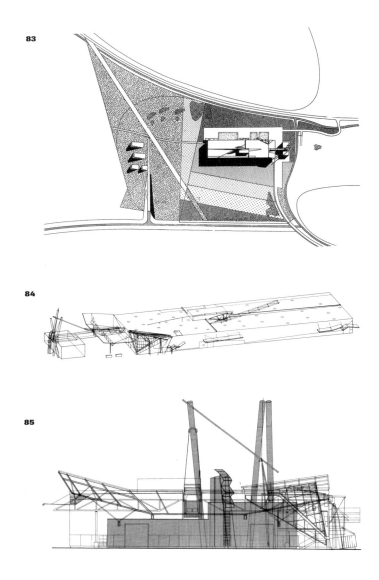

83

84

85

86

87

83 St.Veit/Glan, Carinthia, Austria, Funder Factory 3, 1988–89, site plan **84** Funder Factory 3, isometric drawing **85** Funder Factory 3, cross section through the head of the hall **86** Funder Factory 3, first sketch 1987 **87** Funder Factory 3, view with energy control room and "dancing chimneys" in the foreground **88** Funder Factory 3, interior view of the office and lab wing

86
87
180
181
182
183

long distances as a fifth facade, effective for advertising purposes. The three slanting chimneys are the most striking feature, as thin as dancing spillikins, and linked to the concrete energy control room by stays. A 13 metre cascade of sheet metal and grid frames is an additional "object" near to the chimneys. The media bridge, which cuts through the flying roof, rests partly on the power control room roof, but climbs towards the finishing shop as a bent bridge structure. Half of it is covered with sheet metal panels like the rest of the complex, and the other half is clad in acrylic panels. The flying roof is supported by a protruding truss from the hall and two additional supports. Statically and formally the media bridge, flying roof and energy control centre are held together by two large stays from the chimney. The flat-roofed production box consists of 20 steel trusses whose walls are clad with prefabricated reinforced concrete parts suspended in front in the lower area and with sheet metal panels in the upper section. Only the edge of the south-west facade breaks out of this system with explosive force. It appears as a corner made of glass and steel, dynamically tilted upwards and downwards. Roof trusses, diagonal supports and a number of other apparently vibrating rods and cables thrust through or structure the exposed skin of the building.

Of course the Funderwerk management, rather like their colleagues from the Vitra company in Weil am Rhein, were able to combine elements of patronage and advertising. Regardless of the fact that this kind of architecture could be used to project their own corporate identity effectively (not only with this building, but in other branches as well), the general reaction to the work was conflicting – and what else would one expect. Glossy Japanese magazines positively celebrated the completed project, but Charles Jencks reacted like this: "Coop Himmelblau's Funder factory shows the frenzied cacophony of their method. A long low production hall – basically a shed – erupts at certain points with cantilevered canopies punctuating its flat surfaces. The most dramatic eruptions are the front door marked by a zig-zag awning in blood red (favorite colour of the Neo-Mods) and a volume in glass and steel – the main office area which faces south. Here trusses penetrate the skin, the roof tilts up and turns into a trellis and diagonal beams splay into the leaning glass wall. This is the 'violated perfection' of the Deconstructivists: the perfect white cube suddenly smashed, skewed and skewered into a frenzy of oppositional forms. Another such crescendo occurs in the adjacent power house where the chimneys suddenly tilt off the right angle. In both cases a rational predictable solution is partly violated ..."[43]

However justified this criticism may be in terms of individual details, it is not comprehensible in terms of its overall doubts about the basic conception. Surely Prix and Swiczinsky have done nothing other than to take up Robert Venturi's theory of the "Decorated Shed" (1972)? Instead of sticking on historical quotations, which would have led to nothing but head-shaking in the case of a historical building, they have positively larded their neutral shed with symbolic particles – as demonstrated for them by Venturi with his Basco showroom (1979) or the SITE group with their Best showrooms (from 1972). And they have coarsened them to the extent that they can even be seen from a passing car, as if in slow motion. The particles as such all have a classical Modern pedigree. The "anti-Modern" feature is that they are robbed of their stability and context and placed in new surroundings that are subversive to narrative. Scarcely anyone would doubt that there is a considerable sense of childlike delight in deliberate confusion here. But this makes the result seem all the more important: the idea of a by no means sad "body in pieces" for a regular pariah among architectural commissions!

Coop Himmelb(l)au have reason to be grateful that their most spectacular and perhaps most controversial project to date has been realized. Frans Haks, a Dutch museum director in Groningen and kitsch-obsessed *enfant terrible* of the art agency scene, gave Alessandro Mendini, the high priest of schlocky design, a direct commission to build a new municipal museum for Groningen in 1988. Mendini put a shrill architectural "pleasure steamer" together for himself on the site, as was of course to be expected. Anchored in the canal basin between the trivial Modernistic station area development on one side and old Groningen on the

94
194
195
196

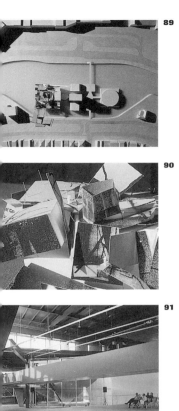

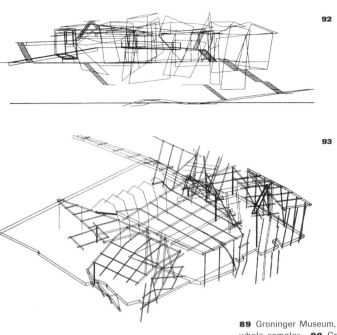

89 Groninger Museum, The Netherlands, 1993–95, model of the whole complex **90** Groninger Museum, East Pavilion, working model with design sketch printed on **91** Groninger Museum, East Pavilion, interior view **92** Groninger Museum, East Pavilion, perspective representation of the spatial structure **93** Groninger Museum, East Pavilion, isometric representation of the support structure

other, this raft-like new building was not only an extraordinarily skilled urban bridge but typologically speaking also a city-within-a-city in its own right. But this was about the only productive feature of this building. And no wonder, as Frans Haks and Alessandro Mendini – who also took it upon himself to appoint "guest designers" like Philippe Starck, Michele De Lucchi and Frank Stella – were both protagonists of the shrill and extravagant and came up with an unparalleled post-Modern pot-pourri. Michele De Lucchi designed the square West Pavilion to accommodate the archaeological collection and Philippe Starck the rotunda above it for the porcelain display. Mendini himself conceived the bridge, the central area around the tower of the gilded "treasure house" and the bastion-like lower sections of the East Pavilion. He also came up with the glorious idea of "sticking" decorative laminated veneer borrowed from furniture design to the last. But anyone who thought that householder Haks and "court architect" Mendini were merely flirting with their openly displayed, shrilly and garishly exaggerated interior and exterior trivialities was quickly taught a lesson after "reading" the brilliant duo's spaces and handwriting. Just as Haks had never allowed a distinction to be made between sacrosanct and trivial works of art in the past, and was concerned only with visual sensation, Mendini has also for decades now constantly campaigned for a culture of the trivial and the acceptance of kitsch.

But whatever has all that got to do with Coop Himmelb(l)au? The answer is as simple as it is amazing. The American sculptor Frank Stella was originally intended to build the East Pavilion for the collection of old master paintings, but he hadn't got round to submitting a binding plan by December 1992, and so had more or less voluntarily thrown in the towel. Prix and Swiczinsky were appointed as his successors within a few days. It is still absolutely staggering today: Mendini and Coop Himmel(b)lau, Coop Himmelb(l)au and a collection of old masters, however can all that fit together? The key to the fundamental change of architects and paradigms of the East Pavilion was that the Viennese team were known as reliable partners from their Groningen video pavilion, and they also had keen supporters in Arie Wink, the director of the Groningen town planning office, and Niek Verdonk. Nevertheless: if one thinks that building started as early as summer 1993, and that the building opened to the public in October

197
198
199

47

1994, it still leaves one somewhat at a loss for words. At a loss for words about how Coop Himmelb(l)au possibly managed to get a project that involved 1,000 square metres of exhibition space from the first sketch to complete working drawings within six months.

"Our idea," said Prix in an interview in 1994, "was to create a museum like a head. A hard shell and, inside, the brain. The shell is the architecture, the brain the art. The fluids, the electrical currents, are the circulation, the routing. The principle of the different viewpoints and the metaphor of the head were the basis."[44] But how does this become architecture within so short a time? Coop Himmelb(l)au used a twin-track, speeded-up procedure to bring this about. First there was a spontaneous, informal design sketch as usual, this time called "liquid architecture", to which I shall return. But they also went straight into the model, in other words embarked on abstract three-dimensional volumetric studies on the subject of "artificial and natural lighting options". Something that was effectively a psychogram or illustration of the first emotional "imprint" gradually crystallized out of continuous superimposition of sketch and model studies to provide an ever more concrete working model. The declared aim of the procedure from then on was to retain the liveliness of this model, which actually owed much to chance, and to adapt it to the functional requirements without sacrificing it to them. The model was digitalized and gradually enlarged to a scale of 1:1, with structural and spatial details becoming increasingly more concrete. As the tight budget and time-frame left little room for manoeuvre, they decided to have all the structurally important elements of the east wing made and fitted by a local shipyard, in the best marine tradition. The data for the geometrically very complicated cut of the wall and ceiling sheets could be taken directly from the computer model. Thus the shipyard was in a position to produce precise double-wall steel panels without concrete sets of plans. The red-painted panels were delivered by boat, completely prefabricated, i.e. provided with insulation, utility fittings, colour coatings and connection details, and not welded together until they were on site. And so essentially there are only welding seams! The result was then more like an alternative steamer welded together against all the guild rules that a seriously assembled museum wing. And then the first design sketch was greatly enlarged and transferred to the outer surfaces of the red steel plates with the help of liquid tar. "The concept of the museum," commented Prix and Swiczinsky ironically, "is theoretically this: steel rusts. It takes 100 years for 4 mm of steel wall to rust way. The drawing, applied in tar, will not rust. And so after 100 years there will not be a museum any more. All that there is left to be seen will be the drawing."[45]

Essentially the concept for the old masters' wing is based on further extending the idea of interplay between spaces and cavities that develop positively and negatively. And actually it is again nothing other than a roof extension (even though on a monumental scale). Certainly the structure is not as extensive as planned, but it still metastasizes clearly and discernibly across the water to the canal bank. Coop Himmelb(l)au wanted at least their part of the museum to extend rampantly into the town. Inside they were not just interested in handling light, but above all that visitors could experience the art from different levels. The way in which the flexible exhibition areas shed their skin and the heterogeneous tissue of linked and horizontally layered circulation levels make it possible to come closer to the art works exhibited in totally unexpected ways.

The superficial result of all this is, according to taste, either a heap of red-painted ice (or iron) floes that is apparently completely out of control or an outlandish ironic tribute to the Dutch De Stijl movement, or more precisely to Rietveld's "Exploded Diagram" for the Schröder House in Utrecht. According to Thomsen, the Coop Himmelb(l)au section explodes "... the aesthetic conventions established on the site, forcing the viewer to see the entire project from a fresh perspective. Coop crush Alessandro Mendini's chocolate box, whose windowless exterior is decorated in the style of Paul Signac's pointillistic paintings ... The deconstructivist part of the building attacks the post-modernist candy-box architecture and steals the show. Coop Himmelb(l)au mobilize Deconstructivism's entire repertoire of principles, materials, and conventions and violate them, reversing the familiar and pressing it to perform new functions. This is expressed in asymmetrical forms, shapes piercing one another, cutting through one another, and pervading one another, all indicating a metaphorical layer which is violently sexual... This is expressed in the articulation of the building's interior: ramps, sloping staircases that turn off at odd angles, galleries, suspended ceilings, asymmetrical windows, floating platforms, jutting ledges, and rooms interpenetrated by sharp comers. This cacophony of disparate effects embodies the boldness to establish an aesthetics of force, even of brutality, and – by normal standards – of apparent ugliness. It is a boldness which eyes this pretty post-modernist ensemble, made out of a do-it-yourself Disneyland kit with all of its cleverly conceived details, then jumps it from behind an rapes it." [46]

Disregarding the sexual connotations, which seem extremely forced, Thomsen is surely right to point out that the fragmented, collapsing container only reveals as much of its interior life from the outside as is needed to arouse curiosity about the inside. In fact the inside is the actual sensation of the building. Has anyone ever seen a more exciting, more labyrinthine iron monster with flying old masters, suspended walkways, twisting ramps, tilting walls, glazed abysses or cryptic light slits? And as in other work by Coop Himmelb(l)au, weaker structural elements attack or penetrate the stronger ones. We should not try to hide the fact that penetrations of this kind created considerable problems at first. If double T girders thrust through glass or steel from the inside to the outside without thermal insulation then there will be drips in winter. And here in northern Europe there were not inconsiderable problems with draught-proofing such "extreme" architectural forms. Thomsen points out that considerations of this kind shifted the museum curators away from their original plan of showing old arts and crafts from 1500 to 1950 here, and decided they would prefer to use the unusual to unwanted heap of space for contemporary touring exhibitions and events that drew a wider public. But that was no longer the case once all the problems had been solved. The East Pavilion was temporarily devoted to the old masters, despite all the prophecies of doom. When Prix delivers lectures today he tends to remark sarcastically that the building took a little over a year to complete, but it took the curators almost two years to work out how to "play" the space, which is a task of similar difficulty to learning to play the organ. [47] He is not so much trying to put an ironic gloss on the structural mistakes, which have since been rooted out; he is much more concerned to point out seriously that ideas about function and actual usefulness are two completely different matters in all Coop Himmelb(l)au's buildings and projects: Prix and Swiczinsky have questioned and broken down classical Modernism's traditional concept of function from the outset.

Adolf Behne said as early as 1923: "The utilitarian subordinates himself to purposes in a commonsensical way that the citizen of today indeed knows and recognizes. He can, as a result, easily become a materialist. The functionalist is clearly no less decisive in approving of purpose, but he does not see it as something complete, unalterable, rigidly prescribed; rather, it is a means to broaden and refine, intensify and sublimate, move and mould human beings." [48] Prix and Swiczinsky also broke away from the utilitarianism that was making a stronger and stronger mark, but not to build "without a function". They wanted to allot a regular abundance of further function to the Vitruvian concept of "utilitas": tactile functions, for example, like touching or pushing away, being able to look away or having to look at something, making certain physically, being directly frightened, feeling something hot or cold, approaching and shutting oneself away, mediation – all these, but unimaginable things as well. All functions that cannot be measured in cubic metres of built space or cents and dollars. As they gain more building experience, Coop Himmelb(l)au try harder and harder to squeeze considerable "added value" from buildings that are supposedly unambiguously functional, whether by artistic subversion or quite concrete utilitari-

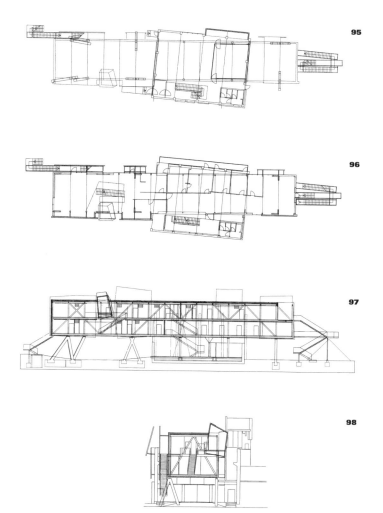

95

96

97

98

95, 96 Seibersdorf Research Center, Austria, 1993–95, ground and 1st floor plans   97, 98 Seibersdorf Research Center, longitudinal and cross-section   99 Seibersdorf Research Center, view from the south-west

99

an economies. In fact this added value is the very essence, the "soul" of their work. This and only this, both practically and theoretically, can convey the transgressions that liberate visitors even from the purgatory of the "red hell of Groningen", purify and emancipate them. Without this sense of purging the museum annex in Groningen would be nothing more that affirmative, post-Modern tittle-tattle, a traumatized box. And this is probably why international critics can still not agree whether the Groningen building is to be seen merely as a redundant confirmation or an avant-garde usurpation of post-Modernism. But there is one thing they all agree about: there can probably be nowhere else in the world where you could find a noisier, more multi-layered, more labyrinthine, more allegorical "art cave" (just think of Zumthor's Kunsthaus in Bregenz as a counter-example).

This makes the subsequent U-turn all the more surprising, Himmelb(l)au's road to Damascus conversion! There next building, for the Seibersdorf Research Center in 1993–95, was structured considerably more subtly and above all more comprehensibly. The brief was to convert and extend an existing hall in the grounds of the institute for office use. Three different disciplines conduct research in Seibersdorf, simultaneously and on an interdisciplinary basis in different spheres: mathematicians, environmental technicians and system analysts. And so it was Coop Himmelb(l)au's declared aim to express the "simultaneity of the systems in the architecture as well". Old and new construction systems were used with equal value and simultaneously for conversion and extension purposes, and this can be read from the various structures, volumes and skins. The facades are carefully layered and slightly fanned out, thus creating impressive transitional zones and gaps that can be seen as providing added visual and tactile value.

200
201
202

The linear extension stands on open supports and is conceived as a large two-storey framework construction with suspended concrete planking. This high bar thrusts through the old building with a very slight transverse turn. The turn is used to give access to the ground floor of the old building, which seems like a gate. The two-storey, elevated extension was built as a partly open, partly closed loft structure, at the users' request. Vertical division into fireproof sections produced open emergency staircases. "Open architecture" was pragmatically displayed here and condensed as a convincing image of the "simultaneity of interior and exterior space",[49] linked up with the transitions and peripheral zones, overbuilt and projecting terraces, open and closed volumes.

The two-storey support structure is largely supported by X- or V-shaped, diagonal reinforced concrete members that are thus the only "loud", dynamic elements. The space-creating covering of the extension building rises perceptibly in differently staggered layers, starting with the inner shells, then moving via the heat- and sound-insulation shells to end in the blue outer walls, which are clad in trapezoid corrugated sheet metal. Some of the galvanized grating elements that are placed in front on the sunny side can be adjusted diagonally. These are large curtains rising through the full height of the building, and are linked to the body of the structure as if floating. They function as providers of shade or light, and as an additional foil for quiet sensation of being "in-between". And so this is a graceful, lightly skipping building, not one that has been violently exposed; not so much a body in pieces as a happy, disciplined new edition of "Walking City". This is a building that is extraordinarily quiet in its effect, and yet extraordinarily dense atmospherically. With it Coop Himmelb(l)au proved compellingly that they could control the balance between stability and instability with increasing professionalism, beyond muscular gestures and slogans whose rhetoric had become increasingly blunted. This approach was also clearly part of the programme for the subtly layered extension for the Austrian pavilion (built by Josef Hoffmann) on the Venice Biennale site (1995), a poetically transformed box.

Coop Himmelb(l)au's first building that was neither a roof project nor a conversion or extension, but a "whole new building", as it were, was a domesticated, that is to say very cultivated and yet hardly less spectacular variation on the Groningen "cultural building" theme. This was the UFA-Palast in Dresden in the Prager Straße area, finished in 1998. Unlike Groningen, the key issue here was addressing the public space. Prix and Swiczinsky, like many of their colleagues, blamed "the financial position of cities" for the fact that this issue is constantly being pushed into the background in Europe. They say that lack of finance "forces local authorities to hand public spaces over to developers who try to make the maximum profit from land with new, single-function buildings. If this single-function structure can be broken up and urban functions are added, then a city can acquire new urban quality; but this is not defined merely by spatial sequences, it needs media events as well."[50] And so there is not more talk about the "poetry of despair" in the desolate slab-construction areas around Prager Straße and Prager Platz – they are looking for escape routes instead! Thus the design grew very precisely out of the urban conditions on the spot. Prix and Swiczinsky were particularly fascinated by the striking interface created by the building site east of Prager Straße and St. Petersburger Straße and the old round UFA cinema from the GDR period. This was a distinguished site halfway through the pedestrian area between the old town and the main station, right on the edge of one of those draughty GDR main show streets of the GDR rebuilding period, far too wide, and even before the fall of the Wall looking like a strangely late rehabilitation of the kind of inhuman vision dreamed up for Berlin by Ludwig Hilberseimer before the Second World War. And so after reunification there had to be increased density, whether people liked it or not. Construction in existing buildings and extensions, smaller sizes and shapes for squares, arcades and other types of public interior spaces had to be created to restore urban density and quality around the centre of Dresden. For this reason Prix and Swiczinsky also refused to devise their new cinema complex as a single-function casing, simply a large container! This sounds good, but it is only half the truth in terms of their client's original intentions. In fact Coop Himmelb(l)au had once again to put in some careful work before gaining the added value they needed to sponsor and urban space, a public "city-in-the-city".

106
107
108
109
110
111
112

Prix and Swiczinsly were able to accumulate the added value they needed in the first place by building the "cinema block" at a very reasonable price; it consists of eight cinemas with a total of 2,600 seats. One of them can even function as a straight theatre. But anyone who jumps to the conclusion that the cinema block became a plain accumulation of boxes piled one on top of the other on financial grounds would definitely be making a mistake. The concrete cinema block is sharply tilted at its ends, diagonally bevelled and dynamically cantilevered, but otherwise rectangular, and is in fact much more strongly reminiscent of Konstantin Melnikov's "Rusakov" workers' club in Moscow (1927–29) than a traditional contemporary multiplex cinema. On the east side, in other words facing St. Petersburger Straße, the streamlined concrete silhouette – incidentally one of the few vertical parts of the building – has acquired a transparent media skin a few metres away, stretched in front of it in the form of a grid. The dynamic staircase cascades of the emergency and normal exits run visibly between the grid and the concrete wall. The cinema block defines the newly created street space as a clear, intelligible form. The extensive cantilevering makes the complex much more open to pedestrian traffic between Prager Straße and St. Petersburger Straße. The cinema's access system defines the image of the two longitudinal facades. The line of the building facing St. Petersburger Straße is shaped by the cinema exits, stairs and the facade suspended in front, the foyer on the Prager Straße side generates an entrance area, and urban square and forum space in the form of a multi-storey "crystal".

213
214
215
216
217
218
219
220

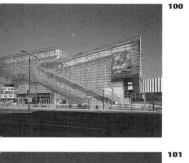

100

101

102

103

100 Dresden, UFA Cinema Center, 1998, view towards St. Petersburger Straße **101** UFA Cinema Center, Crystal, interior view of entrance area **102** UFA Cinema Center, view from the south-west at night **103** UFA Cinema Center, Crystal, interior view of entrance area

The crystalline, glazed volume of the foyer, rising through the full height of the building, shows visitors breathtaking layers of stairs, ramps and platforms moving freely through the space, emphasized by streams of visitors gliding up and down. Inserted "sculptures" work like "editing cuts", with the effect that the spatial sequences constantly intersect and dissolve into each other like video clips. This completely eliminates any experience of the space from a central perspective. The sculptures include the bent concrete tower for the lift, a sloping counterpart, also in concrete, for the media tower and a floating pyramid in the form of an awning that divides the flow of visitors and at the same time serves as a screen for film trailers. The last striking sculpture in this room full of striking things is the "floating double cone" of the "Skybar". This actually does float, and is a vertical cable net structure in the shape of a diabolo, the toy that children used to make spin around its own axis using a cord between two little sticks that they flicked up and down. The transparent cable net supports a circular "orchestra" at its lower end as a bar area. Throughout Coop Himmelb(l)au tried to submit the whole foyer to the concept of transitory spaces. All the materials that define the space are deliberately rough and left untreated. This is not intended to express "neglect", but we are meant to feel a strong sense of the "hardness" of the urban space as it thrust its way inside.

221
222
223
224
225
226
227
228
229
230
284

But this sort of attempted description can only hint at the fascination, the pull on the public that this building has exerted since it was opened. And descriptions cannot convey an objective assessment either. "Coop Himmelb(l)au's … architecture always breaks splinteringly over the city, tattered by the raw energy of a Stones song, where Gehry swings like a symphony – and where his buildings execute computer-controlled pirouettes, as though they wanted to dance Le Corbusier's pilgrimage church in Ronchamp into the ground, the Viennese bang along on steep wedges.[51] These and similar observations were no rarity.

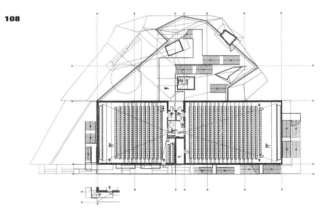

107

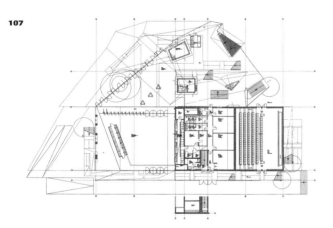

108

110

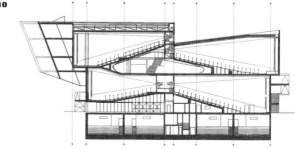

106

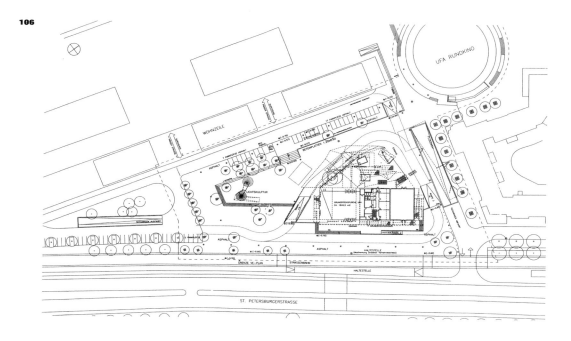

104 UFA Cinema Center, plan of building masses   105 UFA Cinema Center, urban design concept   106 UFA Cinema Center, site plan   107–109 UFA Cinema Center, ground, 1st and 2nd floor plans   110–112 UFA Cinema Center, sections

109

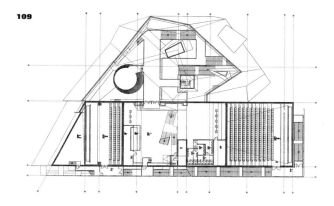

111

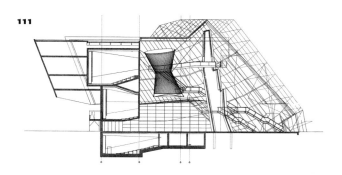

112

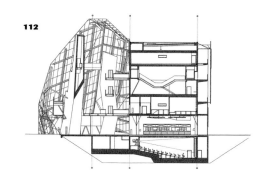

Everyone is free to read some devastating criticism in the local press alongside paeans of praise that are as enthusiastic as they are uncritical in national and international publications. But the results of these new "operations on the box" are now quite openly on show in Dresden, and this is much more revealing. On the one hand we have the cinema box, not a fractured container for images of dreams and deception but a structurally entirely rational device, at most with "sharp edges" and bevelling. And on the other hand we have the "crystal", which is mainly responsible for the fact that the operation on the box in the Dresden UFA-Palast has thrust forward well towards the limits.

218
219
220

This statement is not intended to suggest that the crystal is like a reincarnation of the fictitious crystalline architecture that the revolutionary representatives of the legendary "Gläserne Kette", and above all Bruno Taut, managed to create on paper during the First World War and in the subsequent years of social revolution, but could never build. At most we might remember Paul Scheerbart, the literary mind behind German Expressionism: „Glass architecture will acquire a floating quality", he had said, and drew the questionable conclusion from this that the „influence of glass architecture on the human psyche could thus only be good". Or one remembers a sentence like this „Glass architecture makes human ... places into cathedrals and must have the same effect as these."[52] But merely formal or literary references to architectural history are ultimately just as superficial and hit the target just as little as the recourse taken by some deconstructivists and their critics, and chanted like a mantra, to Soviet Russian architectural utopias.

No, the Dresden crystal comes close to the limits above all because of its levels of perception. Where else has there ever been – with the exception of historical follies – a building that looks entirely different, indeed extremely different, from every angle. But that is precisely the case in Dresden! Seen from one side the "crystal" looks static, towering up steeply; from the next it looks threateningly out of joint, smashed to the ground; and finally from the third side it melts completely, dissolving without contours into light and mirror reflections. This crystalline phenomenon sits in the city in a quite surreal manner, like a planted "*objet trouvé*" as a manifestation of something non-comprehensible that has been conjured up, whose material constitution seems to change ceaselessly as well, from solid to fluid and ethereal. A mutant or hybrid in the middle of the city? Or a being that has left the box a long way behind? Be that as it may, one thing is certain: the Dresden "crystal" could only be realised as a luxurious "waste product" from an entirely secular development project, budgeted cheaply, robustly constructed and solidly built, but on the level of perception it conveys something like the "melting" of the box, or a transformation, reminiscent of Kafka's novels, into an entirely different state. And the transitory element of this process is quite clearly to the advantage of urban quality, or better to the ability of a solid building anchored in urban surroundings to respond to the ceaselessly changing, flowing urban elements around it.

And something similar is even more true of the foyer, the interior of the crystal. The transitory element is put on show in something like a larger-than-life-size glass case, with the showcase removing its own limits through the object exhibited. As Prix and Swiczinsky intended, the space becomes a reflector; it reflects emotions triggered by films or other things that take possession of the emotions.[53] Thus Coop Himmelb(l)au, however strange this may sound, have returned to their roots in the Vienna "Supersommer" (Super Summer) in 1976. The motto then was "taking emotional possession of the city"; admittedly with the small difference that this idea exhausted itself in ephemeral installations at the time, but has now obviously taken on comprehensible architectural form. And in Dresden we are experiencing precisely the exciting moment at which the comprehensible element exhausts itself in the Boullée-like dialectic of ingenious day and night effects while at the same time traditionally safe and solid spaces are starting to dissolve into the ethereal incomprehensibility of media reflectors which contain and convey space. The media concept of the design is to make "the content of the building visible", say Prix and Swiczinsky, "as much as the city is visible from the building. It is an inside-out building which sustains a dialogue with the city. The media event – projected from the interior towards the exterior –

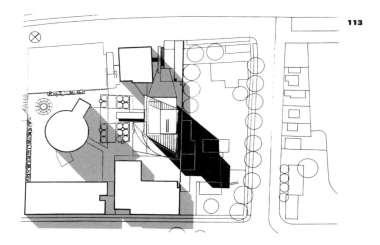

113 Vienna, Austria, SEG apartment tower, 1994–98, site plan

assists in the creation of urban space at night." "[54] Regardless of whether we are inclined to see the Dresden UFA-Palast ultimately as a meteor of failed architectural aspiration that has crashed on the pavement or as an incunabulum of a reflector-oriented building method of tomorrow, analogous to architecture, we are left with the stupendous added value in urban terms that a project fundamentally commercial through and through has left in the middle of the city. All this conceals a fair measure of "corporate identity" for a company, but who could possibly take that amiss?

Coop Himmelb(l)au were able to deliver what is so far their most mature piece of work on the box in a field in which it had long seemed that they were bound to fail whether they liked it or not. This is convincingly refuted in Vienna, near the "Alt-Donau" underground station. The SEG apartment tower is a skyscraper on a European scale that was handed over to its owners in 1998 after four years of planning and building. The 60 metre high tower stands at a key point in the new central Viennese „Donau-City". Its facades are characterized in part by a displacement from the vertical ranging from scarcely perceptible to clearly discernible, but all the more carefully balanced and structurally coherent. It is immediately adjacent to two other towers (one of them designed by Gustav Peichl) and low-rise residential blocks, and this in an outstanding situation. There is a fantastic panorama of the Old Danube from the top. The tower is the proverbial good address, as the Donauzentrum is more or less next door and – this is almost more important – the Großes and Kleines Gänsehäufel, the most popular Viennese excursion destinations are within walking distance. The client was the SEG district housing association. 70 social housing units and some offices and surgeries are housed on 25 storeys. The name "social housing units" confuses the issue somewhat, as these are all owner occupied housing, all financed by the successful Austrian programme for state-subsidized owner occupation for lower income groups.

The SEG tower's striking exterior, which Maak feels is "vaguely reminiscent of a fusion of children's building bricks and 'Blade Runner'",[55] is based on the idea of superimposing two separate tower sections so that a communal space – the "Skylobby" – is created on the dividing line. At least that is what we read in the building report. The reality looked considerably more complex. Coop Himmelb(l)au were able to wrest the volume of the Skylobby from the tower only by pinching a few centimetres of height almost "illegally" from each of the 25 storeys, which then added together to make it possible to "push in" this volume. Why do I say "wrest"? Because it was only through this major effort that Prix and Swiczinsky were once more able to obtain the added value for realizing the Skylobby, for realizing an old dream: this motif, teasing in a communally available, almost urban zone halfway up a residential tower, had already cropped up in the visionary projects of the seventies and eighties. Admittedly there is no scorpion or tongue of flame thrusting through the building here. Instead the

114
115
116
117

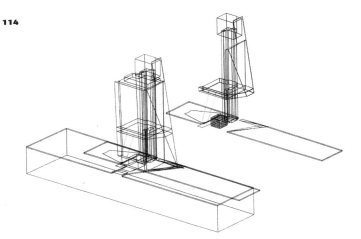

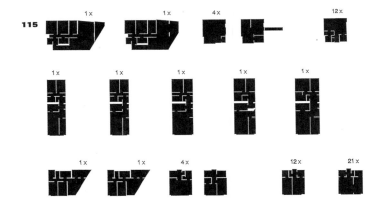

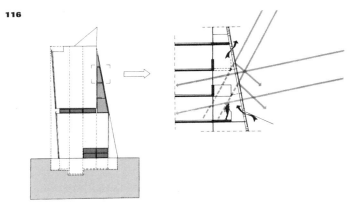

114 SEG apartment tower, structure model **115** SEG apartment tower, range of apartment types **116** SEG apartment tower, structure sections

Skylobby challenges the occupants to bring this "twilight zone" to life as best they can, to make it work for parties and other events or to take active possession of the children's playroom, the Internet café and the sun deck. And so have Coop Himmelb(l)au now finally come to terms with "hot living", finally made peace with the "surrounding despair"? Beware of hasty answers. The diction may have become milder, the architectural language much more professional, but just as little has changed in terms of the key themes or the rigour with which they are implemented. Seen in this way, the Skylobby does nothing more than consistently implement the unbuilt third planning phase for Melun-Sénart. Ultimately they were saying even then that all the loft complexes in the city should be split into two and that the space this created should be set aside for public and social purposes.

The element that combines the two halves of the tower that are concealed in
the interior is the uniform conditioning envelope facing south-east, in the form
of an "intelligent glass apron". This and the huge "Air-Box" on the roof of the
tower and the tower core, which is designed as a heat reservoir, provide coolness and comfort in summer, economical additional heat in winter and sound
insulation. And then the second sensational element of this little skyscraper is
concealed under the prismatic slopes of the glass body. High voids were created in the upper half of the tower, between the oblique glass skin and the terraced residential floors. Each of them covers two to three floors, and in them
are glazed loggias in front of the individual residential units, open belvederes
and even "hanging gardens". And there is also a Cinemascope view of city and
countryside, which is actually beyond price in a large city like Vienna. The tower's
residents had the agonizing choice between fourteen differently tailored dwelling
types, with areas between a minimum of 55 and a maximum of 130 square metres.
All the apartments are laid out as lofts, in other words with open ground plans
and without load-bearing intermediate walls, which guarantees maximum flexibility, i.e. possibilities of individual modifications. The apartments on the entrance
side, which face south-west have a filigree screening wall of glazed loggias rising through the full height of the tower in front of them; if needed these can be
fully opened to the width of the room, even on the 25th floor. You would have
to look a long way today to find a skyscraper loft high in the sky on whose "cloud

235
236
237
238
239
240
241

117 SEG apartment tower, section

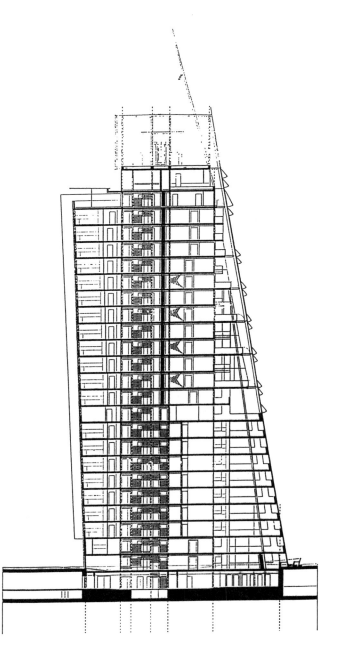

terrace" – it lives up to its name – you can allow the wind to whistle round your ears. The neighbouring residential towers look pretty old in comparison, and not just in this respect. But let us have another look at the south-west facade. Have there been many metal facades since Le Corbusier's "maison clarté" (1930–32) that have reflected the structure of the building, the alternation of different dwelling types, the programme by which they are fitted together in a kind of "répétition différente" as intelligibly as the facade of Le Corbusier's building in Geneva? Probably very few, but this example in Vienna is certainly one of them! Like the legendary Viennese "Superblocks", or more precisely the municipal housing built in "red Vienna" in the early thirties, the SEG tower acquired a prestigious two-storey lobby with a conciergerie. The main entrance is unmistakably identified by a roof that thrusts out like a springboard. Like early skyscrapers by Louis Henry Sullivan and other members of the Chicago School, this contemporary variant also has a plinth (base), a shaft (tower) and a capital (Air-Box). But this exhausts the similarities, because unlike the Chicago skyscrapers the SEG tower contains several skyscrapers at once. There is the "glass tower", the "metal tower", the "stone tower" with punctuated facade, the "service tower", there are "towers within the tower". Although in a much less disturbing way than the dissolving Dresden "crystal", the hard Viennese tower also has many forms and follows the same principle. It looks different from every elevation. And as in Dresden, facades that are strongly to imperceptibly inclined, blurred perspectives and constantly changing material states deliberately disturb the viewer's perceptions. The overall effect is that the tower, although firmly anchored in the ground, seems to vibrate silently, unlike its neighbours, and to change position in the urban fabric almost imperceptibly. Statuesque elements are crossfaded with reactive ones: the tower reflects both the city and its own structure in a striking fashion. It becomes an indicator of the social state of a city that is in flux, something that classical Modernism would like to have achieved, but never brought off in practice. And so in its way the SEG tower is one of the team's most mature achievements; "mature" not because you could say that it is less typically Himmelb(l)au in the popular sense, but because it picks up and transforms substantial motifs from three decades of very hard work on society and the city in a relaxed, indeed almost nonchalant way. Zaha Hadid has been asking in vain for years for people to built "social condensers" rather than forms, and surely this is what has been created here; and in addition it is one that could make history because of its abiding freshness. It remains to be seen whether the thinking for the new city centre in Guadalajara in Mexico, which is so far moving along the same lines, will unswervingly continue to pursue this concentrated freshness and ability to react socially beyond the turn of the millennium.

There are two more projects being planned or under construction that will confirm or reject the image of long-lasting operations on the box. Let us start with the SEG apartment block called "Remise". The building operation was preceded by a study that confronted the familiar disadvantages of a conventionally closed residential block with the advantages of a more open, more differentiated approach. Coop Himmelb(l)au came to the conclusion that blowing up a volume of the same density by injecting internal air pockets of different sizes would not only mean considerable improvements for the residents and the surrounding area, but would also improve the balance of building density and the ratio of open space. The study finally concluded that if block defining structures and silhouettes were raised in this way, thus enhancing residential and urban building quality, it would inevitably have a stimulating effect on future urban development. Coop Himmelb(l)au were then able to prove their thesis, in the form of a U-shaped block-end development between Vorgarten-, Engerth- and Hausteinstrasse, working on the basis of a master-plan drawn up by Boris Podrecca in 1994 for the area around Vienna's Nordbahnhof railway station.

The edge of the block was divided into seven buildings of different heights and widths. The predominant form for the dwellings is linked maisonettes with central access. This means that the glazed residential floors have the best possible lighting. Passive solar energy is used, which means that the building has a low level of energy consumption. Studio to two-bedroom flats complement the

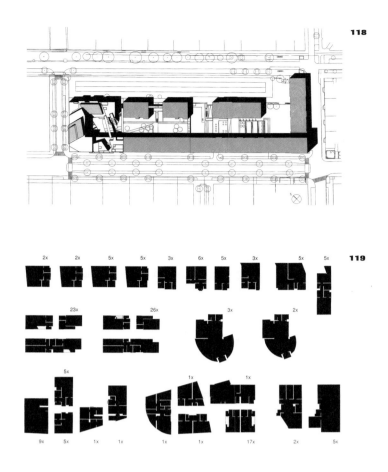

119

118 Vienna, Austria, SEG apartment block Remise, 1994–2000, site plan **119** SEG apartment block Remise, various apartment types

maisonettes, making a total of 140 units. Almost 30 different dwelling types are available. Restaurants, shops, offices and cultural and social facilities are accommodated in the two lower storeys, some of them on both sides of a passage running diagonally through the interior of the block.

The interior of the block marks a high point of the complex. The dominance of the right-angle is broken all the time. But this is no longer achieved by making wilful perforations, but by carefully creating apertures in the floor, skilfully bending walls upwards and inwards, linking and releasing sections of the buildings diagonally, opening and closing inward and outward views with gorge effects or even by implanting an elliptical "alien cell". All this happens both horizontally and vertically in a whole variety of layers, creating a veritable urban landscape. And the outer facades of seven adjacent buildings in the same way look more like geological formations of screen walls and layers of walls – than traditional building facades. There is an abundance of strictly orthogonal facades, including stone ones with punctuation grids and others with horizontal bands of windows, or others again made entirely of glass and metal. The two lower storeys are set back to varying extents, again creating a gorge effect. On the protruding upper floors, supported either on pilotis or V-shaped concrete stilts, punched-out cavities open up restricted views into the interior of the block. More generous pathways, some of them accompanied by powerful diagonal volumes, thrust out above all from the sides of the U-shaped peripheral development and run over the roof gardens of the arcade and the "Remisen" (coach-houses) into the interior of the block, where they help to provide it with daylight. The roof zone, which hops powerfully up and down, and soars up to a height of 42 metres, offers a wonderful view over Vienna and the Danube. Seen from the outside, the SEG Remise block makes a striking fixed point in the urban silhouette of the right bank of the Danube.

120
121
122
123
124
125
126
127
128
129

242
243
244

120

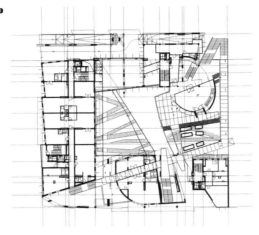

121

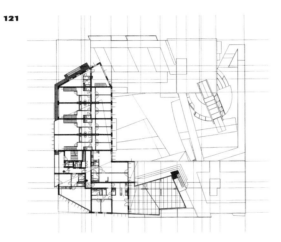

122 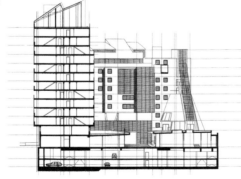 **123**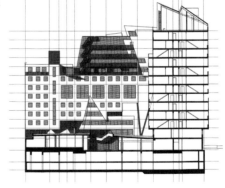

124

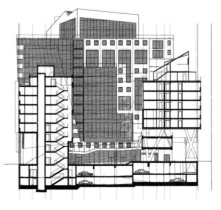

120, 121 SEG apartment block Remise, 1st and 12th floor plans
122 SEG apartment block Remise, section **123** SEG apartment
block Remise, section/north-east elevation **124** SEG apartment
block Remise, section **125** SEG apartment block Remise, mass
model **126** SEG apartment block Remise, model from the south-
west

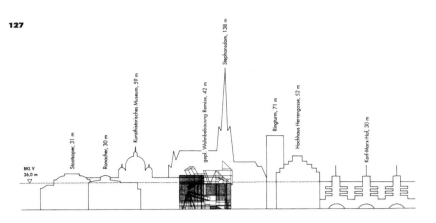

127 SEG apartment block Remise, system section and height comparison **128** SEG apartment block Remise, sketch of elevation **129** SEG apartment block Remise, working model variants

Of course a number of things, like the many different apartment types or the structural interlinking of interior spatial units goes back to experience with the SEG apartment tower. And yet if we look at the structural and material diversity and the complex "landscape structure" and its idyllic games with volumes, one question arises almost inevitably: is this complex a step forward or a step backwards, has it not turned out just a little too "Californian"? Let us not forget that this homogeneous structure, this romantic city-in-a-city or city-landscape was also competed for quite normally, built, profitably sold and let for profit. Once more Coop Himmelb(l)au had to work hard in advance to gain this added value, by using rational building methods, economies and design compromises, and that the "landscape structure" can begin only from the point when this added value is redeemed. With the difference that the added value of the disciplined SEG residential tower (Skylobby and hanging gardens) concentrates here on literally incorporating the "residential" element into the SEG Remise apartment block, and then on expelling the "block" element completely. Once again a closed system was "cracked" and the box transformed into something that wants to become an urban landscape of a quite different kind; in other words a landscape that also contains breaks, rejections, inconsistencies and even shapelessness. "Urban landscape," as Siegfried Kracauer recognised even in his day, "is not posed … The urban image is as little designed as the image of nature, and is like a landscape in that it is not aware that it is asserting itself."[56] Bridging the gulf between unconscious lack of pose and conscious design intentions, overcoming it productively, will be the historic touchstone of this site.

A building that pursues altogether different intentions will cause quite a stir in the east of Vienna. The four listed gasometers in Guglgasse of the first Vienna Gasworks have been waiting to be put to a new use for years. They were built in 1893–99 and clad in the "Windsor Style". Each of them originally had a capacity of 90,000 cubic metres. After the introduction of natural gas the gasometers were decommissioned and gradually dismantled inside, leaving only the masonry rotundas and domes. It subsequently proved extremely difficult to find a use for the gasometers, which are arranged as double pairs, that respects the fact that they are listed and yet is financially viable. Infrastructural change around the gasometers, like the extension of underground Line 3, the new east-west tangent, but also the site's proximity to the Erdberger Brücke city autobahn interchange and the Prater meant that investors started to take an interest in the gasometers. After a whole range of possible uses and financial schemes had been settled by feasibility studies, competitions and expert reports, the local authority agreed to the plan for transforming the four gasometers into a spectacular district centre with housing and leisure facilities. In 1995, Coop Himmelb(l)au were commissioned by the Wiener Wirtschaftsförderungsfond (Vien-

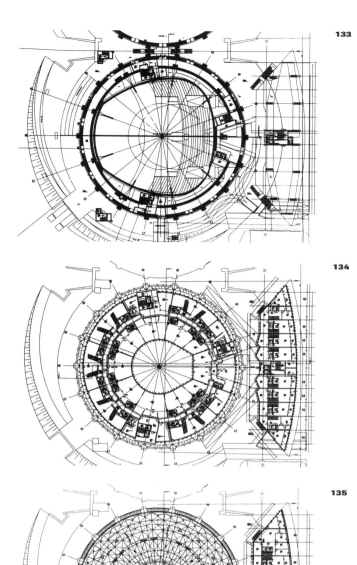

133

134

135

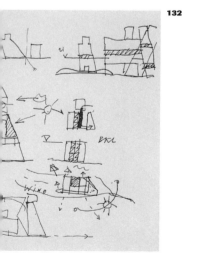

130

131

132

130 Vienna, Austria, Gasometer apartment building, 1995–2001, aerial vew 131 Gasometer apartment building, sketch 132 Gasometer apartment building, concept sketches 133 Gasometer apartment building, ground floor hall plan 134 Gasometer apartment building, upper floor plan, gasometer and shield 135 Gasometer apartment building, upper floor plan, shield with rooftop view of gasometer 136 Gasometer apartment building, section

136

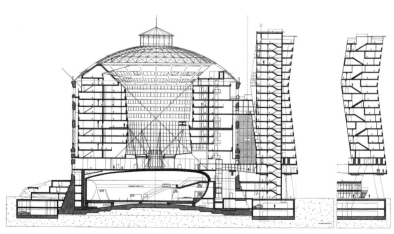

na Financial Promotion Fund; WWF) to put forward their multi-functional concept for Gasometer B in a more concrete form. The present clients are GPA and WPV, a Viennese private employees' trade union and housing association. Commissions for the other three gasometers went to Jean Nouvel, Wilhelm Holzbauer and Manfred Wehdorn.

Coop Himmelb(l)au's complex and refined programme for the complicated revitalization of their Gasometer B consists essentially of three working phases: 1. Fitting a new cylinder into the historical rotunda, 2. adding an external "shield" as a significant district sign, 3. "underpinning" the rotunda with a multi-functional hall in the base area. Housing will be concentrated in the cylinder and the shield. While the cylinder will be lit via a funnel-shaped inner courtyard and the central glass-and-steel dome of the rotunda and also via the historic exterior facades of the gasometer, the shield will be given a north-facing glass facade with loggias. This shield is so wide and high, rather like an elevated screen in an open-air cinema, that it completely covers the historic gasometer, dissolves it. But this shield, delicately balanced on V-shaped supports, only reveals its true subtlety in the vertical section drawings. The structure seems to keep the gasometer slightly at a distance, like a dancer, inclining its trunk gently towards it and turning its torso away. And so the section figure is dynamic and frail, stabilized only by the contact between gasometer and shield. There are a total of 360 residential units in the shield and gasometer respectively, ranging from small apartments and students' accommodation to large maisonettes and loft units. There will also be a deliberate mixture of housing and offices. It is hoped that this will provide innovative exploration of the borders between the worlds of home and work. There will be another "Skylobby" on the sixth floor of the rotunda as a communal communication level. As in the SEG apartment tower the residents are supposed to organize themselves.

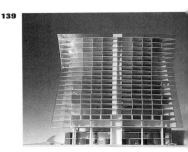

137 Gasometer apartment building, interior simulation, view from the gasometer dome into the interior of the central hall   **138** Gasometer apartment building, interior simulation, view of the gasometer dome from the floor of the central hall   **139** Gasometer apartment building, model of shield, front view   **140** Gasometer apartment building, simulation of the interface between shield and gasometer

Residents and visitors have separate entrances. Residents will be able to come into Gasometer B quite normally from Guglgasse, while visitors can get to the building from the underground station via a shopping mall. This mall links all the other rotundas at first floor level. In Gasometer B's case this broadens out and becomes a kind of anteroom or buffer zone for the hall. The hall itself is a striking bubble-structure, and is inserted into the rotunda as an independent unit. It is a self-supporting shell construction, and not structurally linked with the cylinder. The hall can be reached either from the underground station via the "Night Mall" in the next-door gasometer or directly via Guglgasse. The Night Mall has special restaurants and bars for visitors waiting for events in the hall or wanting to do something else afterwards. Conflicts between housing and work are not anticipated, because the hall can be run entirely separately in terms of both function and access.

But of course the high point, in terms of town planning, construction and formal aesthetics – provided it does not fall victim to the red pencil – will be the dominant, transparent shield. It will be visible from the east motorway and even more directly from Partagonstrasse, which leads straight to Gasometer B. According to the time of day and the weather, people will perhaps see it as a frontispiece for the new district, but more as a transparent leaf in the wind or a gleaming reflector; as a leaf that may be on the ground in front of the gasometer, but is not attached to it. Prix and Swiczinsky, who like many of their colleagues become extremely taciturn when it comes to theorizing about their work, only help us out with a terse marginal note about a vertical section of the complex: "The existing wall becomes an osmotic membrane."[57] And so however clear, however poetic, however rational the shield may seem, something of the old eccentricity flashes out of this statement. Coop Himmelb(l)au were not content, simply could not bear, to leave the exterior of a closed body – this time a cylinder and not a box – untouched, simply to rebuild the interior. Of course the Viennese were quick to shout hands off the monument. But this did not prevent Prix and Swiczinsky from declaring that the dead old building is a living cell. And as the cells in living creatures are surrounded by semi-transparent membranes, which constantly make water-content adjustments until things are in balance, they have transferred this principle of osmosis to their architecture. Their membrane, the shield, presents a picture of osmotic compensation between the "fluids" in the heart of the gasometer hardware and the "fluids" in the surrounding urban space. And so can we say that this quite obviously takes them back to the roots of their creative work, I mean to body-warm, pneumatic, cloud-light architecture? This being said, there is no question that understanding and presenting landscape, city and building as components that are not static, but react to each other like biological, chemical or physical processes is something absolutely new.

RENAISSANCE OF THE CLOUDS?

I have just aired – admittedly with a question-mark – my suspicion that Coop Himmelb(l)au might have gone back to their original roots, at least in some of their contemporary work. This suspicion is supported above all by the observation that organ-like structures, clouds or at least cloud-like building forms have increasingly frequently been "revitalized" in their more recent designs, essentially as an input to conventional structures. Examples are the competition designs for "Cloud #9" in Geneva (1995), the "Kansai-Kan National Library" in Seika-cho, Japan (1996), the "Perfume Museum" in Cologne (1998) or the new city centre in Guadalajara, Mexico (1999). Let me make it clear from the outset: none of these structures has yet been built. These suggestions were too unpredictable, too elaborate as constructions, too uneconomical, not city-friendly enough, too unusual for them to have had even a ghost of a chance of being built. The result of this is that Coop Himmelb(l)au are waiting with increasing impatience for the first opportunity, a client who really sees himself as a patron, so that this kind of design can finally be implemented. They are ready to be able to so it – and as so often before with similar challenges – they are ready to have to be able to do it. They hoped in vain that "Cloud #9" would be the first test, and now it is to be the "Media Clouds" in Guadalajara.

"The concept for 'Cloud #9'," noted Prix and Swiczinsky in 1995, "takes up our desire to return to our beginnings, but this is so that we can go beyond them." For this reason I am going to pick out this design and look at it more closely. Prix and Swiczinsky have provided a particularly eloquent report essay which is very revealing above this unique project's intended effect: "At the end of the twentieth century, and especially in the context of a competition for the United Nations, the idea of the cloud acquires new significance. The constantly growing and changing instable socio-political structure of our world illustrates the change of paradigm that is taking place on various levels – from genetics to quantum physics. This change can be seen as a shift to seeing the world not in relation to individual objects, but in relation to their context (interplay). This corresponds with the concept reflected in Michel Foucault's remark 'each form is an interplay of constraints'. The cloud itself can be seen as an idea without an appropriate concept; it is a differentiated system rather than an object. As it is a product of a complex tissue of influences in which it constantly recreates itself, it is entirely without identity. Thus the cloud, seen as a method, threatens to

203
204
205
206
207
208
209
210

141 Geneva, Switzerland, Cloud #9, project, 1995, model collages
142 Cloud #9, model simulation, side view

undermine architects' control, but at the same time it opens up a whole new range of spatial possibilities. Just as the shape of a cloud is sensitive to heat, wind and air pressure, the design for the Place des Nations is sensitive to the constraints of the site and the programme – to the strength of the city. The cloud's space ignites at the interface of the town planning, height limitation and circulation vector parameters. The result is a soft, fluctuating enigma – a building that does not want to be a building any more. The cloud envelope becomes a glass-like net structure that loosely defines a semi-public space. The transparency of this shell makes it possible to look at people moving about through the layers of light and colour. The space becomes both a meeting-point for diplomats, students and tourists and also access from the city of Geneva to the United Nations International Zone. In this zone private office buildings for consulates and missions are cantilevered from concrete lift-shafts. The space between the envelope and the fixed structure, which is used for balconies and ramps, yields passive energy and provides cloud-like circulation of air."[58]

In this statement, partly unambiguous and partly euphemistic, there is one thing about which there can be no possible doubt: B(l)au with its emphasis on actual building is no longer Blau with its emphasis on the blue sky – however seductive the allusions to cloud traditions may be! It would be just as absurd to try to link the "Villa Rosa", the "Wolke Himmelblau" or other pneumatic cloud simulations of the sixties and seventies with the "Clouds" of the nineties as it would be to make the proverbial comparison between chalk and cheese. Of course Coop Himmelb(l)au were once tied up with the idea of clouds, with equal degrees of intensity and naïveté, and indeed it became part of their company logo. But today's "Clouds" are derived from quite different material, both theoretically and practically. Unlike the Newtonian universe, which moves to immutable rules and laws, and makes linear calculation of the future possible, the image of nature according to Ullrich Schwarz says „farewell to rigid rules, states of equilibrium and linearity. Catastrophe theory, chaos theory, synergetics and other approaches try to describe the evolutionary movement of nature and its non-linear, non-determinist structural dynamics. In contrast with classical physics, this produces an image of a natural process that is fundamentally dynamic, self-organizing and unpredictable. Chaos and order are no longer seen as contradictions, indeterminate and irregular conditions and events are recognized in their creative, structure-forming potential."[59] In this light, Coop Himmelb(l)au's "Clouds" look absolutely nothing like Newton's balloons. They relate much more closely to the structuring potential of drops running into each other. But above all they illustrate the attempt (just think of the repeatedly invoked image of the leaping whale) to address the dialectic of lightness and heaviness in a completely new way as far as structure is concerned.

Subliminally it would seem that all this represents an inversion of Rudolf Arnheim's image of the cave, which Austrian architect Frederick Kiesler, for example, had tried out in his "endless house" in 1950–60. Just as caves get wider or narrower in passages and chambers according to the thickness of the soil layer, the new types of architecture modelled on clouds or drops are intended to react to light, air and sun, but above all to increasing or decreasing pressure from their urban surroundings. Joseph Hanimann suggests that in this way they can tap into something like the "dynamics with which heavy whales make their way through the water".[60] But let us stay with the cave image for a moment. According to Greg Lynn, the cave is "the easiest type of this architecture that is (difficult) to imagine." And he goes on: "The hypothetical moles that could live in these rooms would indeed float in the condensed and multiple 'depths' of this cave, instead of being fixated on the ideal plane of the surface of the earth." Lynn concludes from this that lightness is not the same as switching off gravity, but that in principle it is more like "equating gravitational fields". Diving under means that the borderlines between "figures and grounds" become blurred, and coverings superfluous. This kind of lightness, Lynn says, offers bodies the possibility "of floating within the mass as in a labyrinth. The result is that floating is transformed from an idealized condition of immateriality into embedding and cushioning masses in material contexts with special qualities and characterstsics – shifting from an ideal space in which bodies are tied to the ground by fixed points to dynamic fields with multiply configured supports."[61] Sanford Kwinter argues very similarly when saying in the context of the "emergence" of new spaces – and thus undoubtedly includes Himmelb(l)au's "Clouds" – that Modern "reductionist" ideas of space have definitely been replaced by new spatial organisms according to a liquified matrix that itself drives and determines events – in urban spaces, for example – instead of continuing to be content with the role of the "passive *substratum*".[62]

This evokes a kind of architecture that some observers see as the actual revolution of this declining century, as the first Modern or avant-garde movement that really deserves the name. They feel that classical Modernism is a kind of blind spot in the 20th century, and that its "heroic buildings" are just perfectly camouflaged fossils of late Vitruvian thinking. The originators of this Modernism, supposedly the first and only Modernism, the protagonists of this ostensible revolution, are architects and theoreticians from the United States who have been at loggerheads with antiquated design processes (including Coop Himmelb(l)au's), which they feel are arbitrary or – metaphorically speaking – "off the top of people's heads". They feel that artistic and subjective design is obsolete under today's socio-economic conditions. Instead they propose processual, socially oriented architecture that is "scientifically" justified. This means that it no longer relies on the ambitions of free artists but on the most up-to-date scientific insights; insights that go beyond sociological and semiotic research and address fundamental geometries "of fluid, solid or paracrystalline conditions", whose structures show those remarkable „qualities of an 'active matrix' in which many people now think they can see one source of all creative, autonomous complex structures, including life itself."[63]

If the New Architecture is not to repeat the mistakes of its classical predecessor, says Jeffrey Kipnis, it must not resort to the awkward logic of extinction and reconstitution in the form of "recombinations" (collages). He says that this is possible only with the aid of a new kind of intensive coherence that is based on non-correspndence. In his view, intensive coherence means that qualities of certain hard (monolithic) arrangements would enable the new architecture to enter into relations that are diverse and even contradictory, but above all "soft".[64] In his essay "The folded, the pliable and the supple", Greg Lynn provided a precise definition of such soft relationships in terms of built work, but also applied the concept of digital "morphing" to architecture.[65] He built his case on a process familiar from film and television that can use digitally produced metamorphoses to fold and smooth out bodies, spaces and gaps as desired, and even to make them flexible. Lynn has been looking at a large number of these morphing processes for many years now, but also at the digital generation of different configurations of spherical bodies, including "blobs", for example, drop-like spatial structures that flow together. Lynn says that "the sphere is exposed as a blob when it demonstrates the capacity of fluid and continuois differentiation based on interactions with neighboring forces with which it can be either inflected of fused to form higher degrees of singularity and multiplicity simultaneously."[66]

When thinking of these explanations and computer simulations of "blobs" something that involuntarily comes to mind is the multi-purpose hall that Frei Otto and Carlfried Mutschler built in 1974/75 for the Bundesgartenschau in Mannheim. Surely this vision of droplet forms flowing into each other had already been realized there? But this compelling image has a massive flaw. The building does embody a projection of "fluid" spaces running into each other, but in reality it is "only" a fixed grid shell and not "animated", interactive spherical architecture. Only the "availability and rapid colonization of architectural design by computer-aided techniques presents the discipline with yet another opportunity to both retool and rethink itself as it did with the advent of stereometric projection and perspective. If there is a single concept that must be engaged due to the proliferation of of topological shapes and computer-aided tools, it is that in their structure as abstract machines, these technologies are animate."[67]

The renaissance of the "Clouds" in Coop Himmelb(l)au's work has a lot more to do with this kind of highly complex research and thinking than with the comparatively naïve pneumatic experiments of the late sixties and early seventies. And this is not surprising when one thinks that Wolf D. Prix taught from 1985–95,

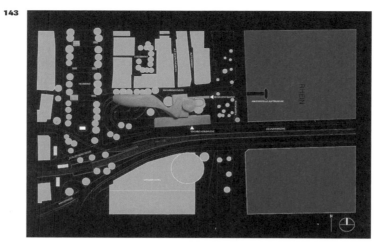

143

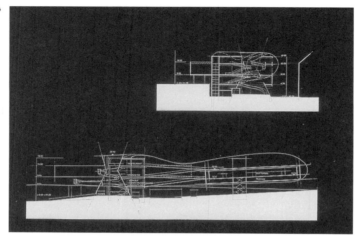

144

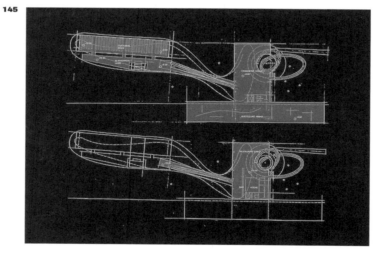

145

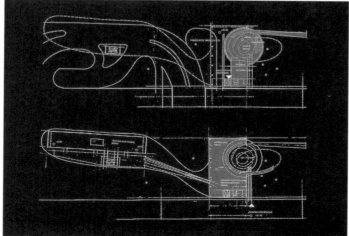

146

for ten years, as Adjunct Professor at the Southern California Institute of Architecture (SCI-Arc) in Los Angeles. During this period he met Karl Chu, an internationally acknowledged expert, a regular magician, in the field of creating breathtaking "animated forms" digitally. Here in SCI-Arc's computer labs cloud analogies had at last taken on the kind of "proto-architectural" form, on the screen at least, that decades ago had to be abandoned for lack of technological and theoretical expertise. The only comforting thing was that even the Americans were not able to construct, to build, anything like this. But now times have changed. The first steps towards realizing "blobs" and other spherical bodies have already been taken in artists' installations, experimental buildings and extensions; and not only in the USA, but also in Japan or Europe, where the Dutch in particular have taken up the Americans' ideas creatively and developed them further. They could be realized technically now as static constructions, as "lightweight structures" made of thin metal ribs and frames, placed on supports and covered with a membrane of shaped glass or other transparent high-tech materials.[68] But Coop Himmelb(l)au's "Clouds", introduced as a "soft fluctuating enigma", as mobile spheres, which in Himmelb(l)au's own words want to be more than buildings, namely floating interactive structures, clouds like these will probably keep us waiting for some time yet.

147

143 Cologne, Germany, Perfume Museum, project, 1998, site plan **144** Perfume Museum, cross and longitudinal section **145** Perfume Museum, floor plans of perfume channel and exhibition, catering facilities **146** Perfume Museum, floor plans of foyer, special exhibition and museum shop **147** Perfume Museum, model, side view

But nevertheless there is still resistance in Europe as well, or perhaps precisely there, to "outdoor experiments" with computer-generated clouds or blobs. And hasn't Jean Baudrillard recently issued a warning against the „virtual clones" of this kind of architecture? Against an increase in „transparent, interactive, mobile, playful architecture on the model of networks and virtual reality, through which a society enacts the comedy of culture, the comedy of communication, the comedy of the virtual "in the same way that it does with the comedy of the political." Baudrillard turns emphatically against „a polymorphic architecture with variable intentions", as it conveys nothing but an impression of emptiness, and gives „the people who walk about in it … no reason to be present any more". The end result is „then an (architectural) object that not only does not go beyond its own project, but not even beyond its own programme."[69] Even a benevolent observer like Andreas Ruby remarks in this context that the actual act of design cannot be directly influenced at the PC, as its logic has already been anticipated in the programming of the computer. According to Ruby the "design possibilities are precisely not in the hands of the 'users'. Instead, the supposed 'interactor' is simply instrumentalized to fill in the blanks in a computer-aided drafting program." But Ruby adds that the "architect naturally does not cease to be an author merely because architecture is increasingly being produced by machines nowadays. Instead, the conditions of authorship are simply being redefined … The author metamorphoses here from a creator of autonomous forms into an organizer of formal processes. Instead of drawing, he now decides which shaping parameters will be taken into account and which software will be used to render them productive for the design. The level of intervention in design thus simply shifts, and the problem of randomness persists along with that of responsibility."[70] In this way Ruby distances himself emphatically and rightly from the "objectivity" of the New Architecture, which is much invoked in the USA in particular, while Kwinter, Kipnis and Lynn feel that this is one of their major theoretical bastions, an indispensable moral driving force in the struggle against the arbitrariness of Deconstructivism. But the severest objections to this development, which are in fact not directed against architecture, come from communications special-

WE ARE FED UP WITH SEEING PALLADIO AND OTHER
HISTORICAL MASKS, BECAUSE WE DO NOT WANT
TO EXCLUDE EVERYTHING IN ARCHITECTURE THAT
MAKES US UNEASY. WE WANT ARCHITECTURE THAT
HAS MORE TO OFFER. ARCHITECTURE THAT BLEEDS,
EXHAUSTS, THAT TURNS AND EVEN BREAKS, AS
FAR AS I AM CONCERNED. ARCHITECTURE THAT
GLOWS, THAT STABS, THAT TEARS AND RIPS WHEN
STRETCHED. ARCHITECTURE MUST BE PRECIPITOUS,
FIERY, SMOOTH, HARD, ANGULAR, BRUTAL, ROUND,
TENDER, COLOURFUL, OBSCENE, RANDY, DREAMY,
EN-NEARING, DISTANCING, WET, DRY AND HEART-
STOPPING. DEAD OR ALIVE. IF IT IS COLD, THEN
COLD AS A BLOCK OF ICE. IF IT IS HOT, THEN AS HOT
AS A TONGUE OF FLAME. ARCHITECTURE
MUST BURN. 1980

» «

148

148 Heart City, installation, 1969 149, 150 Astro Ballon, installation, 1969 151 Cloud, project, 1968–72, model

149

150

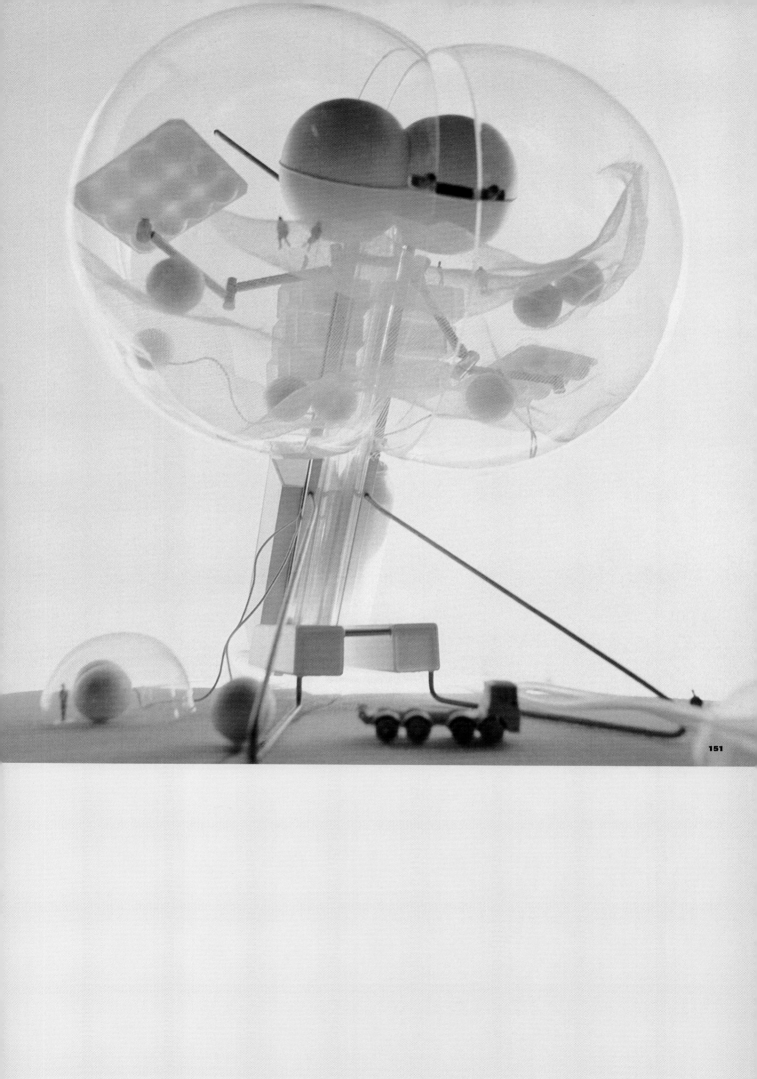

152 London, Great Britain, House with Flying Roof, Changing a
Daily Reality, 1973, photograph of the action

153 Graz, Austria, Blazing Wing, installation in the Technical University 1980   154 Stuttgart, Germany, Merz school extension, project, 1981, model

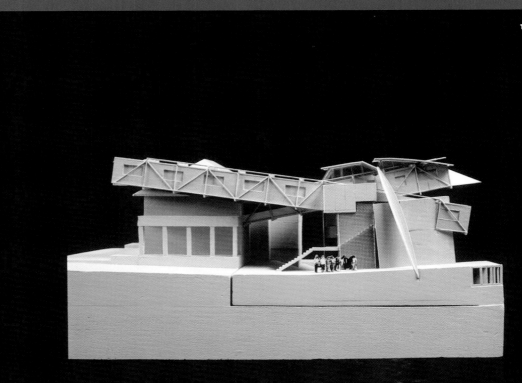

155 Vienna, Austria, Roter Engel Wine Bar and Chanson Theatre, 1981, interior **156–157** Roter Engel, tone line at the ceiling **158** Roter Engel, the body and head of the angel above the stage

155

156

157

158

159

160

162

162 Vienna, Austria, Baumann Studio, 1984–85, gallery and work station **163** Baumann Studio, exterior view at night **164** Baumann Studio, exterior view of entrance and wing sculpture at night **165** Baumann Studio, mezzanine floor with stairs lowered

166

167

166 Baumann Studio, mezzanine floor with stairs raised   167 Baumann Studio, interior with mezzanine floor   168 Baumann Studio, central support in the interior

169 Melun-Sénart, France, The Heart of Melun-Sénart, project, 1987,
full model **170** The Heart of Melun-Sénart

169

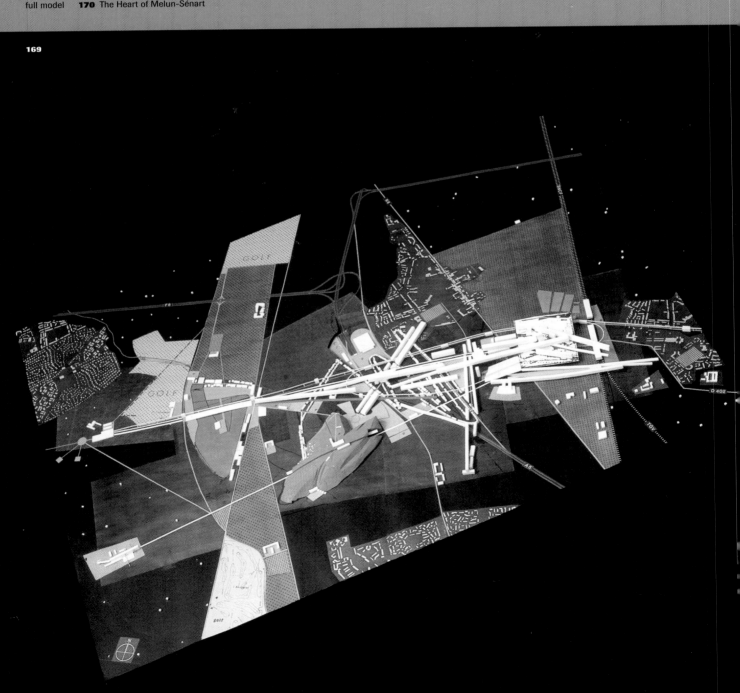

171 Vienna, Austria, Ronacher Theatre refurbishment, project, 1987, section model **172** Ronacher Theatre refurbishment, model, scale 1:100, view from the junction of Seilerstätte and Himmelpfortgasse

171

WHEN WE SPEAK OF SHIPS, OTHERS THINK OF SHI
WHITE SAILS. WHEN WE SPEAK OF EAGLES, THE OT
ABOUT THE WING SPAN. WHEN WE SPEAK OF BL
ANIMALS. WE, HOWEVER, THINK OF THE UNTAMED
OF LEAPING WHALES, OTHERS THINK OF SAURIANS
WE WON'T FIND ARCHITECTURE IN AN ENCYCLO
THOUGHTS MOVE FASTER THAN HANDS TO GRASP

ECKAGE. WE, HOWEVER, THINK OF WIND-INFLATED

RS THINK OF A BIRD. WE, HOWEVER, ARE TALKING

K PANTHERS, THE OTHERS THINK OF PREDATORY

IGEROUSNESS OF ARCHITECTURE. WHEN WE SPEAK

E, HOWEVER, THINK OF 30 TONS OF FLYING WEIGHT.

DIA. OUR ARCHITECTURE CAN BE FOUND WHERE

1991

»   «

175

176

173 Vienna, Austria, Falkestrasse rooftop remodeling, 1984–89, "exterior view of the central construction, beneath which is the conference room. The steel girders are linked by curved glass surfaces. The main girder holds the glass, the underside of which is visible here." 174 Falkestrasse rooftop remodeling, view into the conference room 175 Falkestrasse rooftop remodeling, view from the gallery into the conference room 176 Falkestrasse rooftop remodeling, view into the conference room from the elevated roof terrace 177 Falkestrasse rooftop remodeling, conference room with view of reception area and the gallery above the entrance 178 Falkestrasse rooftop remodeling, view into the foyer 179 Falkestrasse rooftop remodeling, conference room

180 St.Veit/Glan, Kärnten, Austria, Funder Factory 3, 1988–89, partial view with view of media bridge, office and lab wing **181** Funder Factory 3, view with energy control room and "dancing chimneys" in the foreground. **182** Funder Factory 3, interior view of the office and lab wing **183** Funder Factory 3, partial view with "flying staircase", office and lab wing; energy control room in the background

184 Malibu, USA, Open House, project, 1989-1990, model
185, 186 Open House, interior views of the model

185

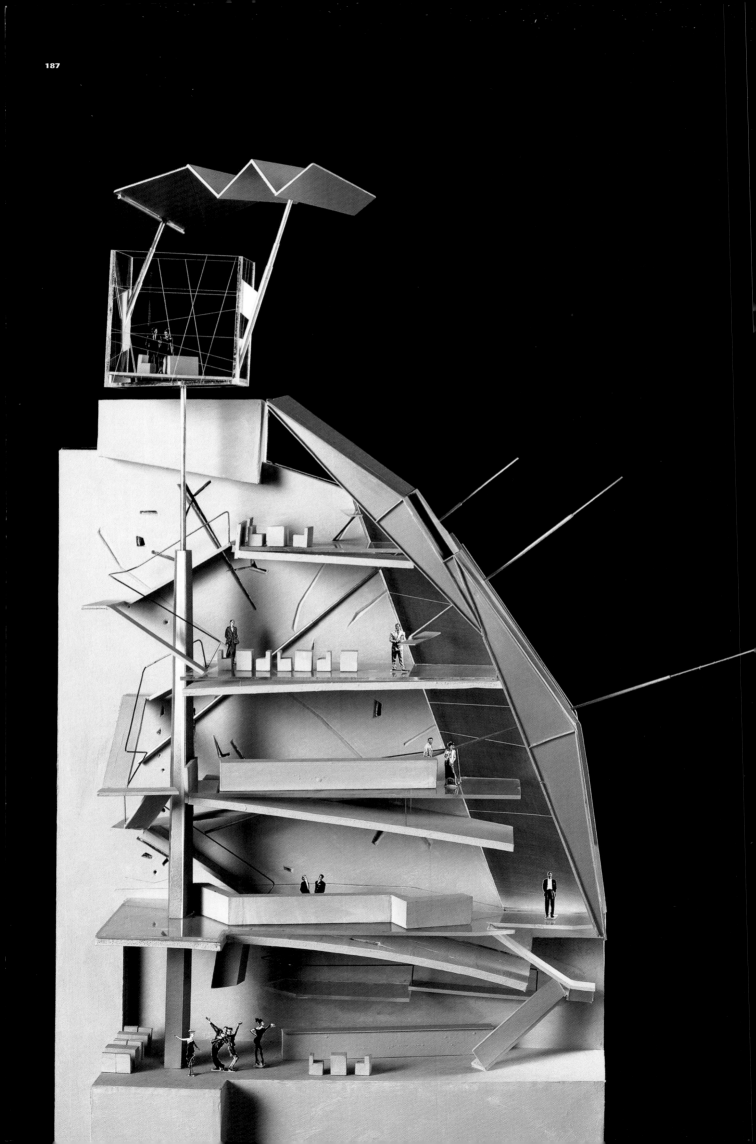

187 Fukuoka, Japan, Jasmac Bar and Restaurant, project, 1989, section model **188** Jasmac Bar and Restaurant, model view

189 Groningen, The Netherlands, Video Clip Folly, 1989–90, side view when closed   190 Video Clip Folly, view from the water when closed   191 Video Clip Folly, side views when open

189

192, 193 St. Pölten, Austria, Europaplatz, project, 1990, mass model

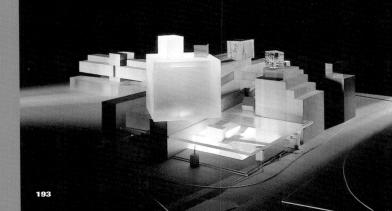

193

195

196

194 Groningen, The Netherlands, Groninger Museum, 1993–95, East Pavilion, partial view from the east   **195** Groninger Museum, East Pavilion, hall with suspended walkway before the exhibits were hung **196** Groninger Museum, East Pavilion, floor dissolved in glass and view of the water   **197** Groninger Museum, East Pavilion, east view **198** Groninger Museum, East Pavilion, partial view from the east **199** Groninger Museum, East Pavilion, interior view with suspended bridge

197

198

199

200 Seibersdorf Research Center, Austria, 1993-95, view from the south-west **201** Seibersdorf Research Center, view from the east **202** Seibersdorf Eesearch Center, view from the north-east

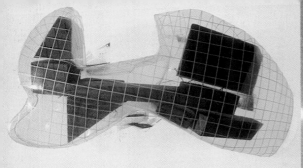

203

203 Geneva, Switzerland, Cloud #9, project, 1995, model simulation, side view and top view **204, 205** Cloud #9, model collages **206** Cloud #9, model collage **207–210** Cloud #9, model simulations, side view

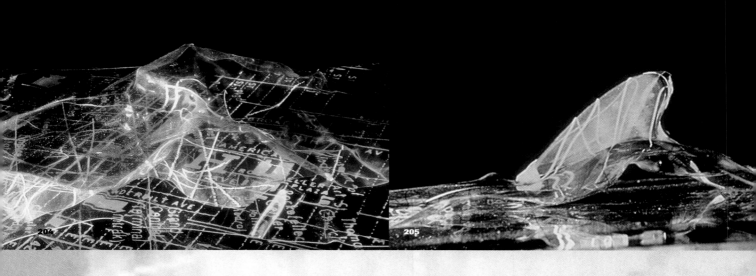

204

205

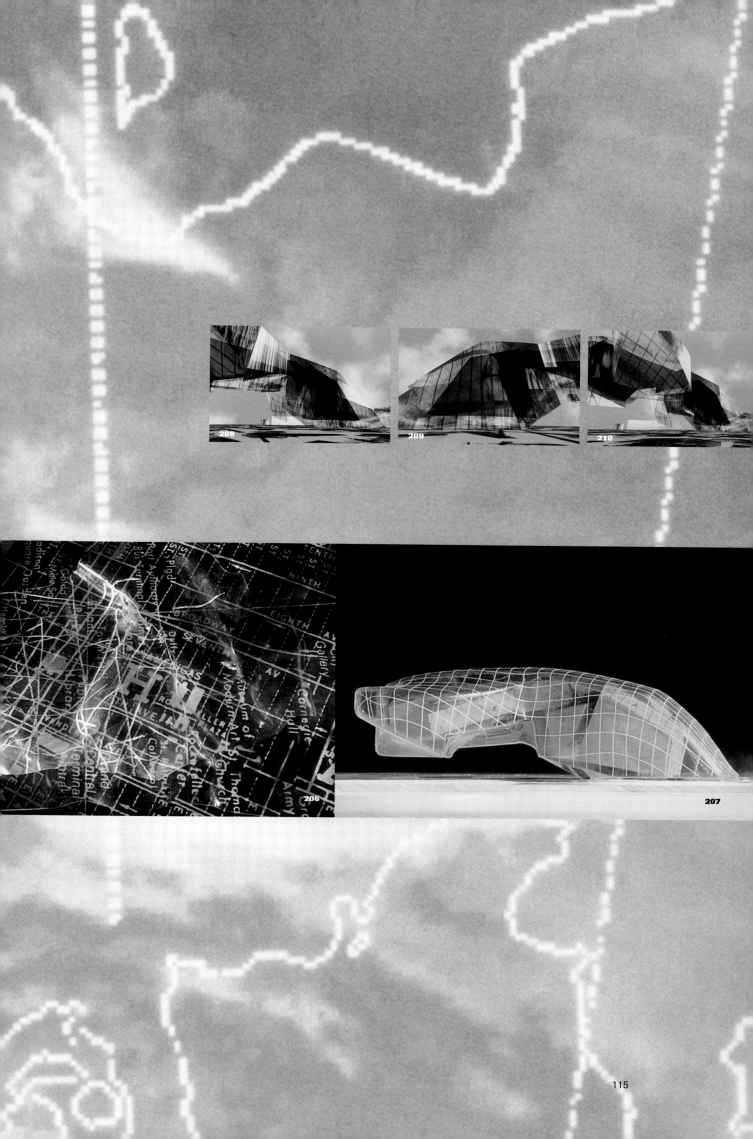

208

209

210

206

207

THE CITY IS LIKE A FIELD

NETWORKED CITY. THE BUILDERS OF THE TOWER

CONCRETE. WE ARE MISSING THE MATERIAL OF TH

IN ORDER TO COMPLETE IT. THERE IS NO SOLUTIO

OPERATE ON THE MATRIX OF DIVERGING IMPOSSI

CLAIM RESPONSIBILITY FOR IT. CLOUDS ARE SYM

FORM AND TRANSFORM THEMSELVES THROUGH TH

VIEWED IN SLOW MOTION THE ARCHITECTURE O

PATCHES OF CLOUDS. THE VOCABULARY OF URBAN

ANTIQUE SHOP AND REPLACED BY PHANTASMS S

LIKE TELEVISION SCREENS AFTER BROADCAST. T

NETWORKED SYSTEM WITHOUT HIERARCHY, IS TH

AND DETERMINE THE IMAGE OF OUR CITIES AND

CENTRE, AXIS AND SPATIAL SEQUENCE WILL HAVE

OF IMAGES. WE SHOULD NOT REGRET THE LOSS O

ATING, NETWORKED MEDIA EVENT. ONE WHICH AC

OF SPACES. THE DEVELOPMENT OF ARCHITECTU

COMPROMISED BY SEARCHING FOR LINES AND F

ANTI-LOGIC AND ANTI-AUTHORITY. BUT THE COIN

MEDIA SPACE – BECOMES THE BASIS FOR NEW DES

MONITION OF A DYNAMIC DESIGN-NET FOR CITI

THAN WHEN YOU ARE GOING TO DISSOLVE FORM

MALISTIC ARCHITECTURE. 1996

OF CLOUDS... THE RUBBER-GRID OF A
BABEL WERE MISSING THE MATERIAL REINFORCED
ONFUSION OF LANGUAGES WHICH WE WOULD NEED
R THE CITY. THE STRATEGIES OF URBAN PLANNING
TIES. THE ARCHITECTS HAVE TO CHOOSE ONE AND
LS FOR CONDITIONS THAT CHANGE QUICKLY. THEY
OMPLEX INTERACTION OF CHANGING SITUATIONS.
RBAN DEVELOPMENT COULD BE COMPARED WITH
NNING SHOULD BE PLACED IN AN ARCHITECTURAL
. TO BE DEFINED, WHICH FLUCTUATE AND FLICKER
HITE NOISE OF URBAN STRATEGY, AS A DIGITALLY
AY OF SUBURB AND PERIPHERY WHICH WILL MOLD
E QUALITY THEY HAVE TO OFFER. THE NOTIONS OF
BE REPLACED BY TANGENT, VECTOR AND SEQUENCE
BLIC SPACE, BUT REINTERPRETE IT AS A FLUCTU-
MORE LIKE A SEMI-CONDUCTOR THAN A SEQUENCE
S ALSO FURTHERED BY STRATEGIES, WHICH ARE
S OF POSSIBILITIES, TIED TOGETHER BY CHANCE,
ENCE OF SYSTEMS – BOTH AS BUILT SPACE AND AS
S AND PROJECTS, THE RUBBER-GRID AS THE PRE-
IKE CLOUDS. YOU CANNOT SCARE PEOPLE MORE,
AT IS ALMOST AN ATTEMPTED MURDER ON FOR-

» «

211, 212 Seika-Cho, Japan, Kansai-Kan National Library, project, 1996, model views

211

213 Dresden, Germany, UFA Cinema Center, 1998, view from the south 214 UFA Cinema Center, view from the north-east 215 UFA Cinema Center, night view towards St. Petersburger Straße 216 UFA Cinema Center, view towards St. Petersburger Straße 217 UFA Cinema Center, view of the Crystal at night

218 UFA Cinema Center, Crystal, view from the north at day **219** UFA Cinema Center, Crystal, view from the north at night **220** UFA Cinema Center, view from the south-west at night

221 UFA Cinema Center, Crystal, view into the Skybar 222 UFA Cinema Center, Skybar seen from below 223 UFA Cinema Center, Crystal, view of the Skybar 224 UFA Cinema Center, view from inside the Crystal 225 UFA Cinema Center, Crystal, interior view of entrance area

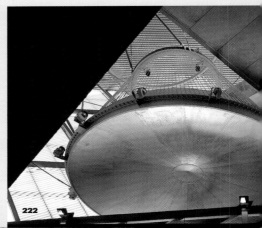

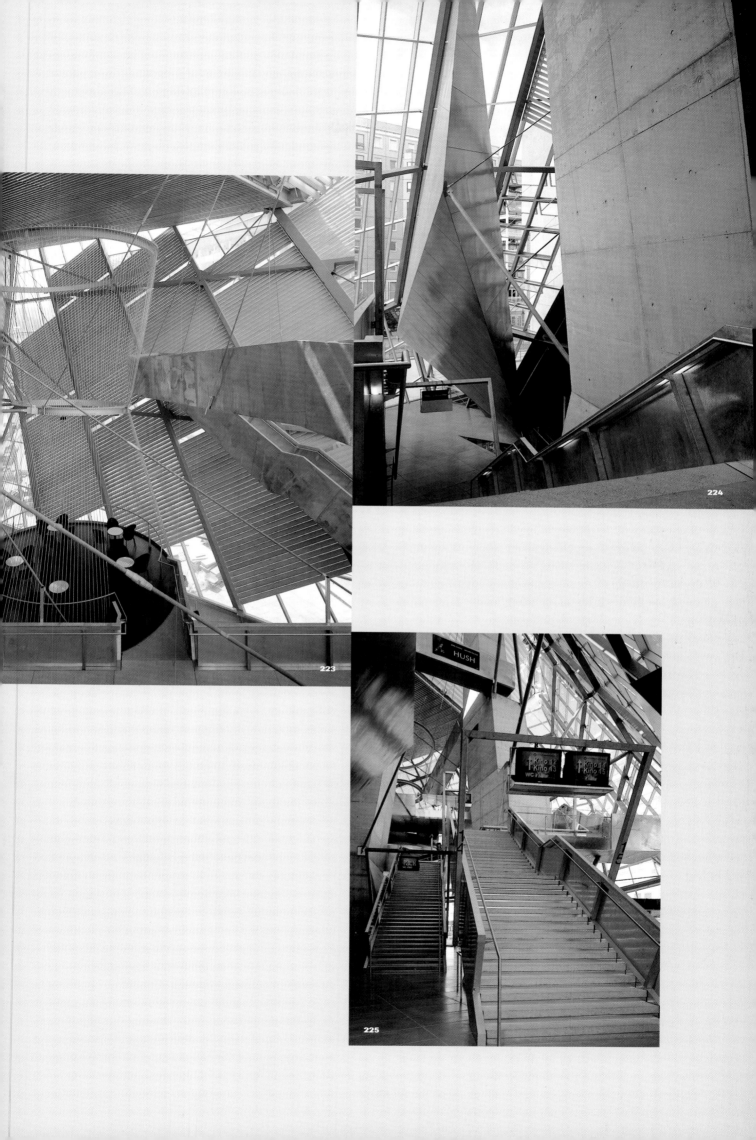

223

224

225

226 UFA Cinema Center, Crystal, spatial screen **227** UFA Cinema Center, Crystal, main staircase, night view **228** UFA Cinema Center, Crystal, media and elevator tower **229** UFA Cinema Center, Crystal, upward access from the ground floor **230** UFA Cinema Center, Crystal, media and lift tower

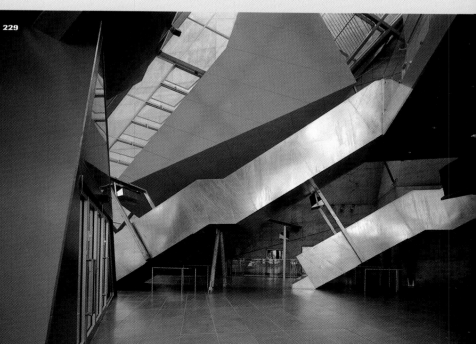

231

232

231–234 Cologne, Germany, Perfume Museum, project, 1998, model, interior views

233

234

235

235 Vienna, Austria, SEG apartment tower, 1994–98, north view from the Old Danube 236 SEG apartment tower, study models 237 SEG apartment tower, view from the south-east

236

238

238 SEG apartment tower, ground floor foyer   239 SEG apartment tower, Orangery in front of the Skylobby   240 SEG apartment tower, air space between apartment and facade   241 SEG apartment tower, Orangery in front of the Skylobby

239

240

241

242

242 Vienna, Austria, SEG apartment block Remise, 1994–2000, working model variants **243** SEG apartment block Remise, model from the north-west **244** SEG apartment block Remise, model from the north-east

243

245 Vienna, Austria, Gasometer apartment building, 1995–2001, model of gasometer and shield, side view   246 Gasometer apartment building, model with adjacent gasometers   247 Gasometer apartment building, simulation of the interface between shield and gasometer   248 Gasometer apartment building, section model

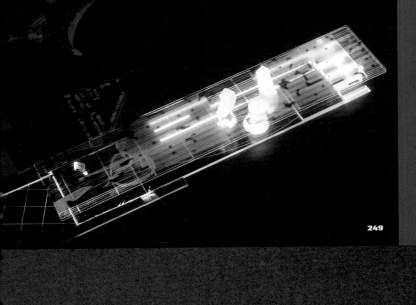

249 Biel, Switzerland, Arteplage, Floating City, 1999–2002, top view of model   **250** Arteplage, Floating City, model view

249

251 Guadalajara, Mexico, JVC The New Urban Entertainment Center, The Simultaneity of Systems, 1999-2003, interior simulations **252** JVC The New Urban Entertainment Center, exterior and interior simulations **253** JVC The New Urban Entertainment Center, simulation of exterior view **254** JVC The New Urban Entertainment Center, perspective simulation of bar und restaurant

251

253

252

254

THE CITY THROBS LIKE A HEART, TH
CITY FLIES LIKE BREATH. AND AN EX
PANDING FEELING FOR LIFE FULFILL
THESE IMAGINARY CITIES. THIS URBA
POETRY WAS SOMETIMES CONFUSE
WITH SCIENCE FICTION. 1968

>> <<

THE BUILT DRAWING

We have already mentioned that Coop Himmelb(l)au start experimenting with still very rough, but already large-scale working models, immediately after they have sketched out their first ideas, in other words long before a project becomes concrete in the form of plans, sections and elevations. If you look closely at these models it becomes suddenly clear how very important the interiors are to Coop Himmelb(l)au. Leaving aside their early work and work that involves building in existing historic stock, some of their most familiar recent projects seem like built "exploded diagrams", built from the inside outwards.

This procedure is not new, it was used in Soviet revolutionary architecture, but above all by the Dutch De Stijl architect Gerrit Rietveld. It is clear from the isometric sketches for Rietveld's *magnum opus*, the Schröder House in Utrecht (1924) how radically and consistently this house was developed in sequence from the centre to the periphery, starting with the smallest piece of furniture in its interior. This consistent logic of developing a "picture" from the inside outwards can be seen with what seems to be complete clarity even in the facade, which taken on its own radiates all the rational austerity and discipline of a Mondrian composition. But seems is the right word, because the image of the interior reflected in the facade also has something threatening, surreal, unstable about it. Could it not be that an "untamed beast" is lurking under the fissured surface? The exterior of the Schröder House, viewed as a snapshot of a "zoomed" interior or a simulation of a spatial implosion only keeps its particles under rational aesthetic and structural control with difficulty as they fly apart. Horizontal and vertical slabs intersect, collide with each other, seem to float, and the viewer is left uncertain as to their materials and statics. Bars, glazed surfaces and primary colours join in with the game, again keeping their balance with difficulty. A glance at the building plans for the house then completely reveals the mixed media *bricolage* that was needed to hold this explosive work together with steel, masonry and timber. It really is surprising that conservative art historians like Sedlmayr preferred to base their fundamental criticism of Modernism on Le Corbusier's Villa Savoye and not on Rietveld's "fly-away image of expansion". Think of the programmatic pictorial montage showing Yves Klein, that magician of the colour blue and French *enfant terrible* of the fifties art scene, on his stomach with arms outstretched, flying freely in front of a facade – would this, although it happened decades later, not have brilliantly suited the expansive force-field of the Schröder House?

Many of Coop Himmelb(l)au's works have taken over the essence of Rietveld's "centrifugal design", an approach actually rooted in the interior, and unconcerned about losses sustained in terms of exterior design. The emergence of this design strategy is most clearly to be found not in the interiors of the embryonic, psychedelic or aggression-bound early phase, but in a group of rooms that can be called something like "built psychograms". Fortunately Prix and Swiczinsky created a real prototype for this group that seems to sum up the most important parameters of their view of space (at that time). In fact the job that produced this seemed scarcely worth mentioning then: it simply involved converting a relatively small working studio on the ground floor of an 1870s building. And yet this project, the Baumann Studio (1985), was to lead to a Coop Himmelb(l)au mind space that is unsurpassed to this day.

A graphic artist friend, who had a collection of works by Attersee, Twombly, Nitsch, Rainer and others, and said that he wanted to live and work with these, commissioned Prix and Swiczinsky to convert his studio, which was much too small. It was hidden away behind three high portal arches of an 1870s palazzo in a room of about 50 square metres in plan, but was almost 5 metres high. "The small size of the premises did not discourage us," Prix and Swiczinsky remembered, "the three portals did not bother us and the height of the room was agreeable to us. We saw high walls and high doors and thought of movable stairs, flying platforms, bridges and galleries. We thought of paintings hanging in three rows one above the other. We thought of collapsed roofs that had turned into frozen wings and sliding glass. In November 1984 the drawing was completed, on July 13th, 1985 it was built."[1] There is every reason here to talk about "build-

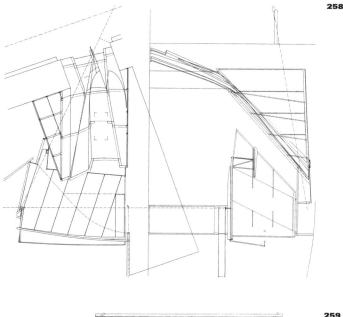

258

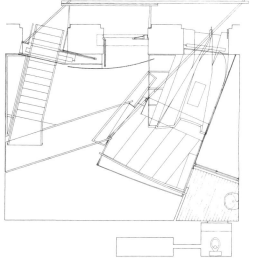

259

255

256

255 Vienna, Austria, Baumann Studio, 1984–85, first sketch 1984
256 Baumann Studio, interior with view of bridge, gallery and work station **257** Baumann Studio, interior with mezzanine floor **258** Baumann Studio, section through the gallery and partial floor plan **259** Baumann Studio, full floor plan of the gallery floor

257

ing a drawing"! Rapidly drawn sketches like this are only rarely to be found: so precisely locating and prescribing everything essential in the virtual space that no further drawing or verbal description is needed to pin things down finally. In principle Scharoun flung the "vineyard terraces" of his Philharmonic Hall in Berlin down on paper in just the same way. Admittedly in that case there was a long way to go before work on such a large building with all its complexity, which was difficult to present, could be set in train. But all that had to be addressed in the Baumann Studio was a single room, and it was a room that already existed. Which in fact did little to harm the expressiveness and depth of focus of this project.

Building the drawing meant not just symbolically installing a fragile mixture of "mobile" and "stable" elements, consisting of platform, bridge, steps and wing, each balancing the other. The space actually was enlarged to 71 square metres by fitting in a mezzanine floor. Admittedly this floor consists only of a platform that was largely detached from the enclosing walls and a bridge-like gallery. The new working area created in this way is reached by a steel drawbridge or flight of steps that can actually be cranked up or down with a cable mechanism. The cable mechanism and mobile steps are not just there for practical purpos-

162
163
164
165
166
167

es, but also for kinetic reasons. The autonomous "function" of the steps in this system that depends so much on balance is taken so far that the bottom step, when it is let down, juts – only just, but bulkily – out of one of the round-arched portals. Then this door can be closed only with the aid of an ingenious sliding device. And if the owner wants to work up on his gallery, he has to go out of the studio into the street first so that he can actually go up the stairs. Then again, when the stairs are raised, they would stick out well beyond the portal and make it quite impossible to shut the door, if it were not for a simple mechanism that automatically folds the bottom-most steps back into the inside of the room. Stairs, bridge (gallery) and platform act both as kinetic vectors that zig-zag diagonally across the room and also appear as overlapping plates or floes in a set of complex tectonic layers.

The second, central portal arch marks the harmless ground floor entrance, but the third is completely displaced by the unfolded aluminium skin of a sculpted wing that curves deeply into the interior. This ventilated, heat-insulated, self-supporting skin with built-in radiator fits on top of the work-space on the gallery like a vertical sight-screen and protective shield. It aids air circulation as a convection surface. A little window in the wing allows a peep out from the workplace. The deep glazing in the spandrels on the right and left of the wing shed muted daylight on to the platform and the bridge. The wing sculpture is a free three-dimensional element that – similarly to the steps when lowered – blurs the clearly marked joint prescribed by the old building between interior and exterior. This gives the studio facade, which is in fact incredibly banal, the surreal quality of an ambiguous phenomenon, especially at night.

260

261

260 Baumann Studio, exterior view of entrance and wing sculpture at night   **261** Baumann Studio, central support in the interior

The statics of the gallery were so important to Coop Himmelblau that a separate chapter was devoted to them in the building report. "The floating state of the design shows a formal state of tension between areas that open up the space and transversely linked lines. The statics and construction interpret this field of tension. The statically determined self-supporting individual elements – like platform, stairs, gallery, and wing sculpture – are braced together by tension members, following the lines of the design drawing, to form a statically indeterminate system. The indeterminate, open system makes it possible to reduce the cross-section of the compressed members. Load is distributed through a cantilever support system in the side walls. Three slender compression columns conduct the remaining vertical loads into the transverse arches of the cellar vaulting. Only one of the columns is visible, the other two are built into the wall. The ground plan remains open. The systems come are brought together on one of the columns. Ideally this node would be stress-free."[2] The key sentence here is the reference to the fact that the tension members in the construction correspond with the lines in the design. Never again was a construction to come so close to a drawing, never again were space-separating elements to create such a high level of floating lightness that was just within the bounds of feasibility. And as far as the free-standing support and its node are concerned, it is tempting to try to follow a very distant line of tectonic descent; let us start, for instance, with Antoni Gaudí's branching treetop-like supports for the Sagrada Familia in Barcelona (1883–1926), then move via Victor Horta's unconcealed iron support with non-positive "whip-crack capital" on the attic floor of his Hôtel Tassel in Brussels (1897), Ludwig Mies van der Rohe's apparently immaterial, "symbolizing" support for the German Reich's pavilion at the Barcelona World's Fair (1929) and ending with this spindly "crutch" with its node welded in an apparently dilettante fashion, in which heterogeneous systems are linked together. Like the supporting rod, like its node the whole space is just one bit of *bricolage*, but admittedly one that presents its force and inner logic quite calmly as a virtuoso balancing act.

Now and again Prix remarks ironically in lectures that Coop Himmelblau and the client had amazingly enough become great friends, despite this "incompetent" conversion that seemed so outlandish to him. "At first," the client said, "the Himmelblaus wanted to punish me with this design because I found their plans so ugly."[3] In fact sketches can only mutate uninterruptedly to such dense "mind spaces" because Prix and Swiczinsky strictly forbid any interference with their work. They sometimes even go against their client's wishes or quite simply try to undermine them subversively. Sometimes that works well, but it very often goes wrong, as shown by the endless story of the conversion project for the German Hygiene Museum in Dresden (1992–98), which was cut down more and more and then finally cancelled after all. But Erich Baumann, who commissioned the studio conversion, is now very enthusiastic about his room, because he says that it turned out to be far more "competent", more efficient that he said he could ever have imagined. And so we see it again, the "added value" that Coop Himmelb(l)au had to fight for at the beginning from job to job – even if it ran openly contrary to the client's will. But one cannot exist like this in the long run. "We believe," say Coop Himmelb(l)au today, "that one can never create a cleft between client and architect",[4] and then go on to say that many projects would not have been realized without a due portion of patronage. Recent large-scale projects, like the SEG apartment tower, for example, also suggest increasingly productive solidarity between architects and clients: ultimately the "added value" does not just benefit the architects' fame and honour, but also pays off well for the investors.

262

263

262 Vienna, Austria, Falkestrasse rooftop remodeling, 1984–89, exterior view   **263** Falkestrasse rooftop remodeling, interior view, foyer

The conference room in the roof extension in Falkestrasse (1988) in Vienna is also one of the "built drawing" spaces, even though here the lines that constitute the space or the structures that control the space are nowhere nearly as delicate as the ones in the Baumann Studio. This is simply because this is practically a new building that has been added on, which also makes an external impact, and is on a considerably larger scale than the Baumann Studio. "The construction model," said Wolf D. Prix with a degree of understatement, "shows that the translation of the spatial idea into architecture was not the simplest of tasks."[5] For the first time the statics were feasable "just so and not even slightly differently", as here ultimately tension and compression forces on a quite different scale had to be focused, collected and dispersed within a "constructive image" through appropriately dimensioned structures. So the cross-sections have become considerably more massive and heavy, exerting a greater load. And so the impression of floating is no longer created by "built lines" but by surfaces that border the space and translucent fields. But the play of dancing surfaces also serves to control the light and the outside view. "We also considered very carefully what view we would facilitate and what view we would block."[6] Outside surfaces blocking sun and sightlines are inserted in the form of sail-like membranes, inside they mutate – above all the sunscreen over the conference table, which is folded like steps – into curious "*objets trouvés*". According to Coop Himmelb(l)au "both views, the view of the interior from outside and the view outside from the interior, captured in one – the first – drawing (define) the complexity of the spatial relationships."[7] And yet on closer consideration attributive elements have come along as well, though in moderation; artificial lighting elements, for example, but of a kind that simply gloss over nodes or penetration points visually. Coop Himmelb(l)au were also very concerned about the effect that would be made at night when they planned the lighting. A system of direct and indirect lighting effects worthy of the theatre, including a specially constructed "arrow of light", intensifies the variable spatial qualities at night, which can be creatively controlled by the users. Transparent sheets of glass are turned into black holes, with closed surfaces placed in front of them like glowing

174
175
177
179

awnings, while the bizarre shadows the structure casts make the space look completely unreal. We must confess, say Prix and Swiczinsky, "that when we saw this building for the first time, a glittering diamond on the roof of the house, we were very proud just of ourselves."[8]

The last largely undistorted space – with just a metre-high beam ploughing through it – that can be included in the "built drawings" group, though with reservations, is: to be found at the front end of the long manufacturing ship in the Funder Factory 3 factory (1989). This was Coop Himmelb(l)au's largest interior until well into the nineties. Admittedly there is as good as no sign of seemingly "provisional" realization of graphic lines in architecture here. The volume is too massive, the tilted support structure too solid, the perforation in the glass skin too unambiguous for the result to be called filigree or even floating in any way at all. Instead, new and different spatial tendencies can be noticed, which were to change Coop Himmelb(l)au's future interiors considerably. Horizontal layers of space criss-cross each other, suggesting the "centrifugal design" from the inside to the outside that we had seen previously in Rietveld's Schröder House. The subliminally surreal effect that this causes will be reinforced in future by the addition of labyrinthine structures. That is to say by the additional installation of complex interlinking systems of motion spaces or "spaces in the space" that can no longer be perceived immediately: we can only take them in by moving in the space ourselves. And so spatial configurations are no longer immediately comprehensible, but can be decoded only by private "mental mapping". Gustav René Hocke suggests in this respect that "the aesthetic of unifying the disparate becomes an anticipated 'surreal' event."[9]

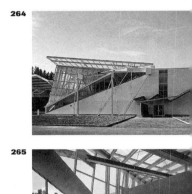

264

265

264 St. Veit/Glan, Kärnten, Funder Factory 3, 1988–89, exterior view with entrance and "glass corner"(office and laboratory wing)
265 Funder Factory 3, "glass corner" interior

BRAINSTORMING

The first realized interior based on this idea is in the East Pavilion of the Groninger Museum (1994), as mentioned above. Two statements by Coop Himmelb(l)au are extremely revealing in terms of "reading" the spatial structure installed there. Firstly, Prix compared the east wing in Groningen figuratively with a head (in the interview with Marijke Martin and Cor Wagenaar quoted above), defining the architecture as the skull and the art as the brain. Incidentally, this is an image that also crops up in the baroque period, in contemporary commentaries on Francesco Borromini's or Guarino Guarini's architecture, for example, or in historical observations on late Baroque baldacchino construction in Germany and Austria. This image also places animate and inanimate, hard and soft, flat and folded, solid and liquid, smooth and labyrinthine elements in a state of delicate balance. And since, when the brain has long since dried out, the hollow skull still exists, hardware and software form an entirely conflicting, ambiguous unity. Coop Himmelb(l)au also ironically call upon another image for Groningen, which is one of the avant-garde's best-known myths, and that is the ship metaphor, the steamer motif. "Built like a ship. Le Corbusier promised it." Prix likes to mention this playfully in his lectures, "Coop Himmelb(l)au held the promise".[10] In fact the nautical idea is not particularly interesting here, because there were very definite reasons for the fact that this building was constructed and welded together like a ship, as already explained. It seems much more revealing that Le Corbusier's person and work are brought in. Prix and Swiczinsky have frequently stressed in interviews that they admire Le Corbusier's work, especially his sculptural late work, but they are not thinking of notably popular buildings like the Ronchamp pilgrimage church (1950), the monastery of La Tourette in Eveux-sur-l'Arbresle (1957) or the Philips Multimedia Pavilion at the Brussels World's Fair (1957). They were much more interested in uncomfortable buildings like the Millowners Association building in Ahmedabad in India (1954), the parliament building in Chandigarh, India (1961) or the Harvard University Visual Arts Centre in Cambridge, Massachusetts (1961). Uncomfortable to the extent that Le Corbusier's "*promenade architecturale*" along ramps that were originally straight becomes more complicated, more "winding", in brief deliberately less immediately comprehensible; and because in Ahmedabad, Chandigarh and Cambridge "the contradiction between Cubist total form and 'organic' individual form is blown up into a sculptural drama".[11] And indeed it was not only Coop Himmelb(l)au who were fascinated by organic spatial structures placed freely inside rectangular buildings as "spaces in the space", and linked by curving pathways. Their influence can still be seen today in designs by Rem Koolhaas, Mecanoo and work by many other architects in the form of "floating objects in space", with dizzying, interactive pathways between them. But apart from aspects of this kind, Prix and Swiczinsky feel drawn to Le Corbusier's person and work because he essentially saw himself as an influential Cubist painter and sculptor rather than a practising architect, and also as a designer he tried to "restore the destroyed link between hand and head".[12]

266

267

266 Groninger Museum, The Netherlands, East Pavilion, 1993–95, hall with suspended walkway and exhibits in place   **267** Groninger Museum, East Pavilion, Exhibition space with stair

The exterior of the east wing in Groningen is actually the final outcome of the centrifugal design described above. But while Rietveld still subjected the peripheral delimitation of his Schröder House to Dutch-Calvinistic self-discipline, Coop Himmelb(l)au actually allowed the "inscribed" sheets of their spacious tectonic landslide to stagger, tilt and fall downwards and apart. The kinetics of decay are then "frozen" as in a video still; ultimately the interior is not intended to reveal itself, but simply to admit enough daylight as is needed for effective use. As in Rietveld's building, the outward drift of the exterior is focused on the interior, but here it is like a cave with many fissures, rather than working from a centred fixed point. Red-painted steel plates stiffened with former-like ribs and double T-girders of all sorts and sizes come together in the familiar measuring up of forces that plays "corporeality" off against "disembodiment".[13] Underlining the apparent chaos of this process, nearly all the lighting, ventilation and heating equipment is all over the place and open, so that it is quite correct to speak of "flying" radiators and "dancing" pipes. As if under high pressure, the spatial flow is checked everywhere by inserted objects, diverted, brought to a standstill or made to deviate. Downward-tilting ceilings and walls, zones of differing height and sections of floor that, dissolved into glass at selected corners, open up dizzying abysses, and produce a markedly cryptic jumble shot through with light-folds of all kinds and daylight chambers. (Incidentally, the motif of glass-covered holes punched threateningly in the floor recurred years later, in 1998, though with quite different atmospheric connotations, in Daniel Libeskind's Felix-Nussbaum-Museum in Osnabrück, in gridded form.) About the only things that contribute a little repose in Groningen are the vertical, white wall panels, which compensate for all diagonals and function as neutral backgrounds for the old master paintings at certain points. Without them there would effectively be no vertical hanging space.

Coop Himmelb(l)au summed up the actual high point of the space in two simple sentences: "The concept helps people to experience art on various planes. Both the inner skin of the flexible exhibition system and also the variable circulation levels make it possible to look at the art objects exhibited from a variety of viewpoints."[14] As in most Himmelb(l)au buildings, flexibility and variation are brilliantly illustrated, but in reality there are limits. However this does not contradict our argument concerning the different circulation and perception levels, as a flying walkway, i.e. a walkway suspended from the ceiling, thrusts through the centre of the spatial structure. It is reached by zig-zagging steps and platforms inserted into little nooks and crannies of space on the periphery. It is this

194
197
198

195
199

196
268

"gangway" floating halfway up the space that forms the actual crux of the whole ensemble. To the right and left of this walkway are floating white panels – looking as though they are hanging on a washing-line. These are miniature cabinets that can be unfolded for paintings to be fixed on them. They are tangibly close here, at eye-level, and yet one cannot reach them. Le Corbusier's "*passage intérieur*" always offers an austere choreography of flowing sequences of movement and perception via partial spaces and intersecting perspectives, then brings them together to form a static whole within the intended image, but Coop Himmelb(l)au offer "multiple choice". Observers are intended to be able to choose individually between different kinds of approach, between different planes of circulation, in fact even between different close-up, distant and even fine focusing of their zooming eye on the art. Horizons of perception that go beyond border or space and time replace an all-embracing whole that has been lost. In old or conventional museums there is a so-called "compulsory tour"; this is replaced here by a mind space that opens up and is accessible from all sides, divided and labyrinthine. Coop Himmelb(l)au are not particularly interested in how good this all is for the conservatorial side of art. This presentation makes it look as though Prix and Swiczinsky are projecting curious slides of random art-works on to unfinished interior walls. Coop Himmelb(l)au's section of the building was violently criticized precisely for this after the opening. It was not just problems with sealing and air-conditioning that aroused the displeasure of custodians and curators. What was attacked above all was their lack of reticence about art, indeed the fact that they more or less disempowered it completely with their "rowdy disaster architecture". In fact it would probably scarcely be possible to imagine a greater contrast today than that between Zumthor's immaculate, ascetic shrine for art in Bregenz and Himmelb(l)au's baroque container for old masters in Groningen, which is almost completely out of joint – to say nothing about Gehry's "dancing" Guggenheim Museum in Bilbao, which was most beautiful without art. But despite all the criticism we should not forget that "design's" predominance over the house exhibits (admittedly largely of local significance only) has been raised to the status of a programme by director Frans Haks and his chief architect Alessandro Mendini, and was thus intended to be the principal leitmotif in the overall composition. "Design is the Message", was the motto issued as a variant on Marshall McLuhan's familiar slogan. Mendini, Starck and De Lucchi obeyed, and their museum wings distanced themselves from the aura of the particular exhibits, generously to ingeniously. What is much more interesting is the fundamental question of whether Coop Himmelb(l)au succeeded in pulling a project that was drowning in superficiality out of the swamp of the canal basin almost by its own forelock? Whether the tireless agitators for "open spaces", by working on one of the most "closed" projects of populist architecture, have not willy nilly substantiated the suspicion that Deconstructivism is ultimately nothing but a disguised variant on late post-Modernism? Whether Himmelb(l)au's achievement in Groningen was not just "a concentrated design of accessories ... which ends up in the completely wrong place"?[15] Leaving aside critical questions of this kind, does not Himmelb(l)au's approach mean that in reality they have decorated Mendini's ideal world with a "city-crown or a crown of thorns" in steel that has burst apart, and in the interior have made the most important exhibition item a cracked landslide of space that does not worry much about compatibility between itself and the "old masters". According to Ulf Jonak, "the motifs of the broken, the semi-finished, the shaky and the scratched become allegories of human existence and, indeed, describe a feeling of 'being deeply affected' by the world as well as, at the same time, of having an effect on the world. Appropriation appears as self-assertion."[16]

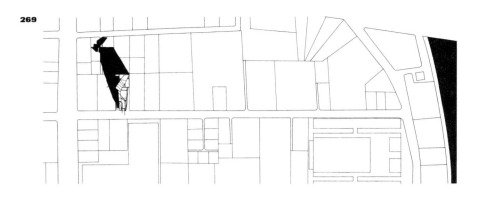

269 Fukuoka, Japan, Jasmac Bar and Restaurant, project, 1989, site plan **270** Jasmac Bar and Restaurant, model view

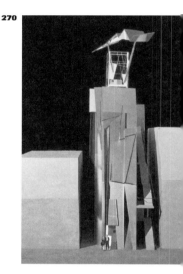

THE LIBERATED LABYRINTH

187

188

Coop Himmelb(l)au had already provided a foretaste of what Hocke calls "surreal event architecture" in 1989 with their unbuilt design for the Jasmac Bar and Restaurant building in Fukuoka, Japan. Here a very small gap between the existing buildings was to be filled with a structure housing restaurants and bars only. Practically speaking, all there was room for was a five-storey "promenade wall". The Japanese client had already seen the roof extension in Falkestrasse in Vienna, and had felt that its transparent quality was not suitable for his project, and so the Fukuoka facade was completely closed with a breast-like curved shield in folded aluminium. According to Coop Himmelb(l)au, the elements that pierce the facade are "the signs for this bar building. Inside they form the constructive elements, which support the entire body of the bar and the fittings. On the left the fire-escape moves diagonally urwards. And for the right lateral facade we have proposed a huge drawing."[17] Parts of this were to be glazed, and open up a lateral lighting slit on the side. Fundamentally the cave-like interior would have seemed like a vertically placed labyrinth, almost like a claustrophobic cage with shelves. Plunging ceilings and diagonally escaping edges were to have blurred the spatial reference and orientation points in the stairwell-like, compressed tangle of narrow, double-floored landings, flying staircases and ramps. The limited extent of the rigid volume would thus have been imperceptible. It would have made way for a dynamic of bodies floating freely in the space. This dynamic would have been further emphasized by a mobile bar container that rather like a "building within a building" would have "penetrated" the roof hydraulically and provided a prominent lookout point high above the town. In the best capitalist manner, the consumption of food and drink would have become socially more exclusive, i.e. more expensive the higher one got and the more restricted the space became.

Coop Himmelb(l)au would have been more than pleased to build walkways, but also ramps and "floating objects" into their spaces a lot earlier. But it was not until they planned the conversion for the German Hygiene Museum in Dresden (from 1992), a prize-winning competition project that has since been shelved, that an X-shaped ramp system with complex criss-crossing was to link various exhibition areas. X-shaped skylights were intended to act as powerful vectors, reinforcing spatial flow and penetration of the body of the building. Transparent roofing was also planned for the central inner courtyard of the Academy of Fine Arts in Munich (from 1995), another prize-winning competition entry that remained unbuilt. This would have produced an additional usable area, which would have served as a nucleus for the agglomeration of heterogeneous spaces in the old building. The concept of a hall space that was open at the front but

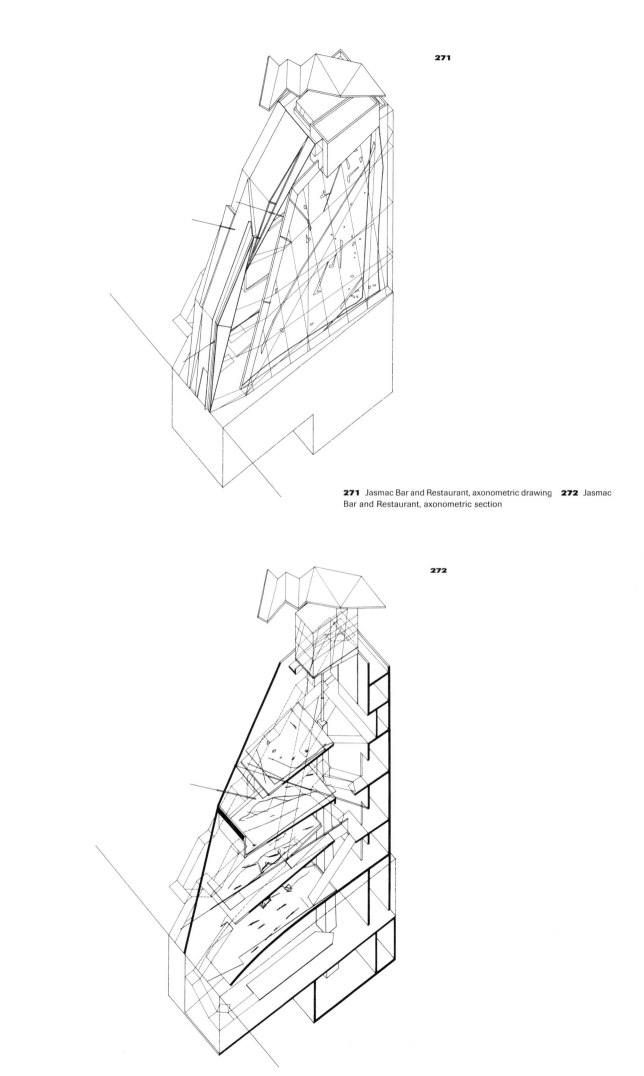

271 Jasmac Bar and Restaurant, axonometric drawing   **272** Jasmac
Bar and Restaurant, axonometric section

276
278

glazed in several layers went back to the theme of the suspended bridge in Groningen, but it was raised to a higher power. Here they were proposing a space in which several sets of stairs, ramps, walkways and bridges were suspended one above the other, and led off in all directions, some suspended, some supported rather less than more by spindly pilotis, climbing up and down in relation to each other and intended to fit together in a single, oscillating image; an image that was faintly reminiscent of Fritz Lang's film "Metropolis" or the Italian Futurists' lively scenarios. In the model, the pictorial projection of a labyrinth in the casing was rather more fascinating that the metaphor of the building that is supposed to be like a small town, which goes back to Alberti. This would mean that we would have arrived not only at one of the most important topoi in the history of Western art and culture, but probably also at the quintessence of Himmelb(l)au-esque spatial creation, linking inside and outside together.

"If it had been the task of history," says Dietmar Kamper, "to turn the inside out and extricate it (Hegel), then it has succeeded; the human environment corresponds to the hyper-complexity of the human brain which serves, morphologically and functionally, as the model for all labyrinths."[18] This statement not only deciphers the origins of the Groningen spatial structure, which according to Prix is supposed to embody a built "brain". It also tries to find a convincing interpretation of the link between inside and outside in the "labyrinthine model": "outwardly strange, fascinating, and horrible… inwardly familiar, fascinating, and sacred, and always conforming to a consciousness which grew out of a crossing of boundaries and an affirmation of life beyond death. Perhaps the easiest way for us to understand this interlacing of inside and outside is in reference to that transsubjective structure of longing which Freud has tentatively termed the 'unconscious'."[19] Of course we have to ask whether the labyrinth's symbolic enclosing walls have not already fallen today, and whether linking inside and outside has not acquired a quite different meaning because beyond the outside there is hidden nothing but the empty desert that philosophers Gilles Deleuze and Felix Guattari have described so powerfully. This would have driven away all the hopes of redemption that have been associated with labyrinths from time immemorial. "Because the labyrinth, as a symbol that creates completeness, powerfully and unambiguously points to a single way, it is also as such a figure that is entirely in keeping with the period."[20] This comforting statement by Hermann Kern may still apply to Le Corbusier's labyrinthine design for the "endless museum", which offers a path to redemption through Modernism, but a redemption formula of this kind misses Coop Himmelb(l)au's labyrinths by miles. More recent theoreticians, for similar reasons, question very severely the image of the world as a labyrinth, which is particularly deeply rooted in Italian Mannerism and has been repeatedly put forward since then. "The artist follows his lines:" writes Wolfgang Max Faust, "nomadic lines, migrant lines, sedentary lines. There is no goal, only wandering. But are not those painting metaphors, too, meant to be forgotten? Labyrinth, desert, and …".[21]

There has been harsh criticism of labyrinthine, dissonant, surreal concepts of architecture in the second half of the 20th century on another plane as well, where the labyrinth is seen as the absolute epitome of dissonant, surreal architectural concepts. Thus the Italian architectural theorist Manfredo Tafuri analysed the so-called "neo-avant-garde" of the sixties and seventies very closely. There was as yet no talk of post-Modernism at the time, but Tafuri was alluding to its forerunners. He did not just include architects like Rossi, Venturi or Stirling, but also visionary or revolutionary groups like Archigram or Superstudio. His essays are still seen as milestones of architectural criticism. In them he denied in principle the ability of the supposedly new avant-garde to overcome the crisis of late capitalist architecture by "linguistic" aesthetic shock tactics, drawn out of itself, as it were, or by attempts at built architectural criticism. In one of his most

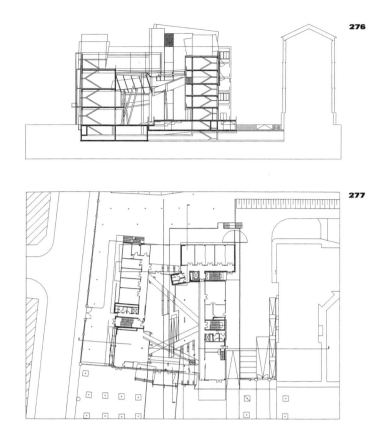

famous essays called "L'architecture dans le Boudoir – The Language of Criticism and the Criticism of Language" he went so far as to give dissonant urban designs by Archigram and Superstudio subtitles like "ceci n'est pas une ville", in allusion to Magritte's "slippery" picture title "ceci n'est pas une pipe".[22] He rejected dissonant, labyrinthine architecture of whatever colour as pure affirmation of existing social structures. Thus he was laying the foundation stones of the critical approach that denies Deconstructivism in particular any critical potential, indeed any ability to be socially "effective" in any way. Tafuri saw the metaphor of the labyrinth as nothing more than an unmistakable sign of social impotence of this kind. "There is no more 'salvation' to be found within it:" he wrote, "neither by wandering restlessly through 'labyrinths' of images so polyvalent that they remain mute, not by shutting oneself up in the sullen silence of geometries content with their own perfection. This is why there can be no proposals or architectural 'anti-spaces': any search for an alternative within the structures determining the mystification of planning is an obvious contradiction in terms."[23] It was also Tafuri, in his criticism of "incomprehensible", aestheticizing protest architecture, who associated the labyrinthine pictorial words of cubist masterpieces of Modernism with Giovanni Battista Piranesi's labyrinthine spatial distortions.[24] He proved what a close link there was between the way in which Piranesi's architectural dream interpretations and Picasso's pictograms of human behaviour used the device of shock as a design programme. And that despite enlightened commitment and despite the use of critical pictorial techniques, all they had succeeded in doing was to leave social realities out of account in a generalizing and formalizing manner; realities, he points out, that in fact were considerably more complex than they were accepted or perceived to be. Thus Tafuri had effectively apprehended Piranesi as the earliest identifiable originator of the shock-like "meta-language", going beyond time and space, that is supposed to be avant-garde and socially critical, but is in fact entirely ineffective. It was necessary at least to hint at this set of arguments as the spatial effect of Coop Himmelb(l)au's recent work has been increasingly frequently compared with Piranesi and labyrinthine concepts – even if only for the sake of a handy argument. And Giovanni Battista Piranesi's copperplate engravings also seem to offer themselves regularly as models for Himmelb(l)au's spaces, which are without perspective boundaries and deformed cubically. But is it legitimate to use baroque *trompe l'œil* for such up-to-date comparisons? In about 1745, when Piranesi's "Invenzioni capric. di Carceri" were first published and reissued in about 1760 as "Carceri d'Invenzione", these imaginary views of dungeons were for a long time taken to be the figments of a fevered mind. It is only 20th century research that has pointed out that Piranesi "ruthlessly completely reinterpreted the elementary rules of architectural spatial formation," and that "the 'carceri' sequence (has become) an experimental series about the expressive qualities of architectural structure".[25] The complicated process by which this experimental series is decoded means that "conventional perspective sets up expectations only to deny them by introducing fresh patterns", so that "the spectator becomes inescapably involved in the creative process".[26] Piranesi's biographer Wilton-Ely points out that it was not until the classical Modern cubism that a similar challenge was to be delivered. In this case, well away from being tied to any particular time (which is also why the "Carceri" are still comparatively popular today), this revealed a counter-model to nature that obeys its own laws exclusively. According to Norbert Miller, it is an artificial world made up of architecture – opposed to the creation – whose life is concealed in the asymmetry and arbitrariness of built work. He goes on to say that this world is dominated by an "impression of being temporary, of being a frozen moment", and will not tolerate any reality except its own. This is why Piranesi "draws the perspectives backwards by hours of the journey, why he allows staircases and bridges to disappear upwards for both the eye and the mind, but this is why he also pushes – by linking and bracing the architecture in the foreground – space towards the observer and up past him: exposed beams and scaffolding thrust forward out of the picture. They are only partly motivated by a desire to make the space deeper, but mainly to suggest the counter-current … compellingly. It is only in this way that the observer, in accordance with the will of the inventor of this dungeon, is completely delivered into something from which he cannot escape, as now … limiting vaulting and walls give no more purchase and as well as this the insubstantial scenic veils of the subjective nightmare have materialized to become an overwhelming presence."[27]

Would it not be possible, without any beating about the bush, to apply such carefully formulated remarks on Piranesi's spatial concepts to what is probably the most impressive interior that Prix and Swiczinsky have so far created? In fact we are not talking about "carceri", but simply about the above-mentioned foyer of their UFA-Palast multiplex cinema in Dresden (1998). However, this space does undoubtedly push towards the observer and up over him, and the exposed beams and scaffolding in this room do also thrust powerfully into the foreground. And besides, it is not possible to see the foyer in terms of a central perspective, not just because the foreground is permanently distorted and the space ceaselessly spreads out into new perspectives, but above all because of the tilting, twisting and pushing of its crystalline spatial mantle. If thick walls were not replaced by a light glass mantle, it would be possible to believe for a moment that one was standing in the labyrinthine monastery library in Umberto Eco's "Name of the Rose". In just the same way, the eye can find nowhere to rest, to say nothing about points of reference. Instead the foyer, which is as much fissured in depth as in height, develops a strong pull and literally ingests the visitors. This is not done particularly gently: they follow the motto "praise be to anything that makes us hard", and so the materials are borrowed from urban space and thus deliberately left rough and coarse. Concrete and metal predominate, with the ungainly form of the concrete sections coming up hard against the filigree steel and glass skin of the crystal. Parts of this folded skin acquired a finely structured second layer for protection against the sun. Otherwise only the double cone of the "Skybar", formed by cables, introduces a markedly filigree

280 Dresden, Germany, UFA Cinema Center, 1998, perspective structure of the Crystal seen from the entrance facade **281** UFA Cinema Center, perspective structure of the Crystal seen from the rear facade **282** UFA Cinema Center, perspective structure of the Crystal **283** UFA Cinema Center, axonometric drawing **284** UFA Cinema Center, Skybar double cone, section

280

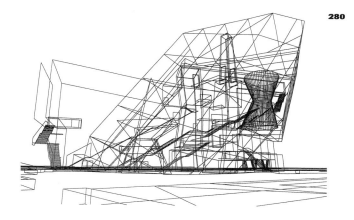

281

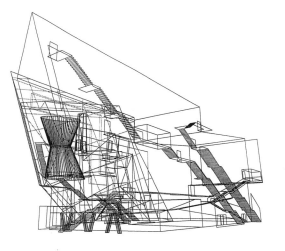

283

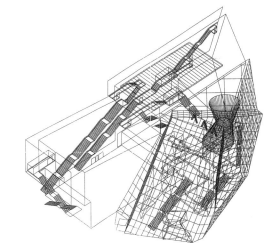

282

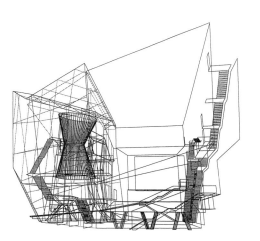

284

note into the divergent structure of massively displayed forces at play. Suspended elements, anchorages, braces, supports and tension rods are manifestly involved, yet scarcely comprehensible in this exhausting interplay of muscle. Deeply folded, largely solid concrete bodies in the ground floor area, looking like brilliant but unfortunately tardy illustrations on the subject of Expressionism, grow out towards the top as slender steles. Steles that seem familiar from Brancusi's studio. They stand in Coop Himmelb(l)au's "Tropical House" like natural formations. The building was so stretched and overstretched to the limits of the structural, the tactile and the visual that it gives the impression that it is well on its way to being transformed into a diffuse state. Here one is involuntarily reminded of the phenomenologist Gaston Bachelard, who established in relation to such quasi-"fluent" overlappings of interior and exterior that we would get no further in our search for the original expression of being by using conventional geometry. Only "by choosing more concrete, more phenomenologically exact inceptions we shall some to realize that the dialectics of inside and outside multiply with countless diversified nuances ... In order to experience (a balance) in the reality of the images, one would have to remain the contemporary of an osmosis between intimate and undetermined space."[28] And here we have it for the second time, the concept of compensation by osmosis. Could it be that built osmosis between town and building is one of the main motifs in Coop Himmelb(l)au's late work?

286

285 UFA Cinema Center, view of the central upward access through the Crystal **286** UFA Cinema Center, Crystal, upward access from the ground floor

In retrospect it is less astonishing that Coop Himmelb(l)au were able to persuade investors to accept such metaphors for the sake of "added value". It is much more surprising that it was ever possible to draw, calculate, fix the details, write out, construct, build and work out the bill for this structure. And all that without the maliciously anticipated structural damage, without the additional costs that were assumed. Much, like the complicated horizontal and vertical sections, could not be drawn conventionally. Here the computer had to come to the rescue, as was also the case for the calculations of mass or the dimensioning, to say nothing at all about the statics. Many sections could only be represented with the help of complicated "patterns", i.e. projections of their surfaces, and a lot of the spatial nodes needed virtual diagrams as illustrations. And anyone who has seen the absolutely oppressive number of drawings and details, which were still additionally needed to keep the whole thing under structural control down to the last detail, will not find it difficult to understand that this was not a particularly lucrative operation for the architects. Nevertheless they not only completely fulfilled their vision, but also provided the city of Dresden with the proverbial thorn in the flesh in terms of ideas.

The steps, ramps, platforms and bridges that perform a mechanical ballet within the glass crystal between the sculptural section of the folded lift tower, the diagonal media tower, the floating pyramid and the suspended double cone of the "Skybar", are elements in a challenging stage set. Its various stations are spread about the space like a matrix for an uncontrolled choreography of human bodies moving freely in the space. But the visitors and the architecture are not just presenting themselves. As the urban surroundings work their way into the glass crystal and the crystalline space itself – above all at night, when film trailers are projected in the urban space – works on the city, then the borders between stage and auditorium, between action and response, are blurred. This makes the foyer, leaving aside the actual use as a cinema, into an "elemental relief map".[29] The foyer becomes a catalyst of urban experience, a transitory scene for events. Its sole task seems to be to make people take an active part in acting out their urban space. Spectators become protagonists.

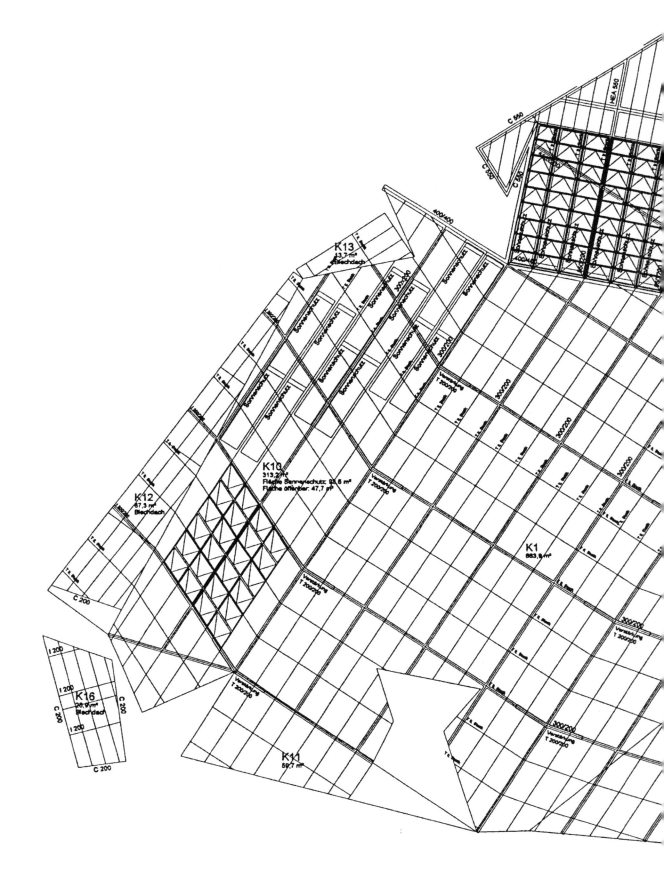

287 UFA Cinema Center, Crystal, projection of facade

For this reason Coop Himmelb(l)au paid particular attention to the lighting and illumination of this "stage". In their earlier work they had striven mainly to create a carefully balanced interplay between covering and exposing, but the proscenium of their multiplex cinema in Dresden is under glass, and thus as good as in the open air. Admittedly this is only true at night: during the day the crystal's innards are largely concealed by the dark veil of the glass covering. During the day the interior is like a negative, defined by layers and intersections, a bizarre play of light and shade that overlays everything like a flickering film and stokes the choreography of moving bodies in space. The intensity and plot of the film are largely left to chance and where the sun is in the sky. But at night the illuminated labyrinthine innards stand out from the amorphous latticework of the crystal. A lighting concept devised with specialist engineers creates effects that make it possible to modulate and control the stage effect made by the foyer. At night the effect of the sculptural bodies under glass becomes part of a permanent urban events show.

288

288 Los Angeles, USA, L.A. County Museum of Art, exhibition architecture for "Expressionist Utopias", 1993

There is much more subtle experience available on the subject of "the psychology of light". Coop Himmelb(l)au had previously been responsible for stage designs (in 1993 for Bruno Taut's "Weltbaumeister" in Graz and in 1994 for "Oedipus Rex" in Salzburg), but they had created exhibition installations as well. The exhibition architecture for "Expressionist Utopias" installed by Coop Himmelb(l)au in the Los Angeles County Museum of Art in 1993 attracted attention in terms of the theme alone. Anthony Vidler felt that this installation was particularly fascinating because it addressed an archaeological reference to the imaginary scenery of historical Expressionism and at the same time a contemporary scenery marked by deliberate distortion. Himmelb(l)au's "copy" contained a mental double coding of the kind described by Freud, who said that it was possible to keep two locations in the same space only in the mind. Vidler says: "Nowhere is this more evident than in the most dramatic event of the installation, in that thick slice of light cut at an angle from one side to the other. Constructed out of real material, it is true, the light is captured between sheets of plexiglass; but as light, it is as if a negative fault line had cracked open the solid fabric of the interior, desplaying its inner substance. Earlier projects of Himmelb(l)au had played with the metaphor of skin, peeled back to reveal the flayed flesh of building beneath; now the building has overcome its organic attachment to the human body, and is revealed as pure desire. In a kind of Rosicrucian metaphor of 'light from within,' this crack of luminosity lures at the same time as it closes itself from accessibility In the ... project the light is in a real sense captured, sliced as if between the two glass slides of a microscopic specimen: light that no longer serves its function of lighting ... deprived of all function, simply to be looked at as an exhibit in a museum. Fetishized light then, and cut uncomfortably close to our own bodies as we move carefully through these uncertain spaces. Where previously Himmelb(l)au's images of desire were figured in the many semi-angelic wings ... in the slice of light any material reference to structure is abandoned. The 'angel' is dissolved, as if in the navel of the dream ... we are literally entered into a scene populated by our doubles, and constructed like our psyche. And, inevitably, the moment we feel we are arriving at the center of this strangely comforting experience, we are suddenly and cruelly cut off from any access to what we want most; that trapped light. Perhaps this is, after all, what 'utopia' is all about; not so much the happy dream of wish-fulfillment, but the anxious dream of blocked desire."[30]

But four years later in Dresden Himmelb(l)au's programmatic light psychology means liberation, and no longer signals denied longings. The period of prohibition is long over. Light is becoming a sign of liberating emancipation. And if

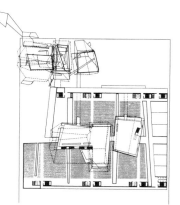

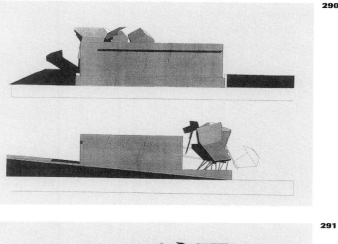

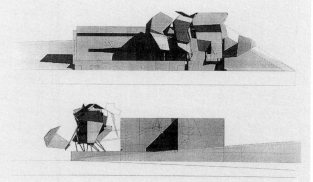

289 Seika-Cho, Japan, Kansei-Kan National Library, project, 1996, floor plan **290, 291** Kansei-Kan National Library, elevations

there is still a double code in Dresden, then the most it is doing is vividly negotiating the dialectic of inside and outside, of private and public life for everyone. According to Niklas Maak, the Dresden cinema takes on the urban role previously played by market-places: "The shimmering welter of views and bridges in the concrete foyer, which rises through the full height of the building, may be reminiscent of Piranesi's visions of space – but it is not the horror of the prison that is evoked here. The hall rips open a new scale in the middle of the world of brooding slab buildings, becoming a labyrinth of light, a light-hearted Piranesi … Coop Himmelb(l)au's building does not just serve Ufa's commercial interests; it also remains aware of the social claims of modern architecture, something that some people had already committed to the ideological scrap-heap of architectural history. This is the idea of creating places for collective experience, for the 'res publica', for public life. The Ufa cinema has become such a place, precisely because of its spectacular form, which sets a sign in the wilderness … An intelligent intervention, inventing a new form of public space after the breakdown of urban quality."[31]

289
290
291

The design for the Kansai-Kan National Library in Seika-Cho, Japan (1996), would have responded to its urban surroundings in the same way. A large volume extracted from the cube of the library block was placed in front of the book container as a free-standing sculptural element. It was defined by Prix and Swiczinsky as a "museum of knowledge" and was intended to be linked with the book stacks and reading rooms by spectacular architectural "conductors" like the synaptic connections between neurones in the human brain. And so Prix and Swiczinsky's task was similar to the one in Groningen: designing "a copy of memory" positioned in front of the plain book container as a symbol of cultural significance. But the spaces in the extremely creased and distorted glass end of the building, which was even provided with extremities, would have thrust much more aggressively into its urban environment than was the case in Dresden. A more restrained variant was the original "Hamburg Crystal" (1997), which has since been considerably changed in terms of function. The diagonally positioned crystal was supposed to stand as a "nocturnal source of energy" for Hamburg, within an extraordinarily difficult mixture of college and student building, a hotel complex and a theatre for musicals. Placing a crystalline shape above a street corner would have been able to present something of the lively use and convey it to the outside world in media terms. Here too a commercial space would have become the kind of urban meeting-place that became reality in Dresden after this design.

292, 293 Kansai-Kan National Library, model views **294** Hamburg, Germany, Hamburg Crystal, 1997- , model view

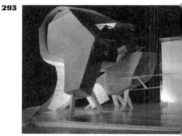

The theatrical character of Coop Himmelb(l)au's Dresden crystal has become a theme in its own right: since then Prix and Swiczinsky have taken the sculptural sections reminiscent of Brancusi's steles out of the glass "Tropical House" and put them under "flying" horizontal roofs everywhere. The final working design for the new city centre in Guadalajara, Mexico or the prize-winning competition entry for the "Arteplage" in Biel, which will be built for the Swiss national exhibition "expo.02", illustrate this new approach. The oscillating labyrinth, the osmotic response of fractured, layered structures to the urban space – never mind whether it is in a cave or under glass – are replaced here by the concentrated use of interactive, three-dimensional bodies at the city's media focal point. Coop Himmelb(l)au's floating raft for the "Arteplage" will project its visitors' movements on to a canvas-covered roof floating high above the raft, while three sculpturally distorted towers with viewing platforms will thrust brutally through this media sky. Here Coop Himmelb(l)au are returning to the "situationist" spaces of their early days, albeit under quite different conditions. And in Guadalajara there will again be cloud-like structures alongside hard and freely-sculpted bodies. So far we can only gain a sense of how its structure and even its interior could look from computer-generated spatial simulations. But there is sure to be a collision here as well between hard (calculating) and soft (experimental) structures. The city as a forum for a disciplined "*jeu magnifique*", for a mixture of fixed and hybrid bodies in the media space, could this be Himmelb(l)au's material for the future?

249
250

74
75
76

But in fact it is still the timeless image of the "Open House" that provides the most conclusive projections of what Coop Himmelb(l)au's motion spaces and mind spaces mean for the small private sphere. In 1990 is was about to be realized on Malibu beach in California. But the client died. And yet as a piece of "unbuilt architectural theory" for housing it is still perhaps one of the most exciting models since Le Corbusier's Villa Savoye in Poissy near Paris (1931) and Mies van der Rohe's Farnsworth House in Plano, Illinois (1950). Its interior involves a symbiosis of "built drawing", "centrifugal design" and "liberated labyrinth". Remembering that the only access to the interior cosmos of the Villa Savoye is by a monocentric "*promenade architecturale*" and the classical-style cella of the Farnsworth House is effectively the zero point of "centrifugal design",

the flow of the "Open House" is articulated in an indeterminate, provisional casing. Although historical comparisons are actually ruled out, this casing seems like nothing other then an optimistic paraphrase of Caspar David Friedrich's oppressive painting "Schiff im Eismeer oder die gestrandete Hoffnung" (Ship in the Sea of Ice or Stranded Hope; 1821). In Friedrich's picture the ice floes are pushing over each other diagonally to one side of a wrecked ship that is crushed in the ice, and forcing their way, threateningly erect, into the centre of the hopeless scenario, but the "Open House" seems to radiate complete optimism. It seems to reflect liberating balance rather than aggression. Cave and crystal, stage and box, exposing and covering, heaviness and lightness, inside and outside seem to fuse in its interior quite effortlessly. If we follow Herbert Muck and define synergy as an "interlaced, overlapping, multi-dimensional form of function, which we can see happening in a whole range of natural spheres … . as being allotted to complex fields of effectiveness" and talk "about synergy between organs and their surroundings, objects and milieu",[32] then the interior of the "Open House" is pure synergy. There is no more labyrinthine claustrophobia, no more staggering through cryptic "carceri", no inhibiting trials of strength between rival structures. Instead of this we are offered a single, light, spacious room, bounded by a few provisional-seeming surfaces and lines. Bridge, ramp, stairs and "springboard", bound into the disciplined confusion of dynamic lines and thin profiles, have something of the charm of fifties swimming-baths. The space seems to react in a lively fashion to sky, beach and sea, to reflect them, like the inside of a makeshift wind-break put together from flotsam and jetsam. You feel that the components of this piece of *bricolage* could be blown away in all directions by the wind at any moment. The labyrinth has liberated itself and become a gleaming white piece of housing for nomads. When this space was drawn – with closed eyes – there was also only a vague sense of concentration on "rays of light and shadow, brightness and darkness, height and width, whiteness and vaulting, the view and the air".[33] Classical Modern architecture promised subjective emancipation but only gave us collective domestication in rank and file; surely this promise could be redeemed here.

186

PROJECTING THE PROJECT

All over the world, young architects in particular swear blind that everyone in the Coop Himmelb(l)au office draws with their eyes shut. In fact Prix and Swiczinsky are not entirely innocent of spreading this myth. Connoisseurs of the scene may shrug their shoulders and forget all about it. But as an image of this kind can bother even generous clients who are interested both in experiment and being patrons, and even be counter-productive in the case of everyday investors, we should perhaps put paid to this kind of nonsense once and for all. Anyone who visits the Vienna office or its offshoot in Los Angeles will find colleagues working at drawing boards and PCs with alert eyes and clear heads. Ultimately Himmelb(l)au's projects are so complex as a rule that they require a far higher degree of professionalism and building management that is generally assumed. It is precisely these qualities that even hardened representatives of investment houses and other authorities trust.

But it is a fact that for Wolf D. Prix and Helmut Swiczinsky the first act of "projecting" a design in the form of a concentrated sketch, quite often reinforced immediately by a further series of drawings still has an importance that goes well beyond the world of everyday architecture. The reason for this can be found in Coop Himmelb(l)au's early days. In the great architectural crisis of the late sixties, when everyone started to escape from the "bourgeois subjectivity" of design drawing into the less suspect world of socialist "datascaping",[1] Prix and Swiczinsky kept faith. While some people were giving up designing and building to concentrate on getting socially more relevant details down on paper, notions other than aesthetic problems, and others were confirming Ernst Bloch's slogan that "utopian fermentation in paper architecture grows stronger in times when the way of building changes",[2] Coop Himmelblau were volubly asserting themselves as a team of "doers". The team were fascinated by the Vitality of Viennese actionism, and would not even have dreamed of starting to work on documents folders rather than plans. But the less there really was to build in those days, the more intensively Prix and Swiczinsky concentrated willy nilly on those feverishly nervous, freehand preconceptions that architecture museums the world over are fighting for today. These were film-like animation sketches for tomorrow's science fiction world. Which of course immediately laid Coop Himmelblau open to the reproach of running some sort of "comic studio", but not an architects' office.

"The drawing is important to us," Coop Himmelblau retorted in 1969. "Although it is often forced to replace the building. But we never make a drawing for ist own sake. It is much more a 'building' of an idea on paper. The first, emotional confrontation with the psychic spaces of the project."[3] And so directly after Himmelblau's pneumatic and actionist phase they produced a body of uncommonly dense "first sketches" made up of a few hard lines and hatching, scribbled in pencil and ground into the paper in stark contrast with the "obstetric forceps cleanness of post-war Modernism".[4] Above all they were full of life, these sketches, as though they wanted to avoid precisely the thing that Ludwig Wittgenstein was complaining about in his "Vermischte Bemerkungen" when looking back on his (and Paul Engelmann's) famous house in Vienna: „My house for Gretl is the product of a resolutely discriminating ear, good manners, it expresses great understanding (of a culture etc.), but primitive life, wild life that wants to have a fling – is lacking. And so one could also say that it lacks health."[5] Borrowing from this, Coop Himmelblau's sketches really are a process of "projecting" a design in the etymological sense of the German word *Ent-Wurf.* Before each one of these births from the head and the hand they tried to concentrate completely on excluding every bit of architectural knowledge, every model and everything that had made its mark, and to plunge down to the absolute "zero point", as it were, into the *terra incognita* of pre-architectural sensibility. This is similar to "Dripping" or "Action Painting" by an artist like Jackson Pollock in the fifties. These drawings coaxed out of the milieu were also uncommonly dense pre-architectural projections, spontaneously thrown-out by their own psyche. You could object that this is quite banal, this is how architectural sketches are always made! But what Coop Himmelblau achieved here in the form of "ideation and imagi-

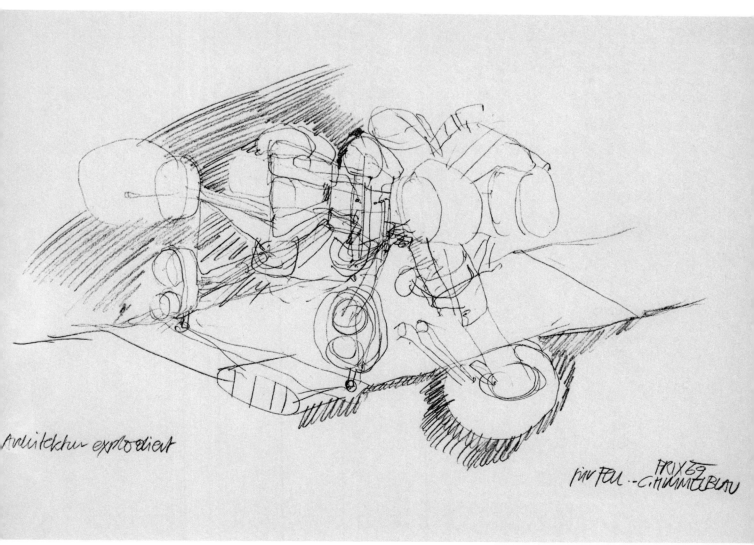

Architektur explodiert

par feu ...C.HIMMELBLAU

PRIX 69

298

300

301

302

nation in the act of drawing"[6] was in fact extraordinary because these were sketches that only seemed to have anything to do with architecture if you looked at them very closely. In this spontaneous process they seem to harden, apparently uncontrolled and fluctuating greatly, into traces that are analogous with architecture, but not in conformity with it. On them you could see either soft condensed space dissolved, distorted or transformed, or sharp-edged, knotted space condensing and hardening. The fact that they were also of a very high aesthetic calibre lent strength to the assumption that Prix and Swiczinsky were indeed "only" artists and not architects; a suspicion that was additionally encouraged by Coop Himmelblau's rowdy, hooligan-like and would-be revolutionary appearance.

MENTAL MAPPING

The importance of the primary sketch in Coop Himmelblau's approach to producing architecture changed when they started to land their first building commissions in the late seventies and early eighties. The pressure of the concrete commission seemed to make the psychograms they committed to paper considerably denser. They became more architectural, but not in the sense that they were now more intelligible in the conventional sense. It was more that concentrating on concrete situations led to the emergence of "mental maps" that effectively embodied the essence of the later design. The process of mental mapping,[7] which was cultivated at a comparatively early stage by Prix and Swiczinsky, in fact condensed all the essential characteristics of a project projected on to scraps of paper in the form of suggestive abbreviations. Most people would have seen these as meaningless, unreasoned scribbles, destined for the wastepaper basket, but for Prix and Swiczinsky they were hypothesis and construction plan in one: "... architecture lives for seconds at the moment of conception. It can never be Past, because at conception it becomes Future. The instant of conception differentiates and decides. Is this instant free from pressure, cliché, ideology and formalism, then architecture becomes free. Then the circumstantial pressures crumble. Cuasality is overturned. Architecture is now."[8] Then in the same year, 1983, Prix and Swiczinsky almost casually wrote a note about design that has pursued them almost as a stigma, right to the present day: "An Open House drawn with eyes closed. Undistracted concentration on the feeling the space will have."[9] And the "action design" that was 'projected' out of this extreme kind of drawing activity was indeed so deeply and – within certain limits – so finally precise that the first working model of the "Open House" was actually developed from this "subconscious figure". The model was thoroughly revised until it could be used as a basis for drawing definitive ground plans, sections and elevations. And even these more objective drawings would turn out to be very different from conventional planning graphics.

"We began to draw elevations and sections on top of each other," noted Coop Himmelblau in 1984, "as if it were possible to see the building with X-ray eyes." It would be appropriate to see them as diagrams of the experience of the specific motion through space. The way in which the building becomes denser and opens up, the overall connections – which can never be seen in their entirety when the building is complete, but only sensed – become sharp and visible on the plan. Themes circling around 'open architecture' and 'project design' became thematic spirals for us. We divided the word 'Entwurf' – project, design – into the prefix 'ent' and the noun 'Wurf'. 'Ent-Wurf'. 'Ent', suggesting something emergent that becomes manifest, and 'Wurf' the act of throwing. Without knowing where this was going to take us we started to condense and shorten the time taken for the design process. This means that we did still have long discussions about the project, but always without thinking of the spatial consequences. And then suddenly the drawing is there, on paper, on the table, and at the same time we make a working model to go with it. It works like this: Coop Himmelblau are a team. While we are drawing the architecture is expressed in words, the drawing is talked through to the others, they are thus able to experience the project and the moment of design as experienced is conveyed. (We cannot prove it, but we think very strongly that the more intensely the design is experienced by the designer, the more the built space will be open to experience.) And this moment, when architecture is experienced, when one has a sense of architecture, is the moment of *'Ent-Wurf'*."[10] Two years later, Prix and Swiczinsky once more confirmed this description in an interview with Peter Noever, the editor of the magazine *Umriss* and director of the Museum für angewandte Kunst (Museum of Applied Art; MAK) in Vienna. " *'Entwerfen'* (designing) like *'Entflammen'* (inflaming, as in passion) suggests a very personal psychological process. We try to shorten the design process into a design moment. Because we work on the basis that the building cannot be different from whatever the architect feels and thinks at the moment of design. The more inhibited, frustrated and cliché-ridden the architect is, the more inhibited, frustrated and cliché-ridden his architecture will be. He is personally responsible for this."[11]

303

303 Groninger Museum, East Pavilion, working model

Passages like this do serve up a considerable portion of mystification, or at least of covering things up. In principle the intention is only that the "mental mapping" in the early design stages should give birth to a spontaneous drawing that takes three-dimensional, situationist, sculptural form immediately afterwards. Both, in other words drawing and three-dimensional work, have more to do with art than architecture. It is only in the successive transformational studies to which the three-dimensional work is submitted that the function and form of the particular building task finally start to shine through, that this sculptural form becomes the touchstone of the archi-tectonic, art becomes an architectural model. And right at the end of this process of mutation things materialize and concretize in the form of plans, and we have the building, "frozen" in one of many possible conditions. Scarcely anything in this process has changed – with the exception of drawing with their eyes closed – right down to the present day. The Groningen museum pavilion is a clear demonstration of this. And it is certainly not alone, as Frank O. Gehry, for example, also scribbles drawings that are at first almost completely unintelligible, and these are then transformed into models by his brilliant "deciphering department". It is only then that the actual task of rejecting and projecting ideas begins. Anyone who has visited Gehry's office in Santa Monica, California, will probably have been struck immediately by the extensive "trophy collections" of rejected working models nailed one above the other on the studio walls. And of course this accumulation of models also makes it clear how great is the danger of failure in this process, how many spatial sculptures have turned out to be architecturally unsuitable in this process of transformation and adaptation.

DESIGN BODIES

But Wolf D. Prix and Helmut Swiczinsky would not be Coop Himmelb(l)au if they had not enriched their design repertoire over the years with other myth-generating techniques. Thus for example in 1987, when they were working on designing "The Heart of a City" for Melun-Sénart, near Paris. A year later the team made a strange admission about how this spectacular design, which won the first prize, had come into being: "Last year, we noticed that we gradually began to emphasize the verbal description of the design with gestures of our hands. And with projects for Paris and Vienna, the language of the body was the better drawing and the first model. And when we began to work on the projects for the cities New York and Berlin, the face and body of these cities became more and more distinct: On a team photo of Coop Himmelblau, we began to see and draw the lines and surfaces of the city. Our eyes became towers, our foreheads bridges, the faces became landscapes, and our shirts site plans. Superimposing the existing city map and the new drawing, the contours, lines and surfaces of the faces and bodies, previously so important, gradually vanished in the whirl of existing planning. Yet the lines, fields and surfaces of the new structure delineate themselves clearly, ever more clearly. They became three-dimensional and cast shadows. Now we are going to enlarge our team photo, step by step, until just the pupils of the eyes are visible. They are the plan of a tall building, and we intend to build it."[12]

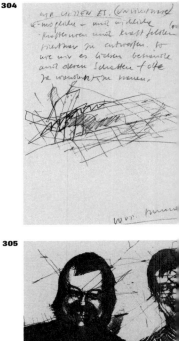

304 Sketch, Our Bodies Dissolving in the City, 1987 **305** Sketch and collage for Melun-Sénart, Our Eyes Become the Ground Plans of Towers, 1987 **306** Collage for Melun-Sénart, The Heart of a City, 1987

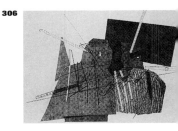

A considerable dollop of scepticism seems in order for this passage as well. At least a critical distinction should be made between truth and stylization. It is true that Coop Himmelblau had experimented with photocopied detailed enlargements of earlier sketches on a number of occasions when working on previous designs, and with photographs of people and actions as well. And there are plenty of precedents for architects using their hands and arms to help them explain certain design or construction problems. For example, Frank Lloyd Wright was famous for ceaselessly using his hands and arms to explain certain construction principles.[13] But Coop Himmelblau's testimony goes a little further by making body and drawing into one. Design means incorporating bodies and vice versa. If this incorporation were to function, it would be a daring move, as it would endow design something like eschatological traits. Admittedly we are quickly back in the realm of fact if the process described is seen merely as an artistic aperçu. As in "Body Painting" with which Yves Klein became so famous in the fifties, in this design – and this design only – "body prints" become abstract "drawing patterns". The bodies lose their characteristics in this process and dematerialize into a strange laying of traces that refers back to them only in "reflection". Incidentally, the Viennese painter Arnulf Rainer's overpaintings of photographs of his own face and body that won him international attention in the sixties also followed similar principles. Bodies disappeared once and for all under violent black brush-strokes, and then referred back to themselves in dematerialized form – completely invisible but reflected into the vacuum of the black surface, as it were. The French philosopher Michel Foucault analysed this reflection effect memorably in one of his lectures: The mirror is "a utopia, in that it is a place without a place. In it, I see myself where I am not, in an unreal space that opens up potentially beyond its surface; there I am down there where I am not, a sort of shadow that makes my appearance visible to myself, allowing me to look at myself where I do not exist ... At the same time, we are dealing with a heterotopia. The mirror really exists and has a kind of come-back effect on the place that I occupy: starting from it, in fact, I find myself absent from the place where I am, in that I see myself in there. Starting from that gaze which to some extent is brought to bear on me, from the depths of that virtual space which is on the other side of the mirror, I turn back on myself, beginning to turn my eyes on myself and reconstitute myself where I am in reality. Hence the mirror functions as a heterotopia, since it makes the place that I occupy, whenever I look at myself in the glass, both absolutely real – it is in fact linked to all the surrounding space – and absolutely unreal, for in order to be perceived it has of necessity to pass that virtual point that is situated down there."[14] Applied to the design for Melun-Sénart, this thesis would reduce Coop Himmelblau's apparently sensational body-reflections to a tolerable scale. The design would return to itself from the depths of virtual space behind these reflections, look at itself and place itself where it had to make its effect. Even though Prix described them later as "better language", as "first models",[15] the bodies that disturb us in this way are objectively speaking nothing other than heterotopias of a social condition, "counter-placings or bearings" that have been marked in. Certainly not everyone would agree with this. For example, the French philosopher Jean Baudrillard never tired of pointing out that nowadays abstraction no longer functions on the pattern of maps, duplicates or mirrors, but exclusively as a result of simulation. He goes on to say that this uses "various models to generate something real that has no origin or reality, i.e. something hyper-real. The territory is no longer situated off the map, and also it no longer becomes outdated. From now on the converse is true: the map is situated off the territory, indeed it produces it".[16] Melun-Sénart would be a perfect projection of hyper-reality in this sense; mental mapping (including the body-pictures) would have existed long before the design and would have created it almost casually, *post festum*.

But let us look harder at what is implied by linking a design with photographs of one's own body, which seems so strange at first sight. It is unlikely that Prix and Swiczinsky were prompted by Foucault's idea of heterotopia, as then as now they are not particularly interested in pre-formulated theories. Even if we wanted to dismiss relating the Melun-Sénart design to pictures of themselves as a mere narcissistic whim, the subject of body-traces as a design justification would still be in the air as one of Deconstructivism's main theoretical and strategic concerns. For example, there is some affinity, though admittedly the approach is much more heavily systematized and theoretically underpinned, in Bernard Tschumi's description in his book "The Manhattan Transcripts" (1981) of the influence of the body and its movements on various levels of a design. Bodies play an extraordinarily important part in Tschumi's research, both in terms of perception and in terms of transformation, combination and deconstruction. In terms of notations, for Tschumi bodies are a key factor in perceiving movement and events. "The movements – of crowds, dancers, fighters – recall the inevitable intrusion of bodies into architectural spaces, the intrusion of one order into another. The need to record accurately such confrontations, without falling into functionalist formulas suggested precise forms of movement notation. An extension of the drawn conventions or choreography, this notation attempts to eliminate the preconceived meaning given to particular actions in order to concentrate on their spatial effects: the movement of bodies in space. Rather than merely indicating directional arrows on a neutral surface, the logic of movement notation ultimately suggests real corridors of space, as if the dancer has been 'carving space out of a pliable substance': or the reverse, shaping continuous volumes, as if a whole movement has been literally solidified, 'frozen' into a permanent and massive vector. Each event or action (a singular moment of a 'program') can be denoted by a photograph, in an attempt to get closer to an objectivity (even if never achieved) often missing from architectural programs."[17] Tschumi also feels that the traces left by bodies or movements also have an important part to play in terms of transformation and combination: "All transformational devices (repetition, distortion, etc.) can apply equally and independently to spaces, events or movements. Thus we can have a repetetive sequence of spaces (the successive courtyards of a Berlin block) coupled with an additive sequence of events (dancing in the first court, fighting in the second, skating in the third, etc.). ... Adding events to the autonomous spatial sequnce is a form of motivation, in the sense the Russian Formalists gave to motivation ..."[18] And finally, in terms of deconstruction Tschumi's ideas lead to a convincing explanation of the desired integration of photographs of bodies or body movements into planning processes: "Photographs of events (as oposed to photographs of buldings): the photograph's internal logic suggests that it can function in varied ways. It first acts as a metaphor for the architectural program, by referring to events or to people. Second, it can be read independently, for these photographs all possess their own autonomy, independent of the drawings juxtaposed to them. Third, the events' allegorical content can powerfully disturb the neutral logic of the game's successive moves, introducing a purely subjective reading. Finally, it can be deconstructed and reorganised in a variety of ways, suggesting the idea of hybrid activities."[19]

Here Tschumi is supplying, albeit indirectly, the reason why Coop Himmelblau transform bodies into urban structures. As well as this, it seems as though Prix and Swiczinsky were intuitively using their own "design bodies" as a practical way of testing a "printing process" that was being researched not just by Tschumi, but by other theoreticians at roughly the same time. However, this should not really change anything about Coop Himmelblau's fundamentally self-referential "Pro-jecting". Thus all Prix had to do was a little light retouching in his lectures. "In the last five to ten years," he said in 1991, "we have begun to shorten the actual process of design, to condense it ... While one of us is putting the drawing down on paper the other is building the model. The model does not have a scale; like the drawing, it is intended to be a preliminary impression of the emergent building. We achieve (our) objective ... better with the method I have just described (which undoubtedly has more to do with art) than with the conventional one-dimensional design rules of today, which date from the nineteenth century. It seems important to us to replace this traditional way of thinking and seeing with a multilayered 'logic' that allows us not only to understand complexity but also to invent it. "Our architecture can be found where thoughts move faster than hands to grasp it. So the first drawing is immensely important for us, it is the first impression of a building. In the last three to four years we have begun to shorten even further this very rapid design process, which can best be compared with coming close to the center of an explosion. We simply started to replace the spoken language, with which we were accustomed to communicate about the projects, with the more rapid language of the body. That is, Helmut and I no longer talk; indications are enough, gestures."[20]

307

307 Body movements (Wolf D. Prix)

As far as the first sketches were concerned, these had now become less inhibited, softer. They actually now consisted only of a few quick strokes, filigree lines, sometime angelic configurations that bore no relation to spatial co-ordinates. Coop Himmelblau had tried in vain to stop this emergence of a more peaceful draughtsman's line before, by attacking their sketches first by tearing them, then even by burning them. Traces of soot, singeing, burns and charred edges were sometimes added later, sometimes built into the creative process. They had in fact only enhanced the morbid aesthetic attraction of such "wounded" preconceptions. Now this was not really what the inventors intended, which was why Prix and Swiczinsky hit upon the above-mentioned language of their own bodies, among other things, in their search for even more striking ways of layering meaning. As they were constantly approached about their somewhat enigmatic design approach Prix came up with another piece of rhetorical foreshortening at an international Deconstructivist meeting in 1992 saying that "we discuss the project for quite some time, but without thinking of the tangible, spatial consequences. Then, suddenly, a design is there ... And always, at the same time, a model is built ... It works like this: Coop Himmelblau is a team. There are two of us. While we draw, architecture is expressed in words; the drawing is then narrated in the three-dimentional model. ... In recent years, we've noted that, slowly but surely, we've begun to emphasize verbal descriptions of our designs by means of the gestures of our hands. Working on projects for Paris and Vienna, we found that it was body language which yielded the superior drawing, and the first model."[21]

Those inclined to mock may object at this stage that Helmut and Wolf have been living together for over three decades now, not like an old married couple, but nevertheless working together almost every day. And surely a few economical silent gestures are sometimes sufficient for people who are so familiar with each other to be able to "tell" each other a whole story? Something that for others would need long-winded explanations can be dealt with in a nod and a wink, as it were, with a few small movements. But does recourse to such minimal gestures not stunt communication? And however much this discordant image might relate to many old married couples, it does not quite cover the case of Prix and Swiczinsky. The fact is that the explanatory gestures mentioned by Prix refer only to the short initial design moment. And so let me immediately put paid in antic-

299

300

ipation to a new myth averring that the Coop Himmelblau team communicate only in gestures. Prix and Swiczinsky not only draw with their eyes open, but also talk to each other in a perfectly normal professional way. Which does not mean that these partners are not particularly well matched: what team could have put up for so long a time with the fact that one of them is extroverted, impatient, quick-tempered, verbally agile and a man of the world, while the other is introverted, careful, soothing and home-based? Wolf D. Prix and Helmut Swiczinsky realized at an early stage that their strength lay mainly in ideas they had in common: about shaping design and models, about creative and reflective thinking, about vision and pragmatism. Sometimes this common approach goes so far nowadays that they both start drawing the same sketch spontaneously and simultaneously, working next to each other with two or four hands, moving towards each other or drawing one on top of the other. Each of the two has found an appropriate position in the office, which has now grown to quite a size – about 40 employees at the time of writing –, Prix as foreign secretary and Swiczinsky as home secretary. While one of them travels around the world, publicizing the office and getting work, or spends weeks in Los Angeles as a design teacher, the other looks after the proverbial shop, making sure that customers are cared for and deadlines met, that planning is calculable and building correctly executed. But they are still both Coop Himmelb(l)au!

The example of the Groningen museum wing (1994) shows very clearly that the effectiveness of this teamwork can be driven to the limits of the possible under certain circumstances. The team was heavily under pressure of time, given that they had little more than nine months for planning and building. They produced a first rapid sketch in late 1992 that really bore no resemblance to architectural pre-planning, and a first model that was definitely nothing like an attempt at three-dimensional projection. At least that seemed to be the case. Even Coop Himmelb(l)au themselves spoke of the challenge "of transferring an almost psychedelic first sketch into the third dimension of a model". In fact many people found that it was nothing more than a meagre set of senseless scribbles on paper. It looked as though it had been scribbled absent-mindedly on a note-pad during a telephone call: scarcely more than a few suggested strokes fitting together to make an entirely meaningless random product. But others saw it as a work of art remotely reminiscent of Cy Twombly, concealing the kind of violent gesture that had been typical of minimalist Informel art in the fifties and sixties. Even today it is amazing to compare this sketch with the final plans, not to see how much or how little of the Informel gesture had flowed into the graphics of the plan, but because the effect of constriction and breadth has survived, of static and flowing space. And so in this case the sketch was not so much architectural pre-figuration as a seismographic reaction to the place as found. Its points of repose, its deflections and interferences had first of all to be "preserved" in the hasty model and then continuously transformed into a three-dimensional image. Wolf D. Prix has himself admitted that they had pushed their specific design approach as far as it would go here, both artistically and in terms of representational technique. "We believe," he wrote, "that this (first) drawing when enlarged will contain everything if it is viewed as a Cubist painting. It is not a section, a facade or an elevation and yet it contains not only the programme but the construction and the sequence of spaces. Each programme has starting points at many levels. Like a Cubist painting, this drawing is a psychogram of the space. ... The starting point was to apply this method with complete consistency to a museum. The first drawing tries to hold on to fluid architecture that is constantly changing. We have used this drawing for three different projects: an exhibition in Los Angeles, where we interpreted it as a ground plan; a stage set, where we treated it as a section which shaped the whole space of the theatre; and the Groninger Museum. There we began by studying the basis on our

310

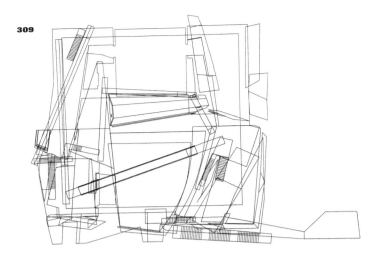

309 Groninger Museum, East Pavilion, three-dimensional structure,
top view   310 First sketch for the Groninger Museum, East Pavilion,
1992

pavilion, which has a very austere form. We tried to define spaces that were lit
by natural and artificial light. This led to a model which, on the basis of Mendini, had different light spaces. We put the drawing over this model. That was the
starting point for the Groninger Museum. The outcome was a model on a scale
of 1 to 200 which already incorporated the next phase. The following step in our
design process consists of enlarging the models to the scale of 1 to 1. ... We
never concerned ourselved with the works to be shown in the pavilion. It was
only when it was finished that we thought about them. A museum only functions properly if it does not go into the art but instead creates art in an atmos-
phere of its own."[22]

Once again, the Himmelb(l)au text conceals more than it reveals. The essence
of what it is saying is that in the case of Groningen the sketch did not precede
the model – as usual – but they were both produced at the same time. The subsequent artistic overlap of abstract model and abstract sketch was intended to
make the sketch more three-dimensional and the model more of an image. As
this could not happen instantly, the overlapping process was repeated until a
viable basis or starting model had been established for concrete development
of the design. This is not the actual sensation contained in the text: the amazing fact is that we are told that the first sketch was used three times for different projects – once as a ground plan, once as a section and finally as an elevation. Of course this is all part of the Deconstructivist presentation technique.
But while plans by Eisenman, Hadid, Moss or Mayne frequently include ground
plans, sections, elevations and isometric designs drawn one on top of the other,
Coop Himmelb(l)au follow Cubist sculptors and twist and turn the same figure
until it fits in with this or that function. This means that the first sketch is (actually "was", because this process has not been repeated since Groningen) removed
from the unique generative process and – robbed of its character as a unique
object and a tool – declared to be a freely available montage figure. We have
known since Lissitzky's "Prouns" or De Stijl buildings at the latest that skilfully
prepared figures of this kind can be transferred to all levels of projection in architecture. Prix and Swiczinsky have shown that the procedure can still be used
today. Whether they have simply developed a more efficient planning economy
for their own office by doing this or have made a productive contribution to reis-
suing and further developing familiar design techniques is a question that is
generally understood to remain unanswered until it can be seen to make sense
and work in terms of a piece of built work. What has been proved beyond doubt
is that the trace image that was the *Ent-Wurf* for Groningen was used again for
the exhibition installation (described above) for Los Angeles and for the stage
set, was entirely viable as a score for performing open space, as part of the struggle again closed space.

DRAWING NARRATED INTO THE MODEL

We have already talked in detail about the adventure of the common ideas, the process of communal design, the emergence of the first sketch. We have also seen that a first pre-architectural model is made in parallel with this process. The statement that "the drawing is narrated into the three-dimensional model" is one of the most precise and poetic that Himmelb(l)au have ever made. Because the more simultaneously the first sketch is narrated into the model after the *Ent-Wurf*, the more the drawing decreases in effect and the model increases in significance. From then on the freely-sculpted model, as a three-dimensional concretization of the narrative, takes on the task of bringing fact and fiction into line to as large an extent as possible, by a process of mutual filtering. Which means that fiction and function have to be made into a stable mixture in the model. This takes whole series of models, as at this experimental stage Coop Himmelb(l)au change suddenly from a very small modelling scale to much larger ones. The pre-architectural, freely sculptural structure is now transformed into an architectural one. As soon as the series of experiments has produced a "stable model condition" for fiction and function the design process moves into its second crucial phase. It is only now that the model is fixed for the particular project. That is to say, until a few years ago it was still recorded photogrammetrically, point by point, so that it could be transferred to conventional drawings by an analytical device, which was expensive in terms of time. Today the fixed model is digitally scanned in next to no time and fed directly into the PC, where it can immediately and very much more precisely be calculated, presented, changed or manipulated in other ways as a 3D image. It has emerged that a great deal of the chance liveliness of the working model survives in the PC. And the precision of the further digital processing increases to the extent that – as in the case of Groningen – it was possible to take the "section patterns" for the steel plates from the working model, process them in the computer and then send them directly to the production plant at the shipyard on a scale of 1:1. Although by no means all the models are as spectacularly tattered and indeterminate as the one for the Groningen project , the hand-made models are the most important instrument for concretizing a design idea, as in Frank O. Gehry's office. It is only in these models that the "power of the first emotional imprint and psychogram" used conceptually to dissolve the space becomes visible. When the first sketch has long since disappeared into the archives, some of the models live for years longer. They live until they have completed their task as interactive links between the agitated imprint of the psyche and the computer-aided model. Then the best thing that can happen to them is that they land up in architectural collections; usually they are just nailed up on the wall or simply disposed of in the wastepaper basket.

A SPECIAL CASE: THE BLOW-UP PROCEDURE

Coop Himmelb(l)au's trust in the model as a tool for creating three-dimensional fractals goes so far that special arrangements of tools are invented for particular tasks. The aim of these unique arrangements is to conduct experiments that fulfil a quite specific task under something like laboratory conditions. In the case of the Groningen museum building the experiment – as described – was to overlay or to harmonize a sculptural model of light-chambers that were thrusting away from each other with the drawn abbreviations of traces of architectural moment. Even before this, another experiment has brought about an even more unconventional arrangement. This was a response to the competition for

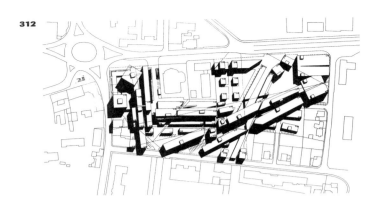

312 St. Pölten, Austria, Europaplatz, project, 1990, definitive site plan after conclusion and evaluation of the "blow-up process"

the new Europaplatz centre in St. Pölten (1990). Here the competition organizers insisted that a natural network of underground watercourses under the selected site should not be built over. This information had been supplied by expert reports. A precise map of the underground water-courses was part of the competition brief. On mature reflection and after various preliminary experiments Coop Himmelb(l)au made a transparent perspex box and transferred the plan of the network of watercourses to its bottom. Then they drilled through the bottom again and again, following the line of the network precisely. Then the square metres of usable area and cubic metres of built space required in the competition brief were translated in small, abstract polystyrene pieces, to scale and separated by function, and the particles of the mass model thus produced put into the transparent box. Finally a blower was fitted under the bottom of the box. The air from this got hold of the pieces of polystyrene as it passed through the drilled holes and spun them around inside the box. When the blower was switched off the model mass was left lying on the floor of the box in a random heap – but always without interfering with the network of watercourses simulated by the holes. This blowing procedure was constantly repeated and the random arrangement of the model masses as they fell together recorded in photographs. After evaluating these photographs they chose the state that was most frequently repeated statisticallyand captured it in the first working model outside the box. This "frozen" heap of building masses, avoiding touching the watercourses as if by a magic hand, formed the concrete starting point for further work on the project, which won a first prize for Coop Himmelb(l)au, even though it was unfortunately not built.

Generating a building idea from a physical reaction in a test-tube like this, concretely inventing a "model machine" to this end, once more illustrates Coop Himmelb(l)au's gift for approaching problems creatively in a quite unorthodox way by using *bricolage* methods. But as well, the process works like a non-political reversal or transformation of the political process proposed by El Lissitzky in his famous children's book "About Two Squares" in 1920. Here, Lissitzky took a composition by Malevich and based a story on it in the form of a sequence of almost film-like moving images. He tells, in readily understandable images, how two squares – a red one and a black one – fly from space towards earth, where conditions are bad. When the two squares hit the surface of the earth everything is destroyed and a new and better order is built up on the basis of the red square. The story ends after "the end" with the word "more", to indicate that the rebuilding process is only just beginning. This relates to the beginning of the book, where Lissitzky challenges the children not just to read, but to be active themselves. "do not read that," he writes, "take little pieces of paper sticks blocks fold them paint them build".[23] While Lissitzky destroys what is already there and builds something new by the collision and coming together of bodies, Coop Himmelb(l)au use air and little blocks that fall together to construct something visible (the desired volume) with the resources of the invisible (the watercourses that cannot be built over). The fact that Prix and Swiczinsky also use film-like resources for presenting and recording in this process is a quite different matter, however, and is almost exclusively about the specific cutting and montage techniques of Deconstructivism. Although in Coop Himmelb(l)au's case the latter are effective only in the short span from the first design to the fixed working model and even then – differently from Tschumi's case – do not become an end in themselves.

CONTROLLED COLLISIONS

And so for more than three decades, Coop Himmelb(l)au have creatively developed a highly personal "maieutic" process for emergence; a process that involves treatment and therapy of their own psyches in the act of *Ent-Wurf*. At first this produces auto-suggestive projections that are scarcely controllable, and these Prix and Swiczinsky have gradually domesticated. Here interactive "dirty models" used effectively as filters between ideation and realization are of considerable help to them; "dirty" because these models serve not so much to look good as to catch the unusable "secretions" of many collisions. For example, if too much light collides with the space or too much space with the light in a model experiment, if an overdose of a means to space delimitation had infiltrated the model, the result would inevitably be a hybrid, unusable for further development because it is no longer open to transformation. In such a case this ineffective model condition would signal a dead end and introduce the step-by-step withdrawal of the overdose of one or the other means of collision, for as long as it takes to achieve a stable condition. But drawings and models have also remained so important until today because (one has only to think of the experience narrated into the model) fluctuation, movement and event are kept so much alive in them that they rub off on even the most feeble structure, on "user and used". Karl Sierek says that "Coop Himmelblau's constructed gesture of the blind lines thrown into their plans without any supporting spatial coordinates ... (is) incorporating an idea of architecture whose central category is the event ... It is determined by a variable approach to the material conceived at that time, and not by the structure or quality of the enclosed spatial development. With rhetorical verve, the movement is attempting to cross space and thinking, structure and acting, seeing and going. It is ... carried out in the real chronotopos of reading, seeing and using. ... Use affects both user and used, and depending on the chemical reaction, precipitates architectonic texture."[24]

Despite the myths and legends that are entwined around Himmelb(l)au's design procedures the first sketches and working models are thus in principle nothing other than tools for breaking open closed systems (including those that are in the mind), generators for producing "anticipated *Heimat*", to use an expression of Ernst Bloch's. There is no doubt that this production method has gone through phases that can be distinguished historically. The technical equipment for this production was laboriously invented phase by phase, developed and adapted to new challenges. But this does not mean that Coop Himmelb(l)au are not always open to a new metaphor. The "beautiful" drawing, the "beautiful" model have long been things of the past. They have made room for ephemeral sketches and paper structures that are like rough tools. The team has now got its tools or generators as effortlessly (and effectively in terms of publicity) under control as the process of breaking open closed systems (reminiscent of the image of the "cracking" a safe), from the practical handling of which it has derived its specific product culture. The countless computers in Coop Himmelb(l)au's office actually just play the part of "auditors" here. In fact none of the projects, however much they seem like products of cyberspace, has yet been computer generated. Even the most recent cloud formations were first sketched and modelled "conventionally" before being digitally scanned and calculated and fed into the computers as simulated bodies. Coop Himmelb(l)au are to this extent quite consciously an "old-fashioned" office, more familiar with brain and hand than with computer-aided creative powers, preferring solid, scratched models that they cut, write on, dent and modify at will, to the smooth perfection of virtual body simulations and keyboard controlled manipulations. Though this does not mean that – as happened with the new design for the Venice Biennale pavilions – there can be no communication between the two levels. "Coop architecture and cyberspace," wrote Peter Weibel in 1995, "together form a dynamic system, variable zones of visibility, and correspond with the variable positions of the subject to the virtual spaces. Pictorial artists and building artists are mutually supportive in their work, in their strategies of dislocation and absence."[25]

The Himmelb(l)au studio needs a team of colleagues who are used to each other and to the Himmelb(l)au approach. The language of the sketches and models is obviously so much in their blood that they can decipher and do further work on even cryptic graphic abbreviations or strangely folded paper structures without needing expert help with interpreting them. Admittedly it is becoming increasingly difficult to train talented young people and keep them in the long term. Kurt Forster tells us in his introduction to the major Gehry monograph[26] that all colleagues move with silent concentration around Frank O. Gehry, then goes on to say that in Gehry's office every question is answered softly and that the quiet is disturbed only by the chirping of the telephones. Which suggests that people know how to handle Gehry's illegible sketches without asking, how to turn them into models and how the next stages of the work are to be set in train. It may be that Viennese temperaments are generally less subdued, and that Prix and Swiczinsky themselves can be particularly loud and bad-tempered, but in one respect the Viennese office is scarcely any different from its "big brother" in Santa Monica: in the professional way in which obvious "curiosities" are recognized, accepted, implemented and worked through. Like its offshoot in Los Angeles, the Vienna office works just as professionally as any other on the international level, and because of the said "curiosities" has to come up with a considerable amount of extra professionalism from time to time. Coop Himmelb(l)au have had a new generation of brilliant partners and project architects for a long time now in Stefan Fussenegger, Markus Pillhofer, Gerhard Rieder, Frank Stepper, Josef Weichenberger and Tom Wiscombe, who are not just executors, but creative workers in their own right. The old cards have been reshuffled, and the old game is going into a new century. It is all very exciting.

HIMMELB(L)AU WITHIN LIMITS

Until the controversial exhibition "Deconstructivist Architecture", mounted by Philip Johnson and Mark Wigley for the Museum of Modern Art in New York, Coop Himmelb(l)au's image was quite firmly fixed in the public eye, and Prix and Swiczinsky were able to live up to their role of "alte Wilde" who had stayed young pretty well unchallenged. After long years of involuntary abstinence from building they had received their first commissions to build and even their first awards from the institutions that their first role had been to fight against. Their view now extended well beyond the confines of Vienna, especially as Prix had been teaching as Adjunct Professor at the Southern California Institute of Architecture in Los Angeles since 1985. His commuting between Los Angeles and Vienna opened up new horizons both theoretically and practically. In Vienna his ideally matched partner had to surpass himself in order to secure day-to-day business and more besides. And independently of this, Coop Himmelb(l)au's reputation had also been firmly established internationally at least since the first prize in the competition for the new town of Melun-Sénart near Paris (1987); so firmly established that Prix and Swiczinsky were able to allow themselves entertainingly provocative remarks like these, at an interview just before the New York exhibition: "The truth is that we are not interested in architecture ... We do more than architecture. We do something that has to do with life. We don't talk about architecture very much in our office – in fact we only talk to journalists about it."[1]

Admittedly the positive public image was not going to conceal the fact that the majority of European architects – to say nothing of large sections of society – still wanted to have nothing at all to do with movements that were not part of the mainstream. This didn't just mean Coop Himmelb(l)au, but also included members of the so-called Graz school and for a time work by architects like Günter Behnisch as well. Even international theorists were at best prepared to allot this "neo-Expressionism" a kind of exotic niche in terms of international architecture. Excluding phenomena of difference and expressiveness in this way has a long cultural and historical tradition – especially in Germany and Austria. For example, the post-Modern rehabilitation of Expressionist achievements and theories before and after the 1918 revolution should not make us forget the fact that these same achievements were very much denigrated in the contemporary context. For example, Helmut Lethen, in his excellent study on "Verhaltenslehre der Kälte", reminds us of Helmuth Plessner, who took up a front-line position against historical Expressionism in 1924. According to Lethen, Plessner "found phenomena" in all varieties of Expressionism "that thrust well into the dangerous zone of the 'ridiculous' because they insisted on disarming themselves. Thus their bodies were defenceless against the attacker, and the cost of the creature's 'expression' is to be abandoned. Consequently the urge to pursue 'expression' can give no indication of humane mind in Plessner's anthropology, on the contrary, he uses this category to divide the humane world off from the animal kingdom."[2] But between 1914 and 1924 only a very few architects pursued expression as an end in itself; in the euphoric mood of a new beginning of the pre- and post-revolutionary phase Wolfgang Pehnt points out that they were much more likely to feel tempted (as many architects still do) "at least as a piece of wishful thinking, to ... break away ... from this antagonism ... between useful purpose and artistic intention, between being allowed to and wanting to."[3] But even an unsuspicious and circumspect observer like Walter Benjamin judged in retrospect: "Fundamentally, Expressionsim reacted pathologically rather than crtically. It was trying to overcome the time when it came into being by making itself the way in which that time was expressed."[4] Today we are all too well aware of what the contemporary rejection of Expressionism produced at the time: nothing other than the emotional coolness of Neue Sachlichkeit, which was celebrated all over the world. According to Lethen, the "cold look" was part of the new heroic attitude of the "active handler", of the celebrated "seizer of the initiative", who protected himself from contacts that penetrated society too deeply and over-emotional reactions. "Is the 'Neue Sachlichkeit' of the twenties," is Lethen's justifiable rhetorical question, "perhaps just to be seen as a failed attempt at a modern 'culture of shame'?"[5] This short flashback on the social polarization of "cold" and "hot" is already hinting at the reasons for the aversion against everything expressive that was to flare up again in the late eighties in the arguments about Deconstructivism. "Utopian fantasy is quarantined," says Susan Buck-Morss succinctly, "contained within the boundaries of theme parks and tourist preserves, like some ecologically threatened but nonetheless dangerous zoo animal. When it is allowed expression at all, it takes on the look of children's toys – even in the case of sophisticated objects – as if to prove that utopias of social space can no longer be taken seriously; they are commercial ventures, nothing more."[6]

By 1988 Prix and Swiczinsky had successfully emerged from all the debates about whether post-Modernism was a good or a bad thing almost as shining heroes of an architecture that was anything but normative and emotionally cool. One of the things Himmelb(l)au has to thank for this image is their tactic of never pinning themselves down theoretically, and being very suspicious of any sort of 'ism'. Instead of this they worked on their image as incorrigible Bad Boys, preferring guitars, whisky and Havanas to wasting even a single word on the content of their songs. These were just two noisy, rustic, really natural lads hacking their way through the jungle of theoretical traps.

THE INTERNATIONAL THEORY TRAP

Once Coop Himmelb(l)au had been placed in the Deconstructivist pantheon by Philip Johnson and Mark Wigley everything was to change at a stroke. The very group that had so far successfully avoided every 'ism' was now suddenly in the midst of one of the most controversial ones. The anticipation of world-wide popularity and the increase in commissions associated with this meant that they could feel more than flattered and cherish erroneous conclusions. Hadn't their ingenious theoretical abstinence paid off in the end? Precisely the opposite was the case, with paradoxical consequences: the more indisputably their buildings were recognized and accepted, the harder and more persistent the beatings became that were meted out to Coop Himmelb(l)au for their woolly attitude to theory. Here we should keep beatings of a social nature and those relating to Deconstructivism separate to as large an extent as possible. And the criticism of Deconstructivism has also to be separated into arguments that come from the outside and others that originate in their own ranks, as it were. And finally we have to consider the reproaches that apply quite directly to Coop Himmelb(l)au's work and its theoretical basis.

We have discussed an unease in principle with "dissonant architecture" and even more with a regular verdict made in a pseudo-critical "meta-language" that developed from architecture itself. Coop Himmelb(l)au thought they were well armed against such reproaches because of their socially motivated sixty-eighters origins and would-be revolutionary rhetoric. But suddenly everything was different because they had been accepted, essentially against their will, into the top ranks of Deconstructivism. Now their critics were hitting out: things that had previously been seen as 'left-wing' were now supposed to be conservative; spontaneity was attacked as contrived, social polemic as naïveté, significance as "exaggerated expression". This was reminiscent of Gustav René Hocke's argument about European Mannerism. He said that "'overcoming expressive inhibitions' not only led to an 'exaggeration of expressive forms', but also to hiding oneself (and rescuing oneself) in precisely enclosed environments, similar to the 'secret academies' in the 16th century."[7] Did this not also apply to Deconstructivism? Was this not also offered in closed "secret circles"[8] like the dubious New York exhibition? Admittedly it was to turn out to be much more serious that the organizers of this exhibition,[9] which was as memorable as it was questionable, had entirely of their own accord placed Coop Himmelb(l)au in a category that derived from linguistic techniques of all things, in other words from techniques relating to reading and the textures of linguistic constitution. Prix and Swiczinsky should have wondered in 1988 at the latest whether they were not been sent off on entirely the wrong trail. Because for them, unlike Peter Eisen-

313 Coop Himmelb(l)au: Wolf D. Prix left and Helmut Swiczinsky right

man, Daniel Libeskind, Rem Koolhaas or Bernard Tschumi, refined theorizing had never been their thing. Belong to one of the 'isms' that was positively bursting with "textual architecture"[10] with appropriate "in-scriptions", and that banged on about Derrida and still more Derrida, this was all a bit much for a team who had so far carried its "anti-intellectual" qualities before it like a banner. So Coop Himmelb(l)au were hit twice, by criticism from outside and from inside; from outside about the theory of Deconstructivism in general, and from inside by the apparent absence of a viable theoretical framework for the Viennese "chaos team".

The criticism from the outside was first of all only a revival of arguments that Manfred Tafuri had advanced against the neo-avant-garde in the sixties and seventies. "As a Mandarin style," wrote Jencks, "Deconstruction is, as Manfredo Tafuri wrote of the New York Five and others in 1974, '*architecture dans le boudoir*'. Like a Rococo *boudoir* it can be sensual and engagingly complex, but it's fundamentally undemocratic. And here is the real contradiction in Deconstruction: in spite of the claims to pluralism, *différence*, 'a war on totality' and defence of 'otherness', this hermetic work is often monist, elitist, intolerant and conveys a 'sameness' ... Because of such suppressions and contradictions one could argue that a real Deconstructionist architecture of variety and humour has yet to exist."[11] Today – a decade later – we can smirk about the unconscious humour concealed behind this compilation of ancient reproaches. Critics like Gert Kähler or Bruno Schindler were to be taken much more seriously here. "If one points out the contradictions of a period," wrote Schindler in the year of the New York Deconstructivism exhibition, in the spirit of the above-mentioned attitude of Walter Benjamin, "by enhancing them aesthetically, then they also become more palatable – literally. Contradictions very quickly become acceptable in this way ... And so the effect is stabilization, and not criticism. Deconstruction is the luxury of articulating unease about a standardized environment in a striking fashion."[12] Which immediately led Gerd Kähler to conclude: "So if Zaha Hadid or Coop Himmelb(l)au were to build a headquarters for a multinational concern, then it would be because of this quality (advertising aesthetic) – and not for reasons of self-criticism by the client ... Our perfectly functioning world of goods can now even swallow, without gagging, things that have been invented to oppose it, provided that they are striking enough. Farrelly sees Coop Himmelb(l)au's architecture as an 'architecture of freedom' – but I think that if the 'Hot Flat' were to be built in Vienna, it would be a precise counterpart to the Hundertwasser building: both first-class tourist attractions."[13] Or, as we read in a fictitious dialogue by Friedrich Achleitner: Himmelblau's work is ultimately only "architecture that stabilizes the system," and thus "Viennese architecture."[14] However, this line of thought is also short of the mark to the extent that all Coop Himmelb(l)au's buildings are concerned with considerably more than surfaces: they seek to establish emancipatory mind spaces and set off osmotic, derestricted processes between building and city. And if a client can use it for advertising purposes, then so much the better!

Michael Müller's and Franz Dröge's skilful criticism of some Deconstructivists' enthusiasm for "the dirty realism of risky public spaces" that would need deconstruction if they were to function as sources of hope for vague social futures[15] does not affect Coop Himmelb(l)au to the extent that the pamphlets in which Prix and Swiczinsky had glorified neglecting urban spaces, in their activist Sturm und Drang phases, were now well in the past. Today their works are anything but anti-urban or anti-contextual. "What makes them disturbing," writes Mark Wigley, "is the way they find the unfamiliar already hidden within the familiar context. By their intervention, elements of the context become defamiliarized."[16] Admittedly things get considerably less comfortable when Coop Himmelb(l)au's work is tested by critics on how much "in-scription" it contains, in other words when criticism shifts to the linguistic, theoretical plane. Just as in the late seventies architectural post-Modernism drew its ideological and tactical ideas from Paul de Man's "Allegories of reading" among other sources, and earlier works, deconstruction processes are also based on literature and linguistics in the first place. For a decade and a half before architects discovered deconstructionist theory for themselves, ideas of this kind were already at the centre of interdisciplinary research, conducted by French structural linguists and philosophers, above all Jacques Derrida. Derrida had been surprised for a long time, indeed he had made fun of the fact that some architects fell on his reading process with such vigour at so late a date – the process of finding the "*différences*" in supposedly sacrosanct textures and others of his theses. For a long time Derrida even doubted that there could be analogies between the composed quality of texts and architecture. It was not until the start of the dialogue with Derrida initiated and persistently stepped up by Bernard Tschumi and above all Peter Eisenman that Derrida's curiosity about such analogies and interferences between philosophy and architecture was awakened – although this also opened up the floodgates to an imitative, trivial deconstruction all over the world. Since then a wealth of literature has addressed the interplay between Derrida and Eisenman, between philosophical hermeneutics and in-scribed architecture.[17] But the greatest difficulty here is that Derrida, like Heidegger before him speaks in architectural concepts when he is actually not talking about architecture. Thus tautologies and inadmissible syllogisms are pre-programmed, as it were. But in the meantime there is practically nothing that works without Derrida. It is almost as though Jean Baudrillard's simulation theories, Marc Augé's "places and non-places" in the context of an "ethnology of loneliness", Paul Virilio's "vision machine" and many other ideas had never existed. The actual crux lies in reading of and by architecture. The task of 'translating' certain states of affairs by using architecture has in fact been deleted and replaced in the deconstruction process by "an anti-hierarchical diversity and arbitrariness" of variant readings. According to Roger Thiel, "architecture and a reading of its signs becomes allegorical and, indeed, an allegory of reading, of unreadability."[18] Not surprisingly, Coop Himmelb(l)au have very little to offer that would fit in with Derrida's head games with architecture (with the exception of announcing the completion of the Tower of Babel).[19] There is probably not a single building in the world that does not show some sort of sign of in-scription, but whether such traces are compatible with Derrida's "translations" is another matter altogether. And building individually intelligible variants which can be read without inevitably becoming unintelligible has always been one of Coop Himmelb(l)au's declared intentions. These are some of Coop Himmelb(l)au's fundamental reservations about an unduly deconstructivist view.

After a considerable number of deconstructive buildings had gone up all over the globe, the international specialist press finally also realized something that experts had already complained about concerning the New York exhibition: that it is not right to tar all Deconstructivists with the same brush. But they now very quickly set about dividing the Deconctructivist camp into "good" and "bad" protagonists. Even such an eminent magazine as "El Croquis", which dedicated a whole lavishly produced issue to Coop Himmelb(l)au in 1989, was not afraid to downgrade Coop Himmelb(l)au's architecture in the accompanying commentary as "limited operations" of "an epigonic phenomenon" and to play Rafael Moneo's supposedly "more referential" work off against them in a somewhat threadbare manner.[20] If things like this still happen today then it is either through ignorance or professional politics.[21] According to this good Deconstructivists would be those who – like Daniel Libeskind, for example – "ennoble" themselves with symbolic building commissions, while bad ones – like Prix and Swiczinsky – "prostitute" themselves with commercial building commissions, which would confirm Kähler's reproach mentioned above. Of course all this is outrageous nonsense; especially the attempt to play morality off against supposed prostitution, against pragmatism, and revolutionary qualities against supposedly being reactionary, would inevitably be a regression to the "architectural cold war" of the twenties and thirties.

Admittedly, when criticism of practising Deconstructivists comes from their own camp, it acquires a quite different meaning, though here one should distinguish to as large an extent as possible between critical voices from the older and the younger generation. Thus in his essay "En terror firma" Peter Eisenman is only repeating familiar old points when he remarks: "A major displacement concerns the role of the architect/designer and the design process. Something my be designed which can be called displacing, but it may be only an expressionism, a mannerist distortion of an essentially stable language. It may not displace the stable language, but on the contrary further stabilise its normative condition. This can be seen in many examples of current architectural fashion. There is a need for a process other than an intuition – 'I like this,' or 'I like that.' When the process is intuitive, it will already be known, and therefore complicit with the repressions inherent in architectural 'knowledge.' Intuitive design can never produce a state of uncertainty, only, at best, an illustration of uncertainty."[22] Although Coop Himmelb(l)au, Libeskind or Hadid are not mentioned by name, they are quite definitely being addressed here. Eisenman stresses concepts like "otherness", "twoness" or "betweenness" that he feels should be "inscribed" in architecture as uncertainties. But because he denies architecture designed and built in the previously available sense any "textuality", because it incorporates "certainty" and excludes "traces of otherness", he rules out Himmelb(l)au's, Libeskind's, Hadid's and other architects' right to be considered "true" Deconstructivists. But as well as this – and this seems much more serious – Eisenman is referring to the fundamental hopelessness, indeed tragedy of true deconstruction ("true" in Derrida's sense). It can either remain in the abstract textuality of inscribed unbuilt ideation, maintaining its innocence, as it were, or lose this once and for all at the moment of designing and capturing in images of "otherness". And even Eisenman cannot escape from this dilemma, as he frankly admits. In fact he tries to find a possible route in another direction than the one followed by Coop Himmelb(l)au: "Ultimately, each of these four conditions provoke an uncertainty in the object, by removing both the architect and the user from any necessary control of the object. The architect no longer is the hand and mind, the mythic originary figure in the design process. And the object no longer requires the experience of the user to be understood. No longer does the object need to look ugly or terrifying to provoke an uncertainty; it is now the distance beweeen object and subject – the impossibility of possession which provokes this anxiety."[23] Eisenman thus denies Himmelb(l)au's mystical cult of *Ent-Wurf*, and even self-doubtingly questions his own buildings. Are these arguments intended to suggest that Prix and Swiczinsky, like many of their friends, should not count as Deconstructivists, and that this "ism" just fell into their hands. Anyone who knows how grumpily most of the so-called Deconstructivists, but above all Coop Himmelb(l)au, usually react to relevant questions about being part of Deconstructivism or any other "ism" will be strengthened in this suspicion. But whom or what do Coop Himmelb(l)au embody then?

Before it is possible even to start trying to answer this question, Coop Himmelb(l)au seem to have been overtaken by certain developments and more recent concepts. If this were true, Prix and Swiczinsky's work would have been shunted off to the old people's home before the two of them had reached the peak of their achievement. In that case – what an irony of fate –would they have been too early in the early days, and then too late? Admittedly a healthy portion of scepticism is appropriate when augurs announce an entirely new kind of architecture, in this case an imminent architectural world revolution. Ulrich Schwarz, an able observer of the scene, is careful to speak only of "so-called New Architecture", or architecture "after" Deconstructivism. Schwarz maintains that the representatives of this movement combined "René Thom's catastrophe theory with Deleuze's analysis of the concept of folding in Leibniz and other theorems, so that they could create something new synthetically. This approach is sometimes accompanied by post-critical political arguments intended to liberate architecture from an – allegedly – confrontative position of isolation as far as society is concerned. And so a kind of undirected excitement about innovation is built up."[24] The representatives of this "New Architecture", who disagree among themselves, in fact agree about only one point, and that is that the pulsating Baroque architecture of architects like Borromini or Guarini and the apparently floating, interpenetrating elements of late Baroque architecture in Germany should be seen as pre-Modernism, or perhaps as "Modernism" itself. All the subsequent building achievements, even the masterpieces of classical Modernism (with the exception of some Russian examples) are nothing for them other than more or less classically aspirant late models, late followers of the Vitruvian school of thought. Here they cite theoreticians like Colin Rowe, who had compared Le Corbusier's work with Palladio's villas as early as 1947, and discovered concealed or suppressed analogies.[25]

Sanford Kwinter, Jeffrey Kipnis, Greg Lynn and other American "inventors of (new) images of liberty" look on Deconstructivism benevolently as a closed historical chapter, as a preliminary phase for their own work. "Upon closer examination," says Kipnis, "it is not more accurate to say that these works (in the New York exhibition) have been executed under the auspices of an implicit contract of disavowal. In other words, is it not the case that these designs are celebrated as auratic, signature buildings of interest only for their irreproducible singularity, rather than as sources of new principles for a general architectural practice. In that sense, the discipline of architecture has recognised them as exotic, precisely so as to suppress their contribution to a New Architecture."[26] Is it possible that Kipnis was thinking of Coop Himmelb(l)au when he wrote this? American exponents of this newest "New Architecture" draw their conclusions from this and concern themselves – as described in a previous chapter – both subversively and pragmatically with feasibility studies for a kind of architecture that refrains from referring to any models in terms of building typology, architectural theory and social history. Up to now this romps around almost exclusively in computer-generated virtual worlds, as at the time of writing it has remained almost entirely on the drawing-board in practical terms. Something that looks like neo-Baroque architecture at first sight is intended to bring undreamed-of social freedoms with it and to do something of which the Baroque could indeed only dream, and that is to react softly, in a way that can easily be reshaped and changed at will in response to all environmental influences. Kipnis therefore updates Le Corbusier's legendary Five Points for a New Architecture by adding five more points: "that it Points, that it is Blank, Vast, Incongruent and Intensively Coherent."[27]

Kipnis's additional points indirectly disempower, indeed criticize classical Modernism and fans the flames of a fairly superfluous debate about the concept of a "Second Modernism",[28] which was introduced by Heinrich Klotz and others, in order to make it easier to understand current trends, including Coop Himmelb(l)au's building achievements, in conceptual terms. And so a compelling debate breaks out about whether there ever was a "First Modernism", and if so, what it was, and if not, why there should be a "Second" such movement.[29]

In addition to this we have another clash in the form of the fundamentalist quarrel between American exponents of "New Architecture" and Dutch members of the group around Rem Koolhaas. Kwinter, as the spokesman for this argument, insists that "the central thesis of this new (Dutch) school was allegedly to be that (global) infrastructure should be recognized as a creative force; the fact is that the majority of Koolhaas's concepts, from which this new work is thrown together, are watered down and trivialized (though sometimes condensed into elegant slogans, like MVRDV's 'datascapes', for example), so that ultimately these works illustrate nothing more substantial than anaemic columns of figures about market behaviour and demographic pressures. Free access is inevitably being offered here to a naïve determinism that rules out the whole range of actual, unordered social processes and their infinitely dense and always inconstant psychological, political, erotic and anthropological individual structures. 'Pragmatism', as propagated by the new Dutch school, … is pragmatism of the worst kind … In the hands of the new Dutch architects … human and social engineering … as a constitutive creative force for our times becomes a triumph of cynicism, a slippery and often merely tourist-style spin through the all-too-familiar media landscape of 'thinfrastructure'… Social imagination has practically said farewell to progressive architecture with an international thrust … This definitely does not mean that our world and our culture are in some way more fixed and more stagnant than before, but the course of their development is not even theoretically the object of architectural intervention any more. This failure is due simply and solely to *our* actions and *our* theories. The new worlds of ideas that we think we are celebrating in new European work and also quite generally in stylistic neo-Modernism, are merely fragments of ideas, rehashed clichés and fiscal propaganda."[30]

Of course the Dutch were not prepared to let reproaches of this kind stick, and equally the dispute is not just a fundamental conflict between academic teaching (USA) and the "dirty hands"[31] of building pragmatists (Holland). Obviously the accusers are much more concerned to assert their supremacy in the world in terms of architectural theory. And as Prix knows all too well from years of being a visiting professor on the American west coast before taking up a chair and directing a master-class in architecture in Vienna, there is also an internal struggle for supremacy in America, between Columbia, the Los Angeles universities and other academic stronghold in the country. There is a certain piquancy in the fact that the Americans of all people are striking a "left-wing" pose, then attacking Koolhaas and MVRDV – representing many young Europeans – as capitalistic "terminators". In fact if America's "New Architecture" is stripped of its progressive social implications, which in reality it still has to prove, then it is anticipated that considerable weaknesses will come to light. For nowhere else at the moment there is such a yawning gulf between theoretical conception and practical implication as in this "New Architecture". All the famous cyberspace architecture by some like Karl S. Chu or Greg Lynn's breathtaking "paperless studios" – however important they may be for the projection of "anticipated *Heimaten*" – cannot conceal the fact that Coop Himmelb(l)au's architecture is much more exciting and stimulating and also more socially relevant than all these – for whatever society they may be intended – synthetically produced Cyberland mirages. Prix and Swiczinsky did pioneering work in this field at a time when many of their Dutch and American colleagues were still in short trousers. And surely their most recent projects have in fact come really close to meeting originators' of "New Architecture's" theoretical demands?

THINKING BEYOND BUILT WORK

This extensive digression is intended to produce an outline of Coop Himmelb(l)au's precarious position within the global constellations of architectural theory from 1988 at the latest. Until then the team were always considered proponents of "open architecture", not exclusively, but in theoretical terms as well. Then they were suddenly attacked as being incapable of theorizing by the old left, and involuntarily linked with one of the most complex "isms" of the century as far as theory is concerned, and at the same time criticized for lack of theoretical awareness; further exacerbating factors were the typical Viennese kind of laboured "invective" and finally a generational conflict with teenage theoretical giants from America. And then considerable annoyance was caused by the fact that Frank O. Gehry's more extensive oeuvre, which in fact has affinities in terms of theory, is credited with clear evolutionary stages of development, while Prix and Swiczinsky are still accused, even though people know better, of self-referential repetition and lack of forward movement.[32] The two architects from Vienna were not even wearing the emperor's new clothes, they were wearing nothing at all. And their reaction to all this mayhem? Prix likes to compare Coop Himmelb(l)au's work with a tennis match: "returns" should be awarded according to where the ball is coming from.[33] Instead of capitulating in the face of the apparently oppressive supremacy of architectural mind games, Prix and Swiczinsky have returned to their "basic position" without any inferiority complexes, in other words they have gone back on to the offensive that has been familiar for decades. With what result? They are building work that others only talk about and thinking beyond what other people are building! The fact that they do not suppress their older work in embarrassment, but are still proud of it, should not lead us to the rash conclusion that Coop Himmelb(l)au are marking time. Clearly outlined working phases emerge from three decades of development, shaped above all by different theoretical aspects that are reflected in words and buildings. And if the latest signs are not deceptive, the team is presently making a great leap forward again. Perhaps the projects for Guadalajara in Mexico and the Swiss "Arteplage" in Biel, related to their work as a whole, could have a similarly liberating effect to the freely-sculpted solitaires in Le Corbusier's late *œuvre*. And we would submit that liberation should be understood as a final

196

rejection of Freudian implications in favour of being calmly ready to seduce people culturally to accept more social peace. But one question is left in the air unanswered: what architectural and theoretical imprints should be concretized in the work, given the basic assumption that the theoretical ideas move directly from Coop Himmelb(l)au's minds into the built work rather than from the written word? What would be the hard core of these imprints?

I assume that is has become clear in the mean time that for some years now Coop Himmelb(l)au have no longer been pursuing excess or trying to capture the monstrous in architectural images. According to Norbert Bolz this monstrous quality can no longer be captured in architectural images, as each image provides comfort about what it is presenting, however terrible it may be. "Thought," says Bolz, "is no longer interested in the monstrous; indeed images are constituted by suppressing it. For this reason they miss the reality in its horror."[34] This does not prevent Prix and Swiczinsky from addressing the monstrous and uncanny factors lurking subliminally behind every facade, in every corner of the city. But now they do not design shock images from these sources, but "comforting images of the monsters".[35] And Coop Himmelb(l)au's comforting images reflect the chaos that surrounds them quite directly. But not so much chaos as described in René Thom's theories as chaos in its original etymological meaning. According to Gigon the word *cháos* is derived from "'fissure or hollow' and belongs to the verb *cháo*, which in its usual forms can apply to the gaping of the mouth or a wound, or a yawning cave in a mountain".[36] Fissure and cave, opening and hiding have remained central themes of their work. And in terms of its application to Himmelb(l)au's buildings the etymological image seems much more convincing that Rudolf Arnheim's image of the cave, which Greg Lynn uses to define his synthetic spaces (including the "blobs"), in which ground and horizon merge. Certainly their alternative architecture no longer burns, bleeds, frays and turns until it breaks. But that it has grown from Freudian therapeutic contexts, that it has put the spirits which it called up itself back in the bottle, that it has now long appeared in professional guise, does not exclude spontaneous and unexpected differences which are lived and presented in the building.

If there are theories that come very close, consciously or unconsciously, to Himmelb(l)au's thinking and actions, surely they may be those of Gilles Deleuze, above all his rhizome theory. Working with Félix Guattari, Deleuze pushed thinking forward by using the metaphor of the "rhizome", a root system for certain plants. Wolfgang Welsch describes the basic features like this: "The paradigm of today is not the classical tree with roots, which includes all differences in its development hierarchically, and not the modern system of small roots based on a number of micro-units, but the rhizome, the root-stem system, in which roots and shoots are indistinguishable, a system that is in a state of constant exchange with its surroundings. The rhizome enters alien chains of evolution and makes transverse links between divergent lines of development. It is … nomadic; it creates unsystematic and unexpected differences; it differentiates and synthesizes at the same time."[37] For example – allowing for tautologies – would this not be a better way of describing Coop Himmelb(l)au's Dresden "Crystal" than analogies with Piranesi's Carceri or the Fluids of the American Cyberspace world? If there is a building that actually does fissure and open, that symbolically abandons and combines, that differentiates and synthesizes in terms of the urban space, then it is this one. And does Coop Himmelb(l)au's concept of "osmosis" not borrow indirectly from the image of the "root system" that is constantly establishing a state of balance with its surroundings?

Over and above the metaphor of the rhizome a series of other Deleuze motifs seems to have influenced Coop Himmelb(l)au's work in the manner of a kindred spirit; motifs that are to be found almost word for word in the short notes on the buildings, or indeed reflected in the buildings themselves. Gilles Deleuze brought motifs of this kind together in a brilliant piece of philosophical *Sprechgesang* on the topic of "territories" and "deterritorisation" and allotted the huge cosmos of sub-themes to particular "plateaux" as levels on which they should be considered. The vast majority of these plateaux are purely epistemological by nature, but in between some constantly occur that relate to architecture quite concretely. For example, he speaks of milieu and liveliness, of lines, of materials in architecture, about the city, but above all about smooth and notched space. "From chaos, *Milieus* and *Rhythms* are born ... Every milieu is vibratory, in other words, a block of space-time constituted by the periodic repetition of the component. Thus the living thing has an exterior milieu of materials, an interior milieu of composing elements and composed substances, an intermediary milieu of membranes and limits, and an annexed milieu of energy sources and actions-perceptions."[38] When enclosing something in architectural materials, the point is no longer "a question of imposing a form upon a matter but of elaborating an increasingly rich and consistent material, the better to tap increasingly intense forces. What makes a material increasingly rich is the same as what holds heterogeneities together without their ceasing to be heterogeneous."[39] If we consider what Coop Himmelb(l)au – in their gasometer-project, for example – perceive conceptually as "reflecting liveliness", in the light of Deleuze's definition of life born out of chaos, the agreements produced are more than random. And as far as the requirement for "more consistent" building structures is concerned, which hold together things that are drifting apart without their parts ceasing to be heterogeneous, than all one needs to do is glance at the roof structure in Falkestrasse in Vienna to see that this requirement has been met. When Deleuze finally defines cities as "circuit-points of every kind, which enter into counterpoint along horizontal lines" and "effect a complete but local, town-by-town, integration",[40] then Himmelb(l)au's images of cities as culmination points of complex social circulation systems, activated lines of movement and controlled spatial collisions even goes a long way beyond this.

THE THEORY OF "SMOOTH" SPACE

But the most important point, which was taken up by friends like Gehry, Mayne, Moss, Woods or Hadid and developed independently, arises from Deleuze's analysis of "smooth" spaces, which he relates to "striated" spaces. "Smooth or nomadic space lies between two striated spaces: that of the forest, with its gravitational verticals, and that of agriculture, with its grids and generalized parallels ... But being 'between' also means that smooth space is controlled by these two flanks, which limit it, oppose its development, and assign it as much as possible a communicational role; or, on the contrary, it means that it turns against them, gnawing away at the forest on one side, on the other side gaining ground on the cultivated lands, affirming a noncommunicating force or a force of *divergence* like a 'wedge' digging in ... One of the fundamental tasks of the State is to striate the space over which it reigns, or to utilize smooth spaces as a means of communication in the service of striated space ... Moreover, there are still other kinds of space that should be taken into account, for example, holey space and the way it communicates with the smooth and the striated in different ways. What interests us ... are precisely the passages or combinations: how the forces at work within space continually striate it, and how in the course of its striation it develops other forces and emits new smooth spaces ... (in order to) to live in the city as a nomad, or as a cave dweller. Movements, speed and slowness, are sometimes enough to reconstruct a smooth space."[41]

As we have already briefly addressed the effect of "holey spaces" on the city, we return with this passage to the point at which we started our *tour d'horizon*: to the question about Coop Himmelb(l)au's architectural leitmotifs. Certainly fold and folding are not among them. But "smooth space" is Himmelb(l)au's most important part of architectural theory. Deleuze's word "smooth" should not concern us here: it corresponds with what the English word "fluid" would define as mobile, changeable, non-geometrical, fluent. Its opposite, "striated" means ordered, geometrical, heavy, inflexible, over-shaped. Perceived in this way, Deleuze suggests that the smooth, non-geometrical modern space is somewhere in between the excessively shaped "striated" spaces, that he can bring together at will, but also drive apart like a wedge. It offers refuge to urban nomads and cave-dwellers, sometimes temporarily, but sometimes permanently. Could it not be said that Coop Himmelb(l)au's work, from the very first design, was actually intended to create room and breathing-space for "smooth", in other words non-geometrical, adaptable spaces within the encrusted petrifaction of the city? At the outset this space-creating aim was pursued aggressively, and today it is more casual, but has certainly not become more harmless. The "smooth space" is a perfect synonym for the "open architecture" that Prix and Swiczinsky have devoted themselves to completely, and that they have inscribed in their work. It is an architecture that, after the "urban breakdown", is looking for and finding new forms for public space, new ways of living together collectively. The steps needed for this, and not work that is formulated in rules, make up their very personal theory of architecture!

It does not go without saying that one has to like Coop Himmelb(l)au's architecture. In fact generally speaking no one in our world has to like this or that architecture, indeed any architecture. In fact you could absolutely hate the architecture that is being introduced here for its strident, egocentric approach. And indeed it would probably scarcely be possible to imagine anything that would have a more polarizing effect than the dubious idea of playing Peter Zumthor's Kunsthaus in Bregenz, for example, off against Himmelb(l)au's Groningen museum pavilion or John Pawson's own home in London against Himmelb(l)au's Bachmann studio in Vienna. "Low temperature architecture" is not what Himmelb(l)au are about, and indeed never was. How would the world look if we were surrounded everywhere by Zero architecture wherever we looked – a question that could also be applied conversely to the horrific scenario of a world deconstructed entirely by oblique first- and second-hand architecture. But – Niklas Maak asks – would a successful abduction to the tropics "not always be better than being forced into asceticism"? Certainly so, but nevertheless: you don't have to like Coop Himmelb(l)au's work. But you should at least understand what a high degree of social (and not formal) quality "open architecture" is able to offer. And we should also recognize how much strength and stamina are and have been needed to swim against the tide for so long; swimming against the tide to secure a future for architecture by revealing surprising alternatives. In fact while the whole world is talking about the gradual disappearance of architecture, architecture still has a lot of mileage for Coop Himmelb(l)au. And so on principle everyone should be resisted who suggests that they have invented the "ultimate" architecture, the only kind that can make people happy. According to Baudrillard, architecture has a future only „because as yet no building, no architectural object has been invented that would mean the end of all others, the end of space – and equally no city that would mean the end of all cities, nor a thought that would mean the end of all thoughts. That is the great dream, but while it does not come true there is still hope."[42]

Coop Himmelb(l)au could perhaps be an architects' office like any other if they did not have an unbroken urge to liberate. Heat not cold, fragmentation not unification, opening not enclosure, change not order, ideas not brilliant drawing, consternation not comfort, expressiveness not submission, these are not yesterday's dialectical emotional formulae but contrasts that are still being pursued, heightened aesthetically but also further developed. It is no coincidence that Coop Himmelb(l)au now subject their buildings to "quieter" osmotic interplay between city and property. They squeeze "added value" out of even the most banal architecture built for profit, and this is then credited to the particular building by staging invasions of the urban space. Anyone who denigrates expressive architecture should be dutifully reminded that this strand of architectural history was using expressive devices, long before buildings by Hugo Häring, Hans Scharoun or Erich Mendelsohn appeared, in order to resist the paralysis of social convention. The "expressive" approach that Lethen and Foucault before him evaluated as a positive form of social behaviour, denoting resistance to the "exclusion of feelings", appears increasingly little in Coop Himmelb(l)au's work as a didactic example or therapeutic prescription. More powerful, less inhibited panoramas, images of hopeful social implications, strong bodies in the space have thrust themselves into the foreground recently, even though it has become a great deal more difficult to make heat and cold into pictorial images. Because, according to Thomas Meyer's formulation, the "perfection of social openness, the virtualization of all traditions, orders and obligations, is the social substrate of the cycle of images." But the "social medium that staged images encounter

NOTES

AGAINST THE IDLENESS OF INERT BODIES OR HANDLING THE "CITY IN PIECES" Pages 7–24

1 Mark Wigley, Fear Not…, in: Peter Lang (ed.), Mortal City, New York 1985, p. 80
2 Gerd Hatje (ed.), Coop Himmelblau, Architecture is Now: Projects, (Un)buildings, Actions, Statements, Sketches, Commentaries, 1968–1983, New York 1983, p. 199
3 Coop Himmelblau, Architektur muss brennen, Graz 1980, p. 8
4 Wolf D. Prix, On The Edge, in: Peter Noever (ed.), Architecture in Transition: Between Deconstruction and New Modernism, Munich/New York 1991, p. 20
5 Günther Feuerstein, in: Visionary Architecture in Austria in the Sixties and Seventies: Inspirations, Influences, Parallels, exhibition catalogue by the Austrian Ministry of Science, Transport and Art for the sixth International Architecture Biennale in Venice 1996, Klagenfurt 1996, p. 9
6 For this see: Arnhelm Neusüß, Utopie-Begriff und Phänomen des Utopischen, Neuwied 1972, p. 222
7 Adolf Loos, Architektur (1909), in: Trotzdem, Innsbruck 1930, p. 107
8 Günther Feuerstein, Prozesse, in: Coop Himmelblau (ed.), Supersommer, Vienna 1976, p. 2 ff.
9 loc. cit., p. 5
10 Wolf D. Prix and Helmut Swiczinsky, Supersommer 76, in: Coop Himmelblau (ed.), Supersommer, Vienna 1976, p. 6
11 Coop Himmelblau, see note 2, p. 107
12 For this see: Gert Kähler (ed.), Dekonstruktion? Dekonstruktivismus? Aufbruch ins Chaos oder neues Bild der Welt?, Braunschweig/Wiesbaden 1990, p. 34; Kähler disputes the idea of liberation and assumes that if Hot Flat had been realized as a counterpart to the Hundertwasser House it would merely have been a "first-class tourist attraction".
13 Aaron Betsky, Violated Perfection, Architecture and the Fragmentation of the Modern, New York 1990, p. 114
14 Walter Benjamin, quoted by Dietmar Kamper, That Older Familiarity, Daidalos no. 3, Berlin 1982, p. 107
15 For this see also: Frank Werner, Constructive, not Deconstructive Work on the City of the 21st Century, in: Georg Büchner Buchhandlung (ed.), Coop Himmelblau, The power of the city, Darmstadt 1988, p. 8 f.
16 Philip Johnson, in: Charles Jencks, The New Moderns: From Late to Neo-Modernism, New York 1990, p. 163
17 Coop Himmelb(l)au, The City…, in: Wolf D. Prix, Helmut Swiczinsky (ed.), Coop Himmelb(l)au Austria, Biennale di Venezia 1996.
18 Jacques Derrida, Labyrinth und Archi/textur, ein Gespräch mit Eva Meyer, in: Senator für Bau- und Wohnungswesen (publ.), Das Abenteuer der Ideen, Architektur und Philosophie seit der industriellen Revolution, Berlin 1984, p. 105
19 For this see the self-satisfied "dialogues" between Charles Jencks and participants in the exhibition in: Charles Jencks, The New Moderns, New York 1990
20 Charles Jencks, The Architecture Of The Jumping Universe, London 1995, p. 33

21 Charles Jencks, Deconstruction: The Pleasures of Absence, in: Andreas Papadakis (ed.), Deconstruction Architecture, AD, vol. 58, no. 3/ 4, London 1988, p. 17
22 Michel du Certau, Umgang mit Raum, Die Stadt als Metapher, in: Ulrich Conrads (ed.), Panik Stadt, Berlin/Braunschweig 1979, p. 18 f.
23 Henri-Pierre Jeudi, Inszenierung der Zerstörung?, loc. cit., p. 75
24 Manfredo Tafuri, Kapitalismus und Architektur, Von Corbusiers "Utopia" zur Trabantenstadt, Hamburg/Berlin 1970, p. 118
25 Peter Eisenman still uses this argument (in a politically "cleaned up" version) today to distinguish his allegedly socially "more relevant" protests from his assessment in terms of affirmative, "system-confirming" positions by Gehry, Hadid, Coop Himmelb(l)au et al.
26 Tilo Schabert, Die Architektur der Welt. Eine kosmologische Lektüre architektonischer Formen, Munich 1997, p. 143
27 Diana I. Agrest, Architecture from Without, Theoretical Framings for a Critical Practise, Cambridge, Mass./London 1991, p. 193
28 Walter Benjamin, The Work of Art in the Age of Mechanical Reproduction, in: Illuminations, edited by Hannah Arendt, translated by Harry Zohn, London and Glasgow 1970, p. 238.
29 Victor Burgin, The City in Pieces, in: Nadir Hahiji and D.S. Friedman (ed.), Plumbing, Sounding Modern Architecture, New York 1997, p. 119
30 For the phrase "upright gait" cf. Frank Werner, Die vergeudete Moderne, Europäische Architekturkonzepte nach 1950, die Papier geblieben sind, Stuttgart 1981, p. 57 f; but for "crooked architecture and upright gait", cf. in particular: Gert Kähler (ed.), Schräge Architektur und aufrechter Gang, Dekonstruktion: Bauen in einer Welt ohne Sinn?, Braunschweig/Wiesbaden 1993 using the title of Adolf Max Vogt's essay; in fact Coop Himmelb(l)au's work is treated essentially ironically in this anthology.
31 Michael Mönninger, Schönheit als Irrtum, Versuch, das Chaos der Städte zu verstehen, in: Karl Markus Michel u. Tilman Spengler (ed.), Städte bauen, Kursbuch 112, Berlin 1993, p. 134
32 Marc Augé, Non-Places: Introduction to an Anthropology of Supermodernity, New York 1995.

MASS AND TRANSPARENCY, CONSTRUCTION AND REMOVING BOUNDARIES – A LABORATORY REPORT Pages 25–72

1 Günther Feuerstein, Aktion, in: Visionary Architecture in Austria in the Sixties and Seventies: Inspirations, Influences, Parallels, exhibition catalogue by the Austrian Ministry of Science, Transport and Art for the sixth International Architecture Biennale in Venice 1996, Klagenfurt 1996, p. 44
2 For this see Günther Feuerstein, Visionäre Architektur, Vienna 1958/1988, Berlin 1988, pp. 51 and 58

3 Hans Hollein, Alles ist Architektur, in: Bau no. 1/2, Vienna 1968
4 Hans Hollein, in: Bau no. 2/3, Vienna 1969, p. 6
5 Warren Chalk, Amazing Archigram 4 Zoom Issue, London 1964
6 Philippe Garner, sixties design, Köln 1996, p. 162
7 For this see: Justus Dahinden, Stadtstrukturen für morgen, Analysen-Thesen-Modelle, Stuttgart 1971, p. 20 ff.
8 Coop Himmelblau, In the Beginning was the City, in: Gerd Hatje (ed.), Coop Himmelblau, Architecture is Now: Projects, (Un)buildings, Actions, Statements, Sketches, Commentaries, 1968–1983, New York 1983, p. 194
9 Coop Himmelblau, Villa Rosa, loc. cit., p. 188
10 Günther Feuerstein, see note 2, p. 97
11 Coop Himmelblau, see note 8, p. 182
12 Elizabeth A.T. Smith, Re-Examining Architecture and its History at the End of the Century, in: Russell Ferguson and Stephanie Emerson (ed.), One Hundred Years of Architecture, Los Angeles 1998, p. 78
13 Aaron Betsky, Violated Perfection, Architecture and the Fragmentation of the Modern, Nw York 1990, p. 104
14 Coop Himmelblau, see note 8, p. 142
15 Coop Himmelblau, loc. cit., p. 73
16 For this see: Andrea Gleininger (ed.), Szyszkowitz+Kowalski 1973–1993, Tübingen/Berlin 1994; A. Gleininger also finds nature analogies of this kind in the work of Karla Kowalski and Michael Szyszkowitz, expressed in "the bird and wing shapes of the window and roof landscape". These "are not to be understood as a symbolic attempt to overcome architecural gravity but rather illustrate the dialectic of above and below, bound to the earth and centrifugal forces, transparency and mass"; ibid. p. 18
17 Peter Blundell Jones, Dialogues in Time, New Graz Architecture, Graz 1998, p. 71 ff.
18 Coop Himmelblau, see note 8, p. 52
19 Archive Coop Himmelb(l)au
20 Coop Himmelblau, in: Galerie Aedes (ed.), Coop Himmelblau, Offene Architektur, Ent-würfe 1980–1984, Berlin 1985
21 Detlef Mertins, Nicht buchstäblich: Der Transparenzbegriff bei Sigfried Giedion, in: Kommende Transparenz, Arch+ 144/145, Aachen 1998, p. 106
22 For this cf.: Colin Rowe and Robert Slutzky, Transparency, Basel/Boston/Berlin 1997
23 Dietmar Steiner, quoted by Benedikt Loderer, in: Hochparterre no. 6–7, Zürich 1999, p. 59
24 Coop Himmelblau, The Poetry of Desolation, in: see note 8, p. 116
25 Coop Himmelblau, The End of Architecture, in: Peter Noever (ed.), The End of Architecture? Documents and Manifestos, Munich 1993, p. 17
26 Archive Coop Himmelb(l)au
27 Charles Jencks, The New Moderns: From Late to Neo-Modernism, New York 1990, p. 277
28 E. Torroja, Philosophy of Structures, Berkeley 1958
29 Hans Sedlmayr, Verlust der Mitte, Salzburg 1948, p. 106
30 Adolf Max Vogt, Das Schwebe-Syndrom in der Architektur der zwanziger Jahre,

in: Eidgenössische Technische Hochschule Zürich, Institut für Geschichte und Theorie der Architektur (ed.), Das architektonische Urteil, Basel 1989 p. 229 ff.

31 loc. cit., p. 232 ff.

32 There is scarcely a single specialist publication that does not make formal and aesthetic references to Russian revolutionary architecture, although established connoisseurs like Selim O. Chan-Magomedov et. al. have repeatedly pointed out the unreliability of such false conclusions. Catherine Cooke is not entirely blameless with respect to this formal and aesthetic evaluation process. She promoted Russian revolutionary architecture, which was known only fragmentarily in the West for a long time, by providing memorable images from an early stage and over long periods, until it could be addressed seriously.

33 Adolf Max Vogt, Mit Dekonstruktion gegen Dekonstruktion, in: Gert Kähler (ed.), Dekonstruktion? Dekonstruktivismus? Aufbruch ins Chaos oder neues Bild der Welt, Braunschweig/Wiesbaden 1990, p. 53 ff.

34 Adolf Max Vogt, Schräge Architektur und aufrechter Gang, Was hat sich nach vier Jahren "Dekonstruktion" in der Architektur verdeutlicht?, in: Gert Kähler (ed.), Schräge Architektur und aufrechter Gang, Dekonstruktion: Bauen in einer Welt ohne Sinn?, Braunschweig/Wiesbaden 1993, p. 16 ff.

35 Wolf D. Prix, On the Edge, in: Peter Noever (ed.), Architecture in Transition: Between Deconstruction and New Modernism, Munich/New York 1991, p. 27

36 Joseph Hanimann, Vom Schweren, Ein geheimes Thema der Moderne, Munich/Vienna 1999, p. 60

37 loc. cit., p. 61 ff.

38 Wolf D. Prix, On the Edge, in: Andreas C. Papadakis (ed.), Architectural Design Profile No. 87, Deconstruction III, London 1990, p. 66

39 Coop Himmelb(l)au, From Cloud to Cloud, Venice 1996

40 Archive Coop Himme(l)blau

41 Christian W. Thomsen, Sensuous Architecture: the Art of Erotic Building, Munich/New York 1998, p. 23

42 Günther Feuerstein, Androgynos, the Male-Female in Art and Architecture, Stuttgart 1997, p. 190

43 Charles Jencks, Wilde Kakophonie, in: see note 27, p. 277

44 Wolf D. Prix in an interview with M. Martin and C. Wagenaar on 11 July 1994, publ. in: Marijke Martin, Cor Wagenaar, Annette Welkamp (ed.), Alessandro & Francesco Mendini! Philippe Starck! Michele De Lucchi! Coop Himmelb(l)au! In Groningen!, Groningen, no year (1998), p. 111

45 Archive Coop Himmelb(l)au

46 Christian W. Thomsen, see note 41, p. 24

47 Wolf D. Prix, Lecture Dresden 1995, in: see note 39

48 Adolf Behne, Der Moderne Zweckbau, Munich/Vienna/Berlin 1923; English edition: Adolf Behne, The Modern Functional Building, Santa Monica 1996, p. 123

49 Archive Coop Himmelb(l)au

50 Archive Coop Himmelb(l)au

51 Niklas Maak, Bizarre Gehäuse, Aufruhr gegen das Mittelmaß, in: Theo Sommer (ed.), ZEITPunkte no. 6/99, Hamburg 1999, p. 53

52 Paul Scheerbart, Glasarchitektur, reprint of the 1914 first edition, Munich 1971, p. 130

53 Galerie Aedes (publ.), Coop Himmelb(l)au, The Vienna Trilogy + One Cinema, Berlin 1998, p. V

54 loc. cit., p. V

55 Niklas Maak, see note 53, p. 55

56 Siegfried Kracauer, Straßen in Berlin und anderswo, Frankfurt 1964, p. 51 ff.

57 Coop Himmelb(l)au, in: Galerie Aedes (ed.), see note 55, p. 44

58 Archive Coop Himmelb(l)au

59 Ullrich Schwarz (ed.), Peter Eisenman, Aura und Exzeß, Zur Überwindung der Metaphysik der Architektur, Vienna 1995, p. 26

60 Joseph Hanimann, see note 37, p. 60

61 Greg Lynn, Leicht und Schwer, in: Arch+ no. 124/125, Aachen 1994, p. 43

62 Sanford Kwinter, Emergenz: oder das künstliche Leben des Raums, loc. cit., p. 91

63 loc. cit., p. 91

64 Jeffrey Kipnis, Towards A New Architecture, in: Folding Architecture, Architectural Design, Vol. 63, no. 3/4, London 1993, p. 43

65 Greg Lynn, Das Gefaltete, das Biegsame und das Geschmeidige, in: Arch+ no. 131, Aachen 1996, p. 64

66 Greg Lynn, Fold, Bodies & Blobs, Collected Essays, Brussels 1998, p. 166

67 Greg Lynn, Animate Form, New York 1999, p. 41

68 For this see: Adriaan Beukers, Ed van Hinte, Lightness, The Inevitable Renaissance of Minimum Energy Structures, Rotterdam 1998

69 Jean Baudrillard, Architektur: Wahrheit oder Radikalität?, Vienna 1999, p. 30 ff. (original edition in German)

70 Andreas Ruby, A Generational Issue. Randomness and Responsibility. Greg Lynn's H^2 Pavillon in Schwechat and NOX's "SoftSite", in: Daidalos no. 69/70, Berlin 1998/99, p. 120 f.

71 For this see: Konrad Paul Liessmann, Philosphie der modernen Kunst, Vienna 1999, p. 120

72 Norbert Bolz, Am Ende der Gutenberg-Galaxis, Die neuen Kommunikationsverhältnisse, Munich 1993, p. 139 ff.

INNER WORLDS Pages 145–167

1 Coop Himmelblau, in: El Croquis no. 40, Madrid 1989, p. 38

2 Archive Coop Himmelb(l)au

3 Erich Baumann, quoted in: Michael Mönninger, Stadtansichten, Architekten, Orte, Häuser, Regensburg 1997, p. 42

4 Wolf D. Prix, On The Edge, in: Peter Noever (ed.), Architecture in Transition: Between Deconstruction and New Modernism, Munich/New York 1991 p. 25

5 loc. cit., p. 24

6 loc. cit., p. 24

7 Archive Coop Himmelb(l)au

8 Wolf D. Prix, see note 4, p. 25

9 Gustav René Hocke, Die Welt als Labyrinth, Manierismus in der europäischen Kunst und Literatur, Hamburg 1987 (new, expanded version of the 1957 edition), p. 350

10 Wolf D. Prix and Helmut Swiczinsky, Coop Himmelb(l)au – From Cloud To Cloud, Venice 1996

11 for this cf.: Stanislaus von Moos, Le Corbusier, Elements of a Synthesis, Cambridge, Mass. 1979; this passage quoted from the original German edition: Le Corbusier, Elemente einer Synthese, Frauenfeld 1968, p. 388

12 loc. cit., p. 305

13 Angela Krewani and Christian W. Thomsen, Virtual Realities, in: Daidalos no. 41, Berlin 1991, p. 121

14 Archive Coop Himmelb(l)au

15 Frank Werner, Will the Future of Civilization have a Style?, in: Lotus international no. 85, Milan 1995, p. 128

16 Ulf Jonak, The Torment of Souls, Construction of the Paranoid Imagination, in: Daidalos no. 31, Berlin 1989, p. 120; for this cf. also: Ulf Jonak, Sturz und Riß, Über den Anlaß zu architektonischer Subversion, Braunschweig 1989

17 Wolf D. Prix, see note 4, p. 29

18 Dietmar Kamper, That Older Familiarity, in: Daidalos no. 3, Berlin 1982, p. 107

19 loc. cit., p. 108

20 Hermann Kern, Labyrinthe, Erscheinungsformen und Deutungen, 5000 Jahre Gegenwart eine Urbildes, Munich 1982, p. 448

21 Wolfgang Max Faust, The Labyrinth, the Desert and ..., in: Daidalos no. 3, Berlin 1982, p. 114

22 for this cf.: Manfredo Tafuri, L'Architecture dans le Boudoir, The Language of Criticism and the Criticism of Language, in: Oppositions 3, May 1974

23 Manfredo Tafuri, Toward a Critique of Architectural Ideology, in: Contropiano 1/1969, reprinted in: K. Michael Hays (ed.), Architectural Theory since 1968, New York 1998, p. 32 ff.

24 for this cf.: Manfredo Tafuri, La sfera e il labirinto. Avantguardie e architetttura da Piranesi agli anni ,70, Turin 1980

25 for this cf.: Bruno Reudenbach, G.B. Piranesi – Architektur als Bild, Der Wandel in der Architekturauffassung des achtzehnten Jahrhunderts, Munich 1979, p. 47

26 John Wilton-Ely, The Mind and Art of Giovanni Battista Piranesi, London 1978, p. 85.

27 Norbert Miller, Archäologie des Traums, Versuch über Giovanni Battista Piranesi, Munich 1978, p. 205 ff.

28 Gaston Bachelard, The Poetics of Space, Boston 1994, p. 216 and 230

29 Gustav René Hocke, see note 9, p. 440

30 Anthony Vidler, Space, Time and Movement, in: Russell Ferguson and Stephanie Emerson (ed.), One Hundred Years of Architecture, Los Angeles 1998, p. 119 f.

31 Niklas Maak, Bizarre Gehäuse, Aufruhr gegen das Mittelmaß, in: Theo Sommer (ed.), ZEITPunkte no.6, Hamburg 1999, p. 54 ff.

32 Herbert Muck, Der Raum, Baugefüge, Bild und Lebenswelt, Vienna 1986, p. 98

33 Coop Himmelblau, The "Open House", Malibu, California, in: Architectural Design Profile, Deconstruction III, no. 87, London 1990, p. 71

THE PROJECT AS PROCESS
Pages 168–186

1 The idea of "datascaping" is a relatively recent one, and was unknown at the time. "Datascaping" links objective data from all disciplines that are relevant to the planning process as intensively as possible, in order to seek out unsuspected niches and open spaces for complex individual reactions. Thus design is once again perceived as research.

2 Ernst Bloch, Principle of Hope, Cambridge, Mass. 1986

3 Coop Himmelblau, , Architecture is Now: Projects, (Un)buildings, Actions, Statements, Sketches, Commentaries, 1968–1983, New York 1983, p. 202

4 Ernst Bloch at the Werkbund "Bild und Gestalt" conference in 1965, in: Die Neue Sammlung (publ.) Zwischen Kunst und Industrie, Der Deutsche Werkbund, Munich 1975, p. 495

5 Kurt Wuchterl and Adolf Hübner, Ludwig Wittgenstein in Selbstzeugnissen und Bilddokumenten, Reinbeck 1979, p. 102

6 for this cf.: Gerd Neumann, in: Kunstbibliothek Berlin (publ.), Architekten Zeichnungen 1960–1978, Berlin 1978, p. 4

7 for this cf.: Fraunhofer-Informationszentrum Raum und Bau, Mental maps – kognitive Karten, Stuttgart 1998; mental maps were an important aspect of perception psychology, social geography, sociology and town planning from the sixties onwards, based on relevant research in the USA. It is not clear when architecture discovered "mental mapping", but it was definitely well before the advent of Deconstructivism.

8 Coop Himmelblau. see note 3. p. 11

9 loc. cit., p. 28

10 Coop Himmelblau, Das Fassen von Architektur in Worte (lecture manuscript), in: Galerie Aedes (publ.), Coop Himmelblau, Offene Architektur, Entwürfe 1980–1984, Berlin 1985

11 Peter Noever, Die Sehnsucht nach schrägen Wänden, Über städtisches Wohnen sprach Umriss mit Coop Himmelblau, in: Architekturgalerie München (publ.), Coop Himmelblau, Offene Architektur, Wohnanlage Wien 2, Munich 1986

12 Coop Himmelblau, The Dissipation of our Bodies in the City, in: Coop Himmelblau, The Power of the City, Darmstadt 1988, p. 14 ff.

13 for this cf.: Edgar Tafel, Apprentice to a Genius, Years with Frank Lloyd Wright, New York 1979; Tafel talks about these movements in detail in his memoirs.

14 Michel Foucault, Other Spaces. The Principles of Heterotopia, in: Lotus international, no. 48/49, 1986, p. 12

15 Wolf D. Prix, On The Edge, in Peter Noever (ed.), Architecture in Transition: Between Deconstruction and New Modernism, Munich/New York 1991, p. 21

16 Jean Baudrillard, Agonie des Realen, Berlin 1978, p. 7 ff.

17 Bernard Tschumi, The Manhattan Transcripts, London 1981, new edition London 1994, p. XXIII

18 loc. cit., p. XXV

19 loc. cit., p. XXVII

20 Wolf D. Prix, see note 15, p. 19 f.

21 Coop Himmelblau, The End of Architecture, in: Peter Noever (ed.), The End of Architecture? Documents and manifestos, Munich 1993, p. 19

22 Wolf Prix, in: Marijke Martin, Cor Wagenaar and Annette Welkamp (ed.), Alessandro & Francesco Mendini !, Philippe Starck !, Michele De Lucchi !, Coop Himmelb(l)au !, In Groningen!, Groningen no year, p. 123

23 Reprint of the Russian first edition, published in 1922 by Verlag Skythen, Berlin, Gerhard Verlag, Berlin, no year

24 Karl Sierek, Regulations and Retrospection: the Rhetorics of Building and Film, in: Daidalos no. 64, Berlin 1997, p. 120 ff.

25 Peter Weibel, lecture manuscript in the Archive Coop Himmelb(l)au

26 Francesco Dal Co, Kurt Forster and Hadley Soutter Arnold (ed.), Frank O. Gehry, The Complete Works, New York 1998, p. 9

MIND SPACES AND THEIR THEORETICAL STRUCTURES
Page 187–201

1 Dirk Meyhöfer, Wiener Brandstifter, in: Architektur & Wohnen, no. 4/1988, p. 114

2 Helmut Lethen, Verhaltenslehre der Kälte, Lebensversuche zwischen den Kriegen, Frankfurt 1994, p. 111

3 Wolfgang Pehnt, Die Architektur des Expressionismus, Stuttgart 1973, p. 9, new expanded edition Stuttgart 1998

4 Walter Benjamin, Fragmente, in: Theodor W. Adorno, Gershom Scholem, Rolf Tiedemann and Herrmann Schweppenhäuser (ed.), Walter Benjamin, Gesammelte Schriften, Frankfurt 1982, vol. VI, p. 177

5 Helmut Lethen, see note 2, p. 37

6 Susan Buck-Morss, The City as Dreamworld and Catastrophe, in: Heinz Paetzold (ed.), City Life, Essays on Urban Culture, Maastricht 1997, p. 113

7 Gustav René Hocke, Die Welt als Labyrinth, Manierismus in der europäischen Kunst und Literatur, Reinbeck 1987, p. 248 (first ed. Reinbeck 1957 and 1959)

8 An example of this: on 12 June 1992 an international architectural conference was held in the Museum for applied Kunst in Vienna on the subject of "The End of Architecture?". Coop Himmelblau, Zaha Hadid, Steven Holl, Tom Mayne, Eric Owen Moss, Carme Pinós, Lebbeus Woods and Peter Noever took part. The author chaired the event. Despite great international interest and the presence of numerous foreign trade journalists the conference was conducted behind closed doors, despite protests from the press. The public were not informed about the results until after the conference.

9 This refers exclusively to the questionable way in which the exhibition came about and the question of why other architects who should definitely be categorized as Deconstructivists were excluded. For this cf. also: Charles Jencks, Charles Jencks, The New Moderns: From Late to Neo-Modernism, New York 1990, especially the chapter on Philip Johnson

10 Jürgen Pahl uses this concept in his book Architekturtheorie des 20. Jahrhunderts, Munich/London/New York 1999, p. 270 ff. Pahl does not place Coop Himmelb(l)au's work in this category.

11 Charles Jencks, Deconstruction: The Pleasures of Absence, in: Andreas Papadakis (ed.), Deconstruction Architecture, AD, vol. 58, no. 3/4, London 1988, p. 31

12 Bruno Schindler, Weiß oder Schwarz?, in: Arch + no. 96/97, Aachen 1988, p. 89

13 Gert Kähler, "Schokolade ja; aber Edelbitter", Dekonstruktivismus, Maschine und Utopie, in: same author, (ed.), Dekonstruktion?, Dekonstruktivismus?, Aufbruch ins Chaos oder neues Bild der Welt?, Braunschweig/Wiesbaden 1990, p. 34

14 Friedrich Achleitner, Dialog über Coop Himmelblau und das Wienerische, was sonst?, loc. cit., p. 113 ff.

15 Michael Müller and Franz Dröge, Museumification and Mediation: Two Strategies for Urban Aestheticisation, in: Heinz Paetzold (ed.), see note 6, p. 162 f.

16 Mark Wigley, in: The Museum of Modern Art, New York (ed.), Deconstructivist Architecture, New York 1988, p. 17

17 Christopher Norris and Andrew Benjamin did in fact illustrate their study "What is Deconstruction?", London 1988, with architectural examples, but they do not mention them at all in the text. Mark Wigley provided an account that is much more precise in terms of architectural theory in "The Architecture of Deconstruction. Derrida's Haunt", Cambridge, Mass. 1993.

18 Roger Thiel, The Art of the Fugue, in: Daidalos no. 48, Berlin 1993, p. 76

19 There are conflicting views of this metaphor,. Norbert Bolz sees Babel as a symbol of pluralism in language styles that has had its sting drawn in the post-Modern era: "Post-Modernism thinks Babel is a happy city".

20 José Luis González Cobelo, The Game of Deconstruction II, Coop Himmelblau or the Magic Outcome, in: El Croquis no. 40, Madrid 1989, p. 87

21 for this cf.: Frank R. Werner, Museum ohne Ausweg – Anfang einer neuen Architektur?, Daniel Libeskinds Felix-Nussbaum-Museum in Osnabrück, in: Bauwelt no. 30, Berlin 1998, p. 1656

22 Peter Eisenman, En terror firma: In Trails of Greatness, in: Aarie Graafland, Peter Eisenman: Recent Projects, Amsterdam 1989 p. 42

23 loc. cit., p. 43

24 Ullrich Schwarz (ed.), Peter Eisenman, Aura und Exzeß, Zur Überwindung der Metaphysik der Architektur, Wien 1995, p. 28

25 for this cf.: Colin Rowe, The Mathematics of the Ideal Villa, first published in Architectural Review, 1947, also in: The Mathematics of the Ideal Villa and Other Essays, Cambridge, Mass. 1976

26 Jeffrey Kipnis, Towards a New Architecture, in: Architectural Design, Vol. 63, No. 3/4, London 1993, p. 41

27 loc. cit., p. 48

28 for this cf.: Heinrich Klotz, Architektur der zweiten Moderne, Stuttgart 1999

29 for this cf.: Die Moderne der Moderne, Entwürfe zur Zweiten Moderne, Arch+ no. 143, Aachen 1998

30 Sanford Kwinter, La trahison des clercs (und anderer Mummenschanz), in: Arch+ no. 146, Aachen 1999, p. 84 ff.

31 Bart Lootsma uses this term in his response to Kwinter, loc. cit., p. 87 f.

32 A typical example of assessments of this kind: Charles Jencks, The Architecture of the Jumping Universe, London 1995, p. 33 and 64 ff.

33 Wolf D. Prix in conversation with the author on 2. August 1999 in Vienna

34 Norbert Bolz, Die Welt als Chaos und Simulation, Munich 1992, p. 23

35 loc. cit., p. 27

36 Olof Gigon, Der Ursprung der griechischen Philosophie, Basel 1968, p. 28

37 Wolfgang Welsch, Unsere postmoderne Welt, Weinheim 1987, p. 142

38 Gilles Deleuze and Félix Guattari, A Thousand Plateaus: Capitalism and Schizophrenia, Minneapolis 1987, p. 313

39 loc. cit., p. 329

40 loc. cit., p. 432

41 loc. cit., p. 384, 385 and 500

42 Jean Baudrillard, Architektur: Wahrheit oder Radikalität?, Graz/Vienna 1999, p. 38

43 Thomas Meyer, Die Inszenierung des Scheins, Frankfurt 1992, p. 133

44 Gilles Deleuze, see note 38, p. 500

SHORT BIOGRAPHIES

COOP HIMMELBLAU was founded in Vienna, Austria by Wolf D. Prix and Helmut Swiczinsky in 1968, and has worked in the fields of architecture, art and design since then. A second office was set up in Los Angeles, California in 1988.

COOP HIMMELB(L)AU is working on international projects in France, Germany, Japan, Mexico, The Netherlands, Switzerland and the USA. COOP HIMMEL-B(L)AU has won various awards in the last five years, and first prizes in international competitions. COOP HIMMELB(L)AU is a member of the European Academy of Sciences and Arts.

COOP HIMMELB(L)AU's work has been and is shown in many international exhibitions. These include the "Deconstructivist Architecture" exhibition in the Museum of Modern Art, New York and an individual exhibition in the Centre Georges Pompidou in Paris, France. COOP HIMMELB(L)AU was invited to represent Austria at the Sixth International Architecture Biennale in Venice in 1996.

WOLF D. PRIX

Born in Vienna, Austria in 1942. Wolf D. Prix studied at the Technical University in Vienna, the Southern California Institute of Architecture (SCI-Arc) in Los Angeles and at the Architectural Association in London, UK.

Wolf D. Prix is Professor of the Masterclass for Architecture[3] at the Hochschule für Angewandte Kunst in Vienna. 1984: Adjunct Professor at the Architectural Association in London. 1990: Visiting Professor at Harvard University, Cambridge, Massachusetts. 1985-1995: Adjunct Professor at the SCI-Arc, Los Angeles. 1995-1997: member of the architecture committee in the Austrian Ministry of Science and Research.

HELMUT SWICZINSKY

Born in Posen, Poland in 1944; grew up in Vienna. He studied at the Technical University in Vienna and the Architectural Association in London.

1973: Visiting Professor at the Architectural Association in London.

314 Helmut Swiczinsky and Wolf D. Prix

INDEX

ACKNOWLEDGEMENTS

All illustrations are courtesy of
Coop Himmelb(l)au.

Hélène Binet, London 224, 226, 230, 285
AnnA BlaU, Vienna 235, 238, 240
Tom Bonner, Venice, California 35, 170, 184,
    185, 186, 295, 297
Burgi Eder, Linz 59
Armin Hess, Vienna 251, 252, 253, 254
Margherita Krischanitz, Vienna 42, 43
Stefan Laub, Vienna 44, 45, 46
Markus Pillhofer, Vienna 89, 90, 139, 236,
    239, 241, 245, 249, 250, 278, 294, 303
Punctum & Schink, Leipzig 213
J. Scott Smith, Santa Monica, CA 288
Margherita Spiluttini, Vienna 91, 94, 194,
    195, 196, 197, 198, 199, 268
Ger van der Vlugt, Amsterdam 73, 191
Elke Walford, Fotowerkstatt Hamburger
    Kunsthalle, Hamburg 296
Gerald Zugmann, Vienna Cover, 2, 16, 26, 40,
    41, 61, 66, 81, 87, 88, 99, 100, 101, 102,
    103, 156, 157, 160, 164, 165, 166, 167, 169,
    172, 173, 174, 175, 176, 177, 178, 179, 180,
    182, 183, 192, 193, 200, 201, 214, 215,
    216, 217, 218, 219, 220, 223, 225, 227, 228,
    229, 237, 256, 257, 260, 261, 262, 263,
    264, 265, 286, 308, 314

ABOUT THE AUTHOR

Frank Werner, b. 1944 in Worms am Rhein,
studied art and architecture. He held the chair
of architecture and design history at the Academy of Arts in Stuttgart, Germany until 1993.
He has been a university professor at the University of Wuppertal, Germany since 1994,
where he directs the Institute for Architectural History and Theory. At the time of writing he
is Dean of the Faculty of Architecture at the
University of Wuppertal. Frank Werner is the
author of numerous books and other publications on 20th century architectural history. He
has held the post of visiting professor at the
SCI-Arc/Los Angeles and other international
schools of architecture. He has been writing
about Coop Himmelb(l)au's work since 1975.

Translation:
Michael Robinson, London

Layout and Cover Design:
Silke Nalbach, Stuttgart

Lithography:
Hahn Medien GmbH, Kornwestheim

Printing and binding:
Freiburger Graphische Betriebe, Freiburg i. Br.

This book is also available in a German
language edition
(ISBN 3-7643-6075-5).

A CIP catalogue record for this book is
available from the Library of Congress,
Washington, D.C., USA

Deutsche Bibliothek Cataloging-in-
Publication Data
Werner, Frank: Covering + Exposing: the
architecture of COOP Himmelb(l)au / Frank
Werner. [Transl.: Michael Robinson]. – Basel ;
Berlin ; Boston : Birkhäuser, 2000
    Dt. Ausg. u.d.T.: Werner, Frank: Covering
    + Exposing: die Architektur von Coop
    Himmelb(l)au
    ISBN 3-7643-6079-8

© 2000 Birkhäuser – Publishers for
Architecture, P.O. Box 133, CH-4010 Basel,
Switzerland

Printed on acid-free paper produced from
chlorine-free pulp. TCF ∞

Printed in Germany
ISBN 3-7643-6079-8

9 8 7 6 5 4 3 2 1